On Core Mathematics

Grade 5

HOUGHTON MIFFLIN HARCOURT

Cover photo credit: Garry Gay/Getty Images

Printed in the U.S.A.

ISBN 978-0-547-57520-9

5 6 7 8 9 10 0982 20 19 18 17 16 15 14 13 12

4500385341 ^ B C D E F G

Table of Contents

Operations and Algebraic Thinking

▶ **Write and interpret numerical expressions.**

Lesson 1 CC.5.OA.1 **Algebra** • Evaluate Numerical Expressions 1
Lesson 2 CC.5.OA.1 **Algebra** • Grouping Symbols 3
Lesson 3 CC.5.OA.2 **Algebra** • Numerical Expressions 5

▶ **Analyze patterns and relationships.**

Lesson 4 CC.5.OA.3 Numerical Patterns 7
Lesson 5 CC.5.OA.3 **Problem Solving** • Find a Rule 9
Lesson 6 CC.5.OA.3 Graph and Analyze Relationships 11

Number and Operations in Base Ten

▶ **Understand the place value system.**

Lesson 7 CC.5.NBT.1 **Investigate** • Place Value and Patterns 13
Lesson 8 CC.5.NBT.1 Place Value of Whole Numbers 15
Lesson 9 CC.5.NBT.1 **Investigate** • Thousandths 17
Lesson 10 CC.5.NBT.2 **Algebra** • Powers of 10 and Exponents 19
Lesson 11 CC.5.NBT.2 **Algebra** • Multiplication Patterns 21
Lesson 12 CC.5.NBT.2 **Algebra** • Multiplication Patterns with Decimals 23
Lesson 13 CC.5.NBT.2 **Algebra** • Division Patterns with Decimals 25
Lesson 14 CC.5.NBT.3a Place Value of Decimals 27
Lesson 15 CC.5.NBT.3b Compare and Order Decimals 29
Lesson 16 CC.5.NBT.4 Round Decimals 31

▶ Perform operations with multi-digit whole numbers and with decimals to hundredths.

Lesson 17	CC.5.NBT.5	Multiply by 1-Digit Numbers	**33**
Lesson 18	CC.5.NBT.5	Multiply by 2-Digit Numbers	**35**
Lesson 19	CC.5.NBT.6	**Algebra** • Properties	**37**
Lesson 20	CC.5.NBT.6	Relate Multiplication to Division	**39**
Lesson 21	CC.5.NBT.6	**Problem Solving** • Multiplication and Division	**41**
Lesson 22	CC.5.NBT.6	Place the First Digit	**43**
Lesson 23	CC.5.NBT.6	Divide by 1-Digit Divisors	**45**
Lesson 24	CC.5.NBT.6	**Investigate** • Division with 2-Digit Divisors	**47**
Lesson 25	CC.5.NBT.6	Partial Quotients	**49**
Lesson 26	CC.5.NBT.6	Estimate with 2-Digit Divisors	**51**
Lesson 27	CC.5.NBT.6	Divide by 2-Digit Divisors	**53**
Lesson 28	CC.5.NBT.6	Adjust Quotients	**55**
Lesson 29	CC.5.NBT.6	**Problem Solving** • Division	**57**
Lesson 30	CC.5.NBT.7	**Investigate** • Decimal Addition	**59**
Lesson 31	CC.5.NBT.7	**Investigate** • Decimal Subtraction	**61**
Lesson 32	CC.5.NBT.7	Estimate Decimal Sums and Differences	**63**
Lesson 33	CC.5.NBT.7	Add Decimals	**65**
Lesson 34	CC.5.NBT.7	Subtract Decimals	**67**
Lesson 35	CC.5.NBT.7	**Algebra** • Patterns with Decimals	**69**
Lesson 36	CC.5.NBT.7	**Problem Solving** • Add and Subtract Money	**71**
Lesson 37	CC.5.NBT.7	Choose a Method	**73**
Lesson 38	CC.5.NBT.7	**Investigate** • Multiply Decimals and Whole Numbers	**75**
Lesson 39	CC.5.NBT.7	Multiplication with Decimals and Whole Numbers	**77**
Lesson 40	CC.5.NBT.7	Multiply Using Expanded Form	**79**
Lesson 41	CC.5.NBT.7	**Problem Solving** • Multiply Money	**81**
Lesson 42	CC.5.NBT.7	**Investigate** • Decimal Multiplication	**83**
Lesson 43	CC.5.NBT.7	Multiply Decimals	**85**
Lesson 44	CC.5.NBT.7	Zeros in the Product	**87**
Lesson 45	CC.5.NBT.7	**Investigate** • Divide Decimals by Whole Numbers	**89**
Lesson 46	CC.5.NBT.7	Estimate Quotients	**91**
Lesson 47	CC.5.NBT.7	Division of Decimals by Whole Numbers	**93**
Lesson 48	CC.5.NBT.7	**Investigate** • Decimal Division	**95**
Lesson 49	CC.5.NBT.7	Divide Decimals	**97**
Lesson 50	CC.5.NBT.7	Write Zeros in the Dividend	**99**
Lesson 51	CC.5.NBT.7	**Problem Solving** • Decimal Operations	**101**

Number and Operations – Fractions

Use equivalent fractions as a strategy to add and subtract fractions.

Lesson 52	CC.5.NF.1	Common Denominators and Equivalent Fractions	**103**
Lesson 53	CC.5.NF.1	Add and Subtract Fractions	**105**
Lesson 54	CC.5.NF.1	Add and Subtract Mixed Numbers	**107**
Lesson 55	CC.5.NF.1	Subtraction with Renaming	**109**
Lesson 56	CC.5.NF.1	**Algebra** • Patterns with Fractions	**111**
Lesson 57	CC.5.NF.1	**Algebra** • Use Properties of Addition	**113**
Lesson 58	CC.5.NF.2	**Investigate** • Addition with Unlike Denominators	**115**
Lesson 59	CC.5.NF.2	**Investigate** • Subtraction with Unlike Denominators	**117**
Lesson 60	CC.5.NF.2	Estimate Fraction Sums and Differences	**119**
Lesson 61	CC.5.NF.2	**Problem Solving** • Practice Addition and Subtraction	**121**

Apply and extend previous understandings of multiplication and division to multiply and divide fractions.

Lesson 62	CC.5.NF.3	Interpret the Remainder	**123**
Lesson 63	CC.5.NF.3	Connect Fractions to Division	**125**
Lesson 64	CC.5.NF.4a	Find Part of a Group	**127**
Lesson 65	CC.5.NF.4a	**Investigate** • Multiply Fractions and Whole Numbers	**129**
Lesson 66	CC.5.NF.4a	Fraction and Whole Number Multiplication	**131**
Lesson 67	CC.5.NF.4a	Fraction Multiplication	**133**
Lesson 68	CC.5.NF.4b	**Investigate** • Multiply Fractions	**135**
Lesson 69	CC.5.NF.4b	**Investigate** • Area and Mixed Numbers	**137**
Lesson 70	CC.5.NF.5a	Compare Fraction Factors and Products	**139**
Lesson 71	CC.5.NF.5a	Compare Mixed Number Factors and Products	**141**
Lesson 72	CC.5.NF.5b	**Problem Solving** • Find Unknown Lengths	**143**
Lesson 73	CC.5.NF.6	Multiply Mixed Numbers	**145**
Lesson 74	CC.5.NF.7a CC.5.NF.7b	**Investigate** • Divide Fractions and Whole Numbers	**147**
Lesson 75	CC.5.NF.7b	**Problem Solving** • Use Multiplication	**149**
Lesson 76	CC.5.NF.7c	Fraction and Whole-Number Division	**151**
Lesson 77	CC.5.NF.7c	Interpret Division with Fractions	**153**

Measurement and Data

▶ **Convert like measurement units within a given measurement system.**

Lesson 78 **CC.5.MD.1** Customary Length **155**

Lesson 79 **CC.5.MD.1** Customary Capacity **157**

Lesson 80 **CC.5.MD.1** Weight **159**

Lesson 81 **CC.5.MD.1** Multistep Measurement Problems **161**

Lesson 82 **CC.5.MD.1** Metric Measures **163**

Lesson 83 **CC.5.MD.1** **Problem Solving** • Customary and Metric Conversions **165**

Lesson 84 **CC.5.MD.1** Elapsed Time **167**

▶ **Represent and interpret data.**

Lesson 85 **CC.5.MD.2** Line Plots **169**

▶ **Geometric measurement: understand concepts of volume and relate volume to multiplication and to addition.**

Lesson 86 **CC.5.MD.3** Three-Dimensional Figures **171**

Lesson 87 **CC.5.MD.3a** **Investigate** • Unit Cubes and Solid Figures **173**

Lesson 88 **CC.5.MD.3b** **Investigate** • Understand Volume **175**

Lesson 89 **CC.5.MD.4** **Investigate** • Estimate Volume **177**

Lesson 90 **CC.5.MD.5a** Volume of Rectangular Prisms **179**

Lesson 91 **CC.5.MD.5b** **Algebra** • Apply Volume Formulas **181**

Lesson 92 **CC.5.MD.5b** **Problem Solving** • Compare Volumes **183**

Lesson 93 **CC.5.MD.5c** Find Volume of Composed Figures **185**

Geometry

▶ **Graph points on the coordinate plane to solve real-world and mathematical problems.**

Lesson 94 CC.5.G.1 Ordered Pairs **187**

Lesson 95 CC.5.G.2 **Investigate** • Graph Data **189**

Lesson 96 CC.5.G.2 Line Graphs **191**

▶ **Classify two-dimensional figures into categories based on their properties.**

Lesson 97 CC.5.G.3 Polygons **193**

Lesson 98 CC.5.G.3 Triangles **195**

Lesson 99 CC.5.G.3 **Problem Solving** • Properties of Two-Dimensional Figures **197**

Lesson 100 CC.5.G.4 Quadrilaterals **199**

Name ______________________

COMMON CORE STANDARD CC.5.OA.1

Lesson Objective: Use the order of operations to evaluate numerical expressions.

Algebra • Evaluate Numerical Expressions

A **numerical expression** is a mathematical phrase that includes only numbers and operation symbols.

You **evaluate** the expression when you perform all the computations to find its value.

To evaluate an expression, use the **order of operations.**

Order of Operations

1. Parentheses
2. Multiply and Divide
3. Add and Subtract

Evaluate the expression (10 + 6 × 6) − 4 × 10.

Step 1 Start with computations inside the parentheses.

10 + 6 × 6

Step 2 Perform the order of operations inside the *parentheses*.

Multiply and divide from left to right.

10 + 6 × 6 = 10 + 36

Add and subtract from left to right.

10 + 36 = 46

Step 3 Rewrite the expression with the parentheses evaluated.

46 − 4 × 10

Step 4 *Multiply and divide* from left to right.

46 − 4 × 10 = 46 − 40

Step 5 *Add and subtract* from left to right.

46 − 40 = 6

So, (10 + 6 × 6) − 4 × 10 = 6.

Evaluate the numerical expression.

1. 8 − (7 × 1) ________

2. 5 − 2 + 12 ÷ 4 ________

3. 8 × (16 ÷ 2) ________

4. 4 × (28 − 20 ÷ 2) ________

5. (30 − 9 ÷ 3) ÷ 9 ________

6. (6 × 6 − 9) − 9 ÷ 3 ________

7. 11 ÷ (8 + 9 ÷ 3) ________

8. 13 × 4 − 65 ÷ 13 ________

9. 9 + 4 × 6 − 65 ÷ 13 ________

Name ______________________________

Lesson 1
CC.5.OA.1

Evaluate Numerical Expressions

Evaluate the numerical expression.

1. $24 \times 5 - 41$
   120 − 41

   79
   ______

2. $(32 - 20) \div 4$

   ______

3. $16 \div (2 + 6)$

   ______

4. $15 \times (8 - 3)$

   ______

5. $4 \times 8 - 7$

   ______

6. $27 + 5 \times 6$

   ______

7. $3 \div 3 \times 4 + 6$

   ______

8. $14 + 4 \times 4 - 9$

   ______

Rewrite the expression with parentheses to equal the given value.

9. $3 \times 4 - 1 + 2$

   value: 11

   ______

10. $2 \times 6 \div 2 + 1$

    value: 4

    ______

11. $5 + 3 \times 2 - 6$

    value: 10

    ______

Problem Solving REAL WORLD

12. Sandy has several pitchers to hold lemonade for the school bake sale. Two pitchers can hold 64 ounces each, and four pitchers can hold 48 ounces each. How many total ounces can Sandy's pitchers hold?

    ______

13. At the bake sale, Jonah sold 4 cakes for \$8 each and 36 muffins for \$2 each. What was the total amount, in dollars, that Jonah received from these sales?

    ______

Name ______________________________

Lesson 2

COMMON CORE STANDARD CC.5.OA.1

Lesson Objective: Evaluate numerical expressions with parentheses, brackets, and braces.

Algebra • Grouping Symbols

Parentheses ( ), *brackets* [ ], and *braces* { }, are different grouping symbols used in expressions. To evaluate an expression with different grouping symbols, perform the operation in the innermost set of grouping symbols first. Then evaluate the expression from the inside out.

Evaluate the expression 2 × [(9 × 4) – (17 – 6)].

Step 1 Perform the operations in the *parentheses* first.

$2 \times [(9 \times 4) - (17 - 6)]$

$2 \times [\ \underline{36} - \underline{11}\ ]$

Step 2 Next perform the operations in the *brackets*.

$2 \times [\ 36 - 11\ ]$

$2 \times \underline{25}$

Step 3 Then multiply.

$2 \times 25 = \underline{50}$

So, $2 \times [(9 \times 4) - (17 - 6)] = \underline{50}$

Evaluate the numerical expression.

1. $4 \times [(15 - 6) \times (7 - 3)]$

$4 \times [9 \times$ ______________]

$4 \times [$ ______________]

____

2. $40 - [(8 \times 7) - (5 \times 6)]$

____

3. $60 \div [(20 - 6) + (14 - 8)]$

____

4. $5 + [(10 - 2) + (4 - 1)]$

____

5. $3 \times [(9 + 4) - (2 \times 6)]$

____

6. $32 \div [(7 \times 2) - (2 \times 5)]$

____

Name ______________________________

Lesson 2

CC.5.OA.1

Grouping Symbols

Evaluate the numerical expression.

1. $5 \times [(11 - 3) - (13 - 9)]$

$5 \times [8 - (13 - 9)]$

$5 \times [8 - 4]$

5×4

20

2. $30 - [(9 \times 2) - (3 \times 4)]$

3. $36 \div [(14 - 5) - (10 - 7)]$

4. $7 \times [(9 + 8) - (12 - 7)]$

5. $[(25 - 11) + (15 - 9)] \div 5$

6. $[(8 \times 9) - (6 \times 7)] - 15$

7. $8 \times \{[(7 + 4) \times 2] - [(11 - 7) \times 4]\}$

8. $\{[(8 - 3) \times 2] + [(5 \times 6) - 5]\} \div 5$

Problem Solving REAL WORLD

Use the information at the right for 9 and 10.

Joan has a cafe. Each day, she bakes 24 muffins. She gives away 3 and sells the rest. Each day, she also bakes 36 cupcakes. She gives away 4 and sells the rest.

9. Write an expression to represent the total number of muffins and cupcakes Joan sells in 5 days.

____

10. Evaluate the expression to find the total number of muffins and cupcakes Joan sells in 5 days.

____

Name ____________________

Lesson 3

COMMON CORE STANDARD CC.5.OA.2

Lesson Objective: Write numerical expressions.

Algebra • Numerical Expressions

Write words to match the expression.

6 × (12 − 4)

Think: Many word problems involve finding the cost of a store purchase.

Step 1 Examine the expression.

- What operations are in the expression? multiplication and subtraction

Step 2 Describe what each part of the expression can represent when finding the cost of a store purchase.

- What can multiplying by 6 represent? buying 6 of the same item

Step 3 Write the words.

- Joe buys 6 DVDs. Each DVD costs $12. If Joe receives a $4 discount on each DVD, what is the total amount of money Joe spends?

1. What is multiplied and what is subtracted?

____

2. What part of the expression is the price of the item?

____

3. What can subtracting 4 from 12 represent?

____

Write words to match the expression.

4. 4 × (10 − 2)

____

5. 3 × (6 − 1)

____

Name ______________________

Numerical Expressions

Lesson 3
CC.5.OA.2

Write an expression to match the words.

1. Ethan collected 16 seashells. He lost 4 of them while walking home.

   16 − 4

2. Yasmine bought 4 bracelets. Each bracelet cost $3.

   ____

3. Amani did 10 jumping jacks. Then she did 7 more.

   ____

4. Darryl has a board that is 8 feet long. He cuts it into pieces that are each 2 feet long.

   ____

Write words to match the expression.

5. $3 + (4 \times 12)$

6. $36 \div 4$

7. $24 - (6 + 3)$

Draw a line to match the expression with the words.

8. Ray picked 30 apples and put them equally into 3 baskets. Then he ate two of the apples in a basket.	$(3 \times 2) \times 30$
9. Quinn had $30. She bought a notebook for $3 and a pack of pens for $2.	$(30 \div 3) - 2$
10. Colleen runs 3 miles twice a day for 30 days.	$30 - (3 + 2)$

Problem Solving REAL WORLD

11. Kylie has 14 polished stones. Her friend gives her 6 more stones. Write an expression to match the words.

   ____

12. Rashad had 25 stamps. He shared them equally among himself and 4 friends. Then Rashad found 2 more stamps in his pocket. Write an expression to match the words.

   ____

Name ______________________________

COMMON CORE STANDARD CC.5.OA.3

Lesson Objective: Use two rules to generate a numerical pattern and identify the relationship between the corresponding terms in the patterns.

Numerical Patterns

A soccer league has 5 teams. How many players are needed for 5 teams? How many soccer balls are needed by the 5 teams?

	Number of Teams	1	2	3	4	7
Add 8.	Number of Players	8	16	24	32	56
Add 4.	Number of Soccer Balls	4	8	12	16	28

Step 1 Find a rule that could be used to find the number of players for the number of teams.

Think: In the pattern 8, 16, 24, 32, you add 8 to get the next term.

As the number of teams increases by 1, the number of players increases by 8. So the rule is to add 8.

Step 2 Find a rule that could be used to find the number of soccer balls for the number of teams.

Think: In the pattern 4, 8, 12, 16, you add 4 to get the next term.

As the number of teams increases by 1, the number of soccer balls needed increases by 4. So the rule is to add 4.

Step 3 For 7 teams, multiply the number of players by $\frac{1}{2}$ to find the number of soccer balls.

So, for 7 teams, 56 players will need 28 soccer balls.

Complete the rule that describes how one sequence is related to the other. Use the rule to find the unknown term.

Number of Teams	1	2	3	4	8	10
Number of Players	15	30	45	60	120	
Number of Bats	5	10	15	20		50

1. Divide the number of players by ______ to find the number of bats.

2. Multiply the number of bats by ______ to find the number of players.

Name ______________________

Numerical Patterns

Complete the rule that describes how one sequence is related to the other. Use the rule to find the unknown term.

1. Multiply the number of laps by **50** to find the number of yards.

Think: The number of yards is 50 times the number of laps.

Swimmers	1	2	3	4
Number of Laps	4	8	12	16
Number of Yards	200	400	600	**800**

2. Multiply the number of pounds by ________ to find total cost.

Boxes	1	2	3	4	6
Number of Pounds	3	6	9	12	18
Total Cost ($)	12	24	36	48	

3. Multiply the number of hours by ________ to find the number of miles.

Cars	1	2	3	4
Number of Hours	2	4	6	8
Number of Miles	130	260	390	

4. Multiply the number of hours by ________ to find the amount earned.

Days	1	2	3	4	7
Number of Hours	8	16	24	32	56
Amount Earned ($)	96	192	288	384	

Problem Solving

5. A map distance of 5 inches represents 200 miles of actual distance. Suppose the distance between two cities on the map is 7 inches. What is the actual distance between the two cities? Write the rule you used to find the actual distance.

____

____

____

____

6. To make one costume, Rachel uses 6 yards of material and 3 yards of trim. Suppose she uses a total of 48 yards of material to make several costumes. How many yards of trim does she use? Write the rule you used to find the number of yards of trim.

____

____

____

____

Name ______________________________

Lesson 5

COMMON CORE STANDARD CC.5.OA.3

Lesson Objective: Solve problems using the strategy *solve a simpler problem.*

Problem Solving • Find a Rule

Samantha is making a scarf with fringe around it. Each section of fringe is made of 4 pieces of yarn with 2 beads holding them together. There are 42 sections of fringe on Samantha's scarf. How many wooden beads and how many pieces of yarn are on Samantha's scarf?

Read the Problem

What do I need to find?

Possible answer: I need to find the number of beads and the number of pieces of yarn on Samantha's scarf.

What information do I need to use?

Possible answer: I need to use the number of sections on the scarf, and that each section has 4 pieces of yarn and 2 beads.

How will I use the information?

I will use the information to search for patterns to solve a simpler problem.

Solve the Problem

Sections of Fringe	1	2	3	4	6	42
Number of Beads	2	4	6	8	12	84
Pieces of Yarn	4	8	12	16	24	168

Possible answer: I can multiply the number of sections by 2 to find the number of beads. Then, I can multiply the number of sections by 4, or the number of beads by 2, to find the number of pieces of yarn. So, Samantha's scarf has 2×42, or 84 beads, and 4×42, or 168 pieces of yarn.

1. A rectangular tile has a decorative pattern of 3 equal-sized squares, each of which is divided into 2 same-sized triangles. If Marnie uses 36 of these tiles on the wall behind her kitchen stove, how many triangles are displayed?

____

2. Leta is making strawberry-almond salad for a party. For every head of lettuce that she uses, she adds 5 ounces of almonds and 10 strawberries. If she uses 75 ounces of almonds, how many heads of lettuce and how many strawberries does Leta use?

____

Name ______________________

Problem Solving • Find a Rule

Lesson 5
CC.5.OA.3

Write a rule and complete the table. Then answer the question.

1. Faye buys 15 T-shirts, which are on sale for $3 each. How much money does Faye spend?

Number of T-Shirts	1	2	3	5	10	15
Amount Spent ($)	3	6	9			

Possible rule:
Multiply the number of T-shirts by 3.

The total amount Faye spends is **$45**.

2. The Gilman family joins a fitness center. They pay $35 per month. By the 12th month, how much money will the Gilman family have spent?

Number of Months	1	2	3	4	5	12
Total Amount of Money Spent ($)	35	70				

Possible rule:
____
____

The Gilman family will have spent ________.

3. Hettie is stacking paper cups. Each stack of 15 cups is 6 inches high. What is the total height of 10 stacks of cups?

Number of stacks	1	2	3	10
Height (in.)	6	12	18	

Possible rule:
____
____

The total height of 10 stacks is ________.

Name ________________________________

Lesson 6

COMMON CORE STANDARD CC.5.OA.3

Lesson Objective: Graph the relationship between two numerical patterns on a coordinate grid.

Graph and Analyze Relationships

The scale on a map is 1 in. = 4 mi. Two cities are 5 inches apart on the map. What is the actual distance between the two cities?

Step 1 Make a table that relates the map distances to the actual distances.

Map Distance (in.)	1	2	3	4	5
Actual Distance (mi)	4	8	12	16	?

Step 2 Write the number pairs in the table as ordered pairs.

(1, 4), (2, 8), (3, 12), (4, 16), (5, ?)

Step 3 Graph the ordered pairs. Connect the points with a line from the origin.

Possible rule: Multiply the map distance by 4 to get the actual distance.

Step 4 Use the rule to find the actual distance between the two cities.

So, two cities that are 5 inches apart on the map are actually 5 × 4, or 20 miles apart.

Plot the point (5, 20) on the graph.

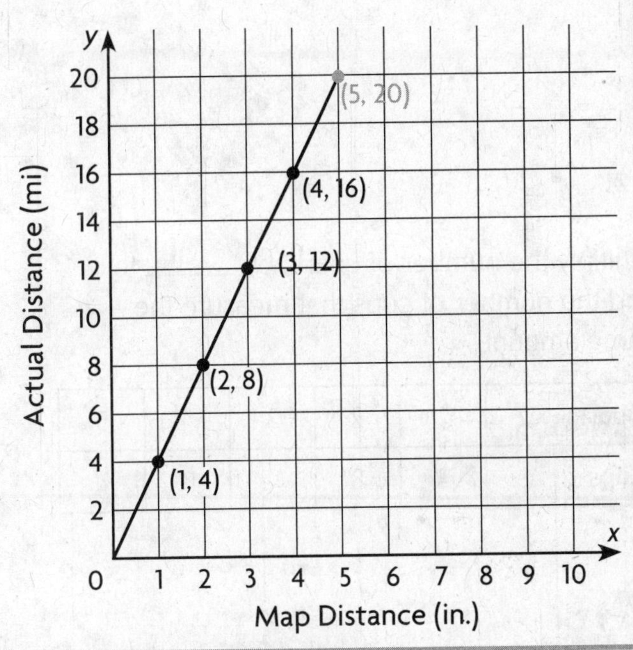

Graph and label the related number pairs as ordered pairs. Then complete and use the rule to find the unknown term.

1. Multiply the number of yards by ______ to find the number of feet.

Number of Yards	1	2	3	4	5
Number of Feet	3	6	9	12	

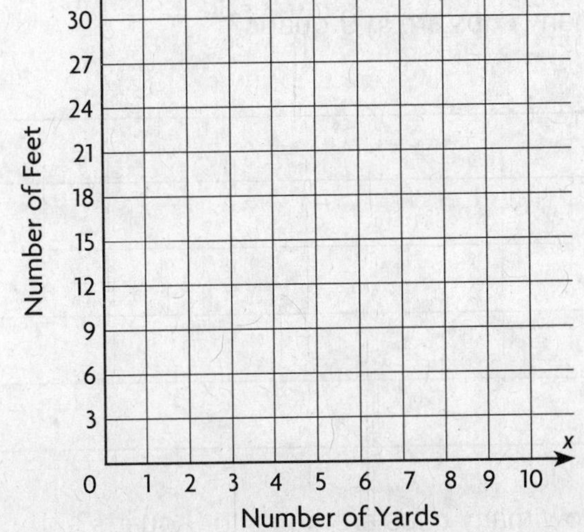

Name ____________________

Lesson 6
CC.5.OA.3

Graph and Analyze Relationships

Graph and label the related number pairs as ordered pairs. Then complete and use the rule to find the unknown term.

1. Multiply the number of yards by __3__ to find the number of feet.

Yards	1	2	3	4
Feet	3	6	9	12

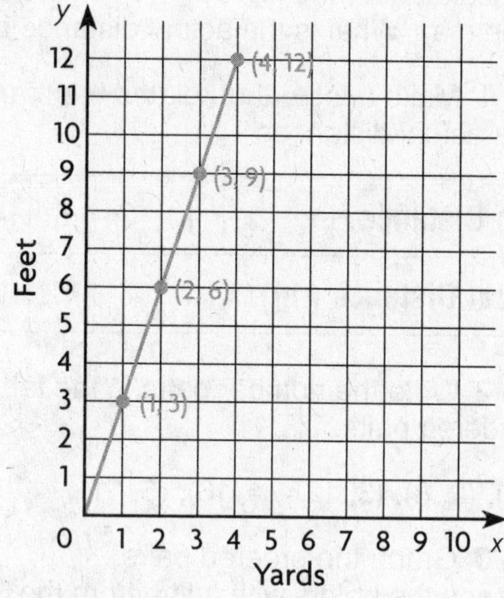

2. Multiply the number of quarts by ______ to find the number of cups that measure the same amount.

Quarts	1	2	3	4	5
Cups	4	8	12	16	

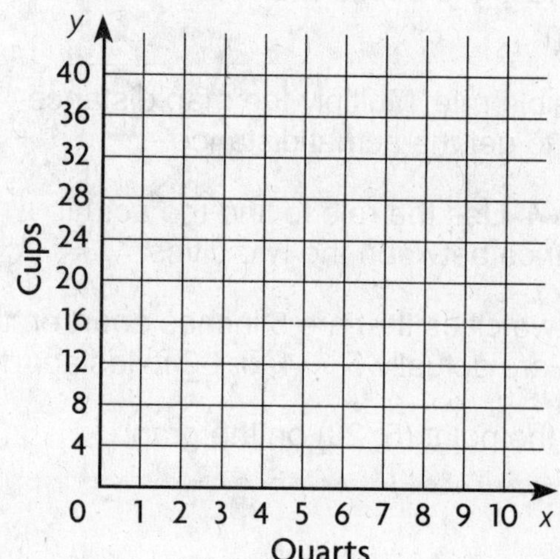

Problem Solving REAL WORLD

3. How can you use the graph for Exercise 2 to find how many cups are in 9 quarts?

____

____

____

____

____

____

4. How many cups are equal to 9 quarts? ______

Name ______________________

Lesson 7

COMMON CORE STANDARD CC.5.NBT.1

Lesson Objective: Recognize the 10 to 1 relationship among place-value positions.

Place Value and Patterns

You can use a place-value chart and patterns to write numbers that are 10 times as much as or $\frac{1}{10}$ of any given number.

Each place to the right is $\frac{1}{10}$ of the value of the place to its left.

	$\frac{1}{10}$ of the hundred thousands place	$\frac{1}{10}$ of the ten thousands place	$\frac{1}{10}$ of the thousands place	$\frac{1}{10}$ of the hundreds place	$\frac{1}{10}$ of the tens place
Hundred Thousands	**Ten Thousands**	**Thousands**	**Hundreds**	**Tens**	**Ones**
10 times the ten thousands place	10 times the thousands place	10 times the hundreds place	10 times the tens place	10 times the ones place	

Each place to the left is 10 times the value of the place to its right.

Find $\frac{1}{10}$ of 600.

$\frac{1}{10}$ of 6 hundreds is 6 tens.

So, $\frac{1}{10}$ of 600 is 60.

Find 10 times as much as 600.

10 times as much as 6 hundreds is 6 thousands.

So, 10 times as much as 600 is 6,000.

Use place-value patterns to complete the table.

Number	10 times as much as	$\frac{1}{10}$ of
1. 200		
2. 10		
3. 700		
4. 5,000		

Number	10 times as much as	$\frac{1}{10}$ of
5. 900		
6. 80,000		
7. 3,000		
8. 40		

Name ______________________

Lesson 7

CC.5.NBT.1

Place Value and Patterns

Complete the sentence.

1. 40,000 is 10 times as much as 4,000.

2. 90 is $\frac{1}{10}$ of ________.

3. 800 is 10 times as much as ________.

4. 5,000 is $\frac{1}{10}$ of ________.

Use place-value patterns to complete the table.

Number	10 times as much as	$\frac{1}{10}$ of
5. 100		
6. 7,000		
7. 300		
8. 80		

Number	10 times as much as	$\frac{1}{10}$ of
9. 2,000		
10. 900		
11. 60,000		
12. 500		

Problem Solving

13. The Eatery Restaurant has 200 tables. On a recent evening, there were reservations for $\frac{1}{10}$ of the tables. How many tables were reserved?

____

14. Mr. Wilson has $3,000 in his bank account. Ms. Nelson has 10 times as much money in her bank account as Mr. Wilson has in his bank account. How much money does Ms. Nelson have in her bank account?

____

Name ______________________________

Lesson 8

COMMON CORE STANDARD CC.5.NBT.1

Lesson Objective: Read and write whole numbers through hundred millions.

Place Value of Whole Numbers

You can use a place-value chart to help you understand whole numbers and the value of each digit. A **period** is a group of three digits within a number separated by a comma.

Millions Period			Thousands Period			Ones Period		
Hundreds	Tens	Ones	Hundreds	Tens	Ones	Hundreds	Tens	Ones
		2,	3	6	7,	0	8	9

Standard form: 2,367,089

Expanded Form: Multiply each digit by its place value, and then write an addition expression.

$(2 \times 1{,}000{,}000) + (3 \times 100{,}000) + (6 \times 10{,}000) + (7 \times 1{,}000) + (8 \times 10) + (9 \times 1)$

Word Form: Write the number in words. Notice that the millions and the thousands periods are followed by the period name and a comma.

two million, three hundred sixty-seven thousand, eighty-nine

To find the value of an underlined digit, multiply the digit by its place value. In <u>2</u>,367,089, the value of 2 is $2 \times 1{,}000{,}000$, or 2,000,000.

Write the value of the underlined digit.

1. <u>1</u>53,732,991

____

2. 2<u>3</u>6,143,802

____

3. 26<u>4</u>,807

____

4. 78,<u>2</u>09,146

____

Write the number in two other forms.

5. 701,245

____

____

6. 40,023,032

____

____

Name ____________________

Lesson 8

CC.5.NBT.1

Place Value of Whole Numbers

Write the value of the underlined digit.

1. $5{,}1\underline{6}5{,}874$

   60,000

2. $2\underline{8}1{,}480{,}100$

3. $7{,}\underline{2}70$

4. $8\underline{9}{,}170{,}326$

5. $\underline{7}{,}050{,}423$

6. $6\underline{4}6{,}950$

7. $37{,}\underline{1}23{,}745$

8. $\underline{3}15{,}421{,}732$

Write the number in two other forms.

9. 15,409

10. 100,203

11. 6,007,200

12. 32,005,008

Problem Solving REAL WORLD

13. The U.S. Census Bureau has a population clock on the Internet. On a recent day, the United States population was listed as 310,763,136. Write this number in word form.

14. In 2008, the population of 10- to 14-year-olds in the United States was 20,484,163. Write this number in expanded form.

COMMON CORE STANDARD CC.5.NBT.1

Lesson Objective: Model, read, and write decimals to thousandths.

Name ______________________________

Thousandths

Thousandths are smaller parts than hundredths. If one hundredth is divided into 10 equal parts, each part is one **thousandth**.

Write the decimal shown by the shaded parts of the model.

One column of the decimal model is shaded.
It represents one tenth, or 0.1.

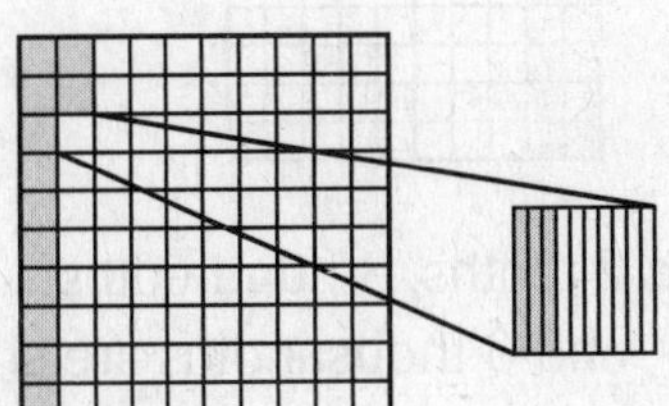

Two small squares of the decimal model are shaded.
They represent two hundredths, or 0.02.

A one-hundredth square is divided into 10 equal parts, or thousandths. Three columns of the thousandth square are shaded. They represent 0.003.

So, 0.123 of the decimal model is shaded.

The relationship of a digit in different place-value positions is the same for decimals as for whole numbers.

Write the decimals in a place-value chart.

Ones	•	Tenths	Hundredths	Thousandths
0	•	8		
0	•	0	8	
0	•	0	0	8

0.08 is $\frac{1}{10}$ of 0.8.

0.08 is 10 times as much as 0.008.

1. Write the decimal shown by the shaded parts of the model.

____

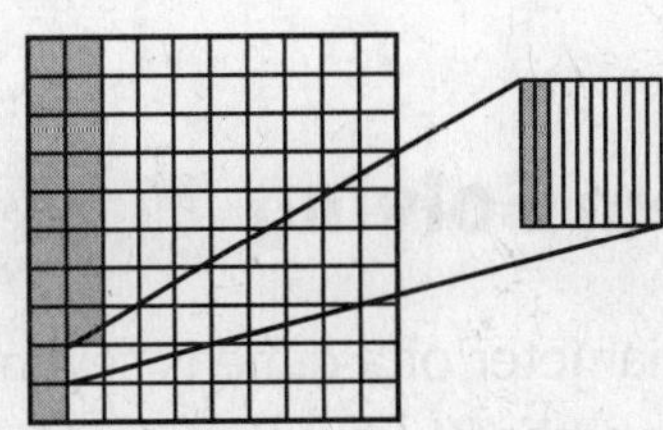

Use place-value patterns to complete the table.

Decimal	10 times as much as	$\frac{1}{10}$ of
2. 0.1		
3. 0.03		
4. 0.5		

Decimal	10 times as much as	$\frac{1}{10}$ of
5. 0.02		
6. 0.4		
7. 0.06		

Name ______________________________

Thousandths

Write the decimal shown by the shaded parts of each model.

1.

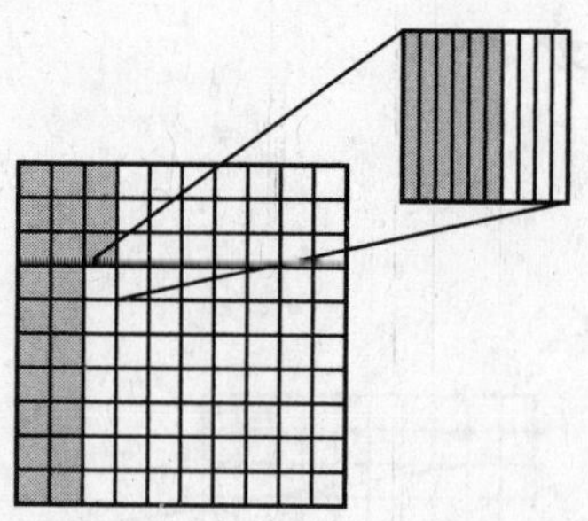

Think: 2 tenths, 3 hundredths, and 6 thousandths are shaded

2.

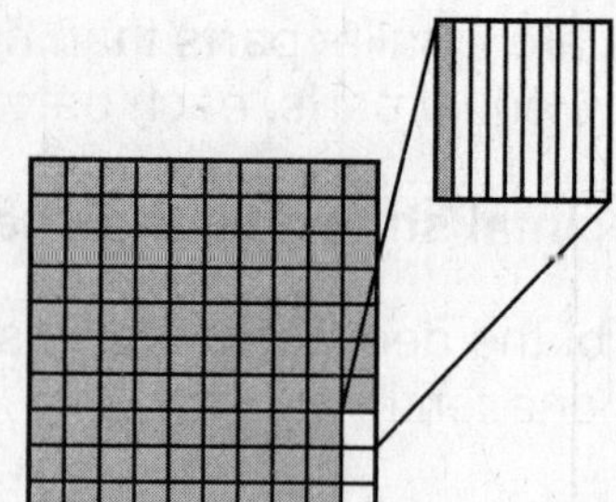

____

Complete the sentence.

3. 0.4 is 10 times as much as ____________.

4. 0.003 is $\frac{1}{10}$ of ____________.

Use place-value patterns to complete the table.

Decimal	10 times as much as	$\frac{1}{10}$ of
5. 0.1		
6. 0.09		
7. 0.04		
8. 0.6		

Decimal	10 times as much as	$\frac{1}{10}$ of
9. 0.08		
10. 0.2		
11. 0.5		
12. 0.03		

Problem Solving REAL WORLD

13. The diameter of a dime is seven hundred five thousandths of an inch. Complete the table by recording the diameter of a dime.

14. What is the value of the 5 in the diameter of a half dollar?

____

15. Which coins have a diameter with a 5 in the hundredths place?

____

U.S. Coins	
Coin	**Diameter (in inches)**
Penny	0.750
Nickel	0.835
Dime	
Quarter	0.955
Half dollar	1.205

Name ______________________

Lesson 10

COMMON CORE STANDARD CC.5.NBT.2

Lesson Objective: Write and evaluate repeated factors in exponent form.

Algebra • Powers of 10 and Exponents

You can represent repeated factors with a base and an exponent.

Write 10 × 10 × 10 × 10 × 10 × 10 in exponent form.

10 is the repeated factor, so 10 is the **base**.

The base is repeated 6 times, so 6 is the **exponent**.

$10 \times 10 \times 10 \times 10 \times 10 \times 10 = 10^6$

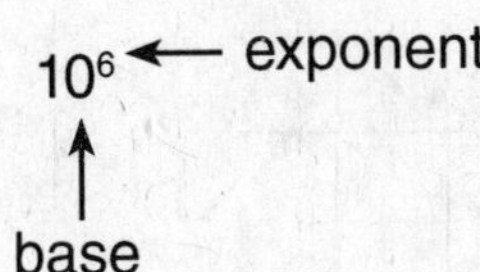

A base with an exponent can be written in words.

Write 10^6 in words.

The exponent 6 means "the sixth power."

10^6 in words is "the sixth power of ten."

You can read 10^2 in two ways: "ten squared" or "the second power of ten."

You can also read 10^3 in two ways: "ten cubed" or "the third power of ten."

Write in exponent form and in word form.

1. $10 \times 10 \times 10 \times 10 \times 10 \times 10 \times 10$

exponent form: ________ word form: ______________________

2. $10 \times 10 \times 10$

exponent form: ________ word form: ______________________

3. $10 \times 10 \times 10 \times 10 \times 10$

exponent form: ________ word form: ______________________

Find the value.

4. 10^4 **5.** 2×10^3 **6.** 6×10^2

______________ ______________ ______________

Name ______________________

Lesson 10
CC.5.NBT.2

Powers of 10 and Exponents

Write in exponent form and word form.

1. $10 \times 10 \times 10$

exponent form: 10^3

word form: the third power of ten

2. 10×10

exponent form: ______

word form: ______

3. $10 \times 10 \times 10 \times 10$

exponent form: ______

word form: ______

Find the value.

4. 10^3 ______

5. 4×10^2 ______

6. 9×10^4 ______

7. 10^1 ______

8. 10^5 ______

9. 5×10^1 ______

10. 7×10^3 ______

11. 8×10^0 ______

Problem Solving

12. The moon is about 240,000 miles from Earth. What is this distance written as a whole number multiplied by a power of ten?

______

13. The sun is about 93×10^6 miles from Earth. What is this distance written as a whole number?

______

Name ______________________________

Lesson 11

COMMON CORE STANDARD CC.5.NBT.2

Lesson Objective: Use a basic fact and a pattern to multiply mentally by multiples of 10, 100, and 1,000.

Algebra • Multiplication Patterns

You can use basic facts, patterns, and powers of 10 to help you multiply whole numbers by multiples of 10, 100, and 1,000.

Use mental math and a pattern to find 90 × 6,000.

- 9 × 6 is a basic fact. $9 \times 6 = 54$
- Use basic facts, patterns, and powers of 10 to find 90 × 6,000.

$$9 \times 60 = (9 \times 6) \times 10^1 = 54 \times 10^1 = 54 \times 10 = 540$$

$$9 \times 600 = (9 \times 6) \times 10^2 = 54 \times 10^2 = 54 \times 100 = 5{,}400$$

$$9 \times 6{,}000 = (9 \times 6) \times 10^3 = 54 \times 10^3 = 54 \times 1{,}000 = 54{,}000$$

$$90 \times 6{,}000 = (9 \times 6) \times (10 \times 1{,}000) = 54 \times 10^4 = 54 \times 10{,}000 = 540{,}000$$

So, 90 × 6,000 = 540,000.

Use mental math to complete the pattern.

1. $3 \times 1 = 3$

$3 \times 10^1 =$ ____________

$3 \times 10^2 =$ ____________

$3 \times 10^3 =$ ____________

2. $8 \times 2 = 16$

$(8 \times 2) \times 10^1 =$ ____________

$(8 \times 2) \times 10^2 =$ ____________

$(8 \times 2) \times 10^3 =$ ____________

3. $4 \times 5 = 20$

$(4 \times 5) \times$ ____________ $= 200$

$(4 \times 5) \times$ ____________ $= 2{,}000$

$(4 \times 5) \times$ ____________ $= 20{,}000$

4. $7 \times 6 =$ ____________

$(7 \times 6) \times$ ____________ $= 420$

$(7 \times 6) \times$ ____________ $= 4{,}200$

$(7 \times 6) \times$ ____________ $= 42{,}000$

Name ___________________________

Multiplication Patterns

Use mental math to complete the pattern.

1. $8 \times 3 = 24$
$(8 \times 3) \times 10^1 =$ 240
$(8 \times 3) \times 10^2 =$ 2,400
$(8 \times 3) \times 10^3 =$ 24,000

2. $5 \times 6 =$ ______
$(5 \times 6) \times 10^1 =$ ______
$(5 \times 6) \times 10^2 =$ ______
$(5 \times 6) \times 10^3 =$ ______

3. $3 \times$ ______ $= 27$
$(3 \times 9) \times 10^1 =$ ______
$(3 \times 9) \times 10^2 =$ ______
$(3 \times 9) \times 10^3 =$ ______

4. ______ $\times 4 = 28$
$(7 \times 4) \times$ ______ $= 280$
$(7 \times 4) \times$ ______ $= 2,800$
$(7 \times 4) \times$ ______ $= 28,000$

5. $6 \times 8 =$ ______
$(6 \times 8) \times 10^2 =$ ______
$(6 \times 8) \times 10^3 =$ ______
$(6 \times 8) \times 10^4 =$ ______

6. ______ $\times 4 = 16$
$(4 \times 4) \times 10^2 =$ ______
$(4 \times 4) \times 10^3 =$ ______
$(4 \times 4) \times 10^4 =$ ______

Use mental math and a pattern to find the product.

7. $(2 \times 9) \times 10^2 =$ ______

8. $(8 \times 7) \times 10^2 =$ ______

9. $(9 \times 6) \times 10^3 =$ ______

10. $(3 \times 7) \times 10^3 =$ ______

11. $(5 \times 9) \times 10^4 =$ ______

12. $(4 \times 8) \times 10^4 =$ ______

13. $(8 \times 8) \times 10^3 =$ ______

14. $(6 \times 4) \times 10^4 =$ ______

15. $(5 \times 5) \times 10^3 =$ ______

Problem Solving REAL WORLD

16. The Florida Everglades welcomes about 2×10^3 visitors per day. Based on this, about how many visitors come to the Everglades per week?

____

____

17. The average person loses about 8×10^1 strands of hair each day. About how many strands of hair would the average person lose in 9 days?

____

____

Name ______________________________

Lesson 12

COMMON CORE STANDARD CC.5.NBT.2

Lesson Objective: Find patterns in products when multiplying by powers of 10.

Algebra • Multiplication Patterns with Decimals

You can use patterns and place value to help you place the decimal point.

To multiply a number by a power of 10, you can use the exponent to determine how the position of the decimal point changes in the product.

	Exponent	**Move decimal point:**
$10^0 \times 5.18 =$ **5.18**	0	0 places to the right
$10^1 \times 5.18 =$ **51.8**	1	1 place to the right
$10^2 \times 5.18 =$ **518**	2	2 places to the right
$10^3 \times 5.18 =$ **5,180**	3	3 places to the right

You can use place-value patterns to find the product of a number and the decimals 0.1 and 0.01.

	Multiply by:	**Move decimal point:**
$1 \times 2{,}457 =$ **2,457**	1	0 places to the left
$0.1 \times 2{,}457 =$ **245.7**	0.1	1 place to the left
$0.01 \times 2{,}457 =$ **24.57**	0.01	2 places to the left

Complete the pattern.

1. $10^0 \times 25.89 =$ ________

$10^1 \times 25.89 =$ ________

$10^2 \times 25.89 =$ ________

$10^3 \times 25.89 =$ ________

2. $1 \times 182 =$ ________

$0.1 \times 182 =$ ________

$0.01 \times 182 =$ ________

Name ______________________

Lesson 12
CC.5.NBT.2

Multiplication Patterns with Decimals

Complete the pattern.

1. $2.07 \times 1 =$ 2.07
   $2.07 \times 10 =$ 20.7
   $2.07 \times 100 =$ 207
   $2.07 \times 1{,}000 =$ 2,070

2. $1 \times 30 =$ ________
   $0.1 \times 30 =$ ________
   $0.01 \times 30 =$ ________

3. $10^0 \times 0.23 =$ ________
   $10^1 \times 0.23 =$ ________
   $10^2 \times 0.23 =$ ________
   $10^3 \times 0.23 =$ ________

4. $390 \times 1 =$ ________
   $390 \times 0.1 =$ ________
   $390 \times 0.01 =$ ________

5. $10^0 \times 49.32 =$ ________
   $10^1 \times 49.32 =$ ________
   $10^2 \times 49.32 =$ ________
   $10^3 \times 49.32 =$ ________

6. $1 \times 9{,}670 =$ ________
   $0.1 \times 9{,}670 =$ ________
   $0.01 \times 9{,}670 =$ ________

7. $874 \times 1 =$ ________
   $874 \times 10 =$ ________
   $874 \times 100 =$ ________
   $874 \times 1{,}000 =$ ________

8. $10^0 \times 10 =$ ________
   $10^1 \times 10 =$ ________
   $10^2 \times 10 =$ ________
   $10^3 \times 10 =$ ________

9. $1 \times 5 =$ ________
   $0.1 \times 5 =$ ________
   $0.01 \times 5 =$ ________

Problem Solving REAL WORLD

10. Nathan plants equal-sized squares of sod in his front yard. Each square has an area of 6 square feet. Nathan plants a total of 1,000 squares in his yard. What is the total area of the squares of sod?

____

____

11. Three friends are selling items at a bake sale. May makes $23.25 selling bread. Inez sells gift baskets and makes 100 times as much as May. Carolyn sells pies and makes one tenth of the money Inez makes. How much money does each friend make?

____

____

Name ________________

COMMON CORE STANDARD CC.5.NBT.2

Lesson Objective: Find patterns in quotients when dividing by powers of 10.

Algebra • Division Patterns with Decimals

To divide a number by 10, 100, or 1,000, use the number of zeros in the divisor to determine how the position of the decimal point changes in the quotient.

	Number of zeros:	Move decimal point:
147 ÷ 1 = 147	0	0 places to the left
147 ÷ 10 = 14.7	1	1 place to the left
147 ÷ 100 = 1.47	2	2 places to the left
147 ÷ 1,000 = 0.147	3	3 places to the left

To divide a number by a power of 10, you can use the exponent to determine how the position of the decimal point changes in the quotient.

	Exponent	Move decimal point:
$97.2 \div 10^0 = 97.2$	0	0 places to the left
$97.2 \div 10^1 = 9.72$	1	1 place to the left
$97.2 \div 10^2 = 0.972$	2	2 places to the left

Complete the pattern.

1. $358 \div 10^0 =$ ________

$358 \div 10^1 =$ ________

$358 \div 10^2 =$ ________

$358 \div 10^3 =$ ________

2. $102 \div 10^0 =$ ________

$102 \div 10^1 =$ ________

$102 \div 10^2 =$ ________

$102 \div 10^3 =$ ________

3. 99.5 ÷ 1 = ________

99.5 ÷ 10 = ________

99.5 ÷ 100 = ________

Name ______________________

Lesson 13
CC.5.NBT.2

Division Patterns with Decimals

Complete the pattern.

1. $78.3 \div 1 =$ 78.3

$78.3 \div 10 =$ 7.83

$78.3 \div 100 =$ 0.783

2. $179 \div 10^0 =$ ______

$179 \div 10^1 =$ ______

$179 \div 10^2 =$ ______

$179 \div 10^3 =$ ______

3. $87.5 \div 10^0 =$ ______

$87.5 \div 10^1 =$ ______

$87.5 \div 10^2 =$ ______

4. $124 \div 1 =$ ______

$124 \div 10 =$ ______

$124 \div 100 =$ ______

$124 \div 1{,}000 =$ ______

5. $18 \div 1 =$ ______

$18 \div 10 =$ ______

$18 \div 100 =$ ______

$18 \div 1{,}000 =$ ______

6. $23 \div 10^0 =$ ______

$23 \div 10^1 =$ ______

$23 \div 10^2 =$ ______

$23 \div 10^3 =$ ______

7. $51.8 \div 1 =$ ______

$51.8 \div 10 =$ ______

$51.8 \div 100 =$ ______

8. $49.3 \div 10^0 =$ ______

$49.3 \div 10^1 =$ ______

$49.3 \div 10^2 =$ ______

9. $32.4 \div 10^0 =$ ______

$32.4 \div 10^1 =$ ______

$32.4 \div 10^2 =$ ______

Problem Solving

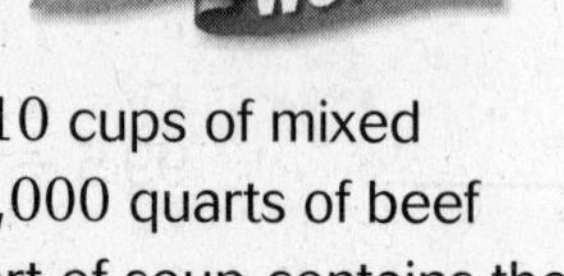

10. The local café uses 510 cups of mixed vegetables to make 1,000 quarts of beef barley soup. Each quart of soup contains the same amount of vegetables. How many cups of vegetables are in each quart of soup?

____

11. The same café uses 18.5 cups of flour to make 100 servings of pancakes. How many cups of flour are in one serving of pancakes?

____

Name ______________________________

Lesson 14

COMMON CORE STANDARD CC.5.NBT.3a

Lesson Objective: Read and write decimals through thousandths.

Place Value of Decimals

You can use a place-value chart to find the value of each digit in a decimal.
Write whole numbers to the left of the decimal point.
Write decimals to the right of the decimal point.

Ones	Tenths	Hundredths	Thousandths
3 •	8	4	7
3×1 •	$8 \times \frac{1}{10}$	$4 \times \frac{1}{100}$	$7 \times \frac{1}{1,000}$
3.0 •	0.8	0.04	0.007

Value

The place value of the digit 8 in 3.847 is tenths.

The value of 8 in 3.847 is $8 \times \frac{1}{10}$, or 0.8.

You can write a decimal in different forms.

Standard Form: 3.847

Expanded Form: $3 \times 1 + 8 \times \frac{1}{10} + 4 \times (\frac{1}{100}) + 7 \times (\frac{1}{1,000})$

When you write the decimal in word form, write "and" for the decimal point.

Word Form: three and eight hundred forty-seven thousandths

1. Complete the place-value chart to find the value of each digit.

Ones	Tenths	Hundredths	Thousandths
2 •	6	9	5
2×1 •		$9 \times \frac{1}{100}$	
	0.6		

Value

Write the value of the underlined digit.

2. 0.7<u>9</u>2 ______________

3. 4.<u>6</u>91 ______________

4. 3.80<u>5</u> ______________

Name ______________________

Place Value of Decimals

Lesson 14
CC.5.NBT.3a

Write the value of the underlined digit.

1. 0.2$\underline{8}$7

8 hundredths, or 0.08

2. 5.$\underline{3}$49

3. 2.70$\underline{4}$

4. 9.$\underline{1}$54

5. 4.00$\underline{6}$

6. 7.2$\underline{5}$8

7. 0.1$\underline{9}$8

8. 6.$\underline{8}$21

9. 8.02$\underline{7}$

Write the number in two other forms.

10. 0.326

11. 8.517

12. 0.924

13. 1.075

Problem Solving

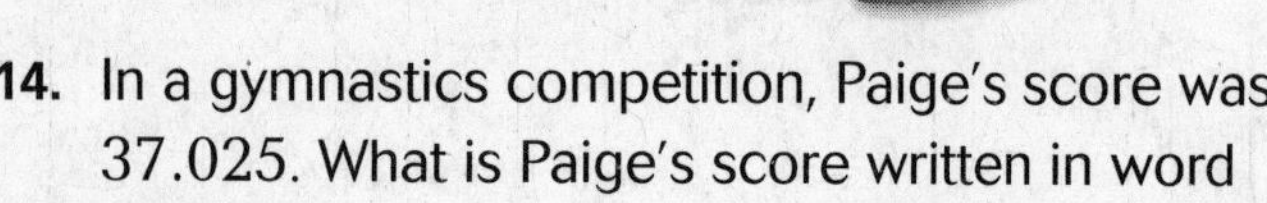

14. In a gymnastics competition, Paige's score was 37.025. What is Paige's score written in word form?

15. Jake's batting average for the softball season is 0.368. What is Jake's batting average written in expanded form?

Name ______________________________

Lesson 15

COMMON CORE STANDARD CC.5.NBT.3b

Lesson Objective: Compare and order decimals to thousandths using place value.

Compare and Order Decimals

You can use a place-value chart to compare decimals.

Compare. Write <, >, or =.

4.375 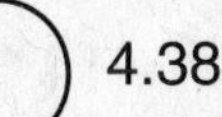 4.382

Write both numbers in a place-value chart. Then compare the digits, starting with the highest place value. Stop when the digits are different and compare.

Ones	Tenths	Hundredths	Thousandths
4 •	3	7	5
4 •	3	8	2

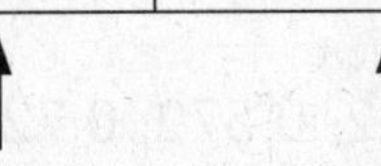

The ones digits are the same. The tenths digits are the same. The hundredths digits are different.

The digits are different in the hundredths place.

Since 7 hundredths < 8 hundredths, 4.375  4.382.

1. Use the place-value chart to compare the two numbers. What is the greatest place-value position where the digits differ?

Ones	Tenths	Hundredths	Thousandths
2 •	8	6	5
2 •	8	6	1

____

Compare. Write <, >, or =.

2. 5.37 ◯ 5.370

3. 9.425 ◯ 9.417

4. 7.684 ◯ 7.689

Name the greatest place-value position where the digits differ. Name the greater number.

5. 8.675; 8.654

____

____

6. 3.086; 3.194

____

____

7. 6.243; 6.247

____

____

Order from least to greatest.

8. 5.04; 5.4; 5.406; 5.064

____

9. 2.614; 2.146; 2.46; 2.164

____

Name ______________________________

Lesson 15
CC.5.NBT.3b

Compare and Order Decimals

Compare. Write <, >, or =.

1. 4.735 (<) 4.74
2. 2.549 ◯ 2.549
3. 3.207 ◯ 3.027
4. 8.25 ◯ 8.250
5. 5.871 ◯ 5.781
6. 9.36 ◯ 9.359
7. 1.538 ◯ 1.54
8. 7.036 ◯ 7.035
9. 6.700 ◯ 6.7

Order from greatest to least.

10. 3.008; 3.825; 3.09; 3.18

____

11. 0.275; 0.2; 0.572; 0.725

____

12. 6.318; 6.32; 6.230; 6.108

____

13. 0.456; 1.345; 0.645; 0.654

____

Algebra **Find the unknown digit to make each statement true.**

14. 2.48 > 2.4 ■ 1 > 2.463

____

15. 5.723 < 5.72 ■ < 5.725

____

16. 7.64 < 7. ■ 5 < 7.68

____

Problem Solving

17. The completion times for three runners in a 100-yard dash are 9.75 seconds, 9.7 seconds, and 9.675 seconds. Which is the winning time?

____

18. In a discus competition, an athlete threw the discus 63.37 meters, 62.95 meters, and 63.7 meters. Order the distances from least to greatest.

____

Name ____________________

Lesson 16

COMMON CORE STANDARD CC.5.NBT.4

Lesson Objective: Round decimals to any place.

Round Decimals

Rounding decimals is similar to rounding whole numbers.

Round 4.682 to the nearest tenth.

Step 1 Write 4.682 in a place-value chart.

Ones	• Tenths	Hundredths	Thousandths
4	• (6)	<u>8</u>	2

Step 2 Find the digit in the place to which you want to round. Circle that digit.

The digit __6__ is in the tenths place, so circle it.

Step 3 Underline the digit to the right of the circled digit.

The digit __8__ is to the right of the circled digit, so underline it.

Step 4 If the underlined digit is less than 5, the circled digit stays the same. If the underlined digit is 5 or greater, round up the circled digit.

__8__ > 5, so round 6 up to 7.

Step 5 After you round the circled digit, drop the digits to the right of the circled digit.

So, 4.682 rounded to the nearest tenth is __4.7__.

Write the place value of the underlined digit. Round each number to the place of the underlined digit.

1. 0.3<u>9</u>2

____

____

2. 5.<u>7</u>14

____

____

3. 1<u>6</u>.908

____

____

Name the place value to which each number was rounded.

4. 0.825 to 0.83

____

5. 3.815 to 4

____

6. 1.546 to 1.5

____

Name ______________________________

Lesson 16

CC.5.NBT.4

Round Decimals

Write the place value of the underlined digit. Round each number to the place of the underlined digit.

1. $0.\underline{7}82$

   tenths

   0.8

2. $\underline{4}.735$

3. $2.\underline{3}48$

4. $0.5\underline{0}6$

5. $15.\underline{1}86$

6. $8.4\underline{6}5$

Name the place value to which each number was rounded.

7. 0.546 to 0.55

8. 4.805 to 4.8

9. 6.493 to 6

10. 1.974 to 2.0

11. 7.709 to 8

12. 14.637 to 15

Round 7.954 to the place named.

13. tenths

14. hundredths

15. ones

Round 18.194 to the place named.

16. tenths

17. hundredths

18. ones

Problem Solving REAL WORLD

19. The population density of Montana is 6.699 people per square mile. What is the population density per square mile of Montana rounded to the nearest whole number?

20. Alex's batting average is 0.346. What is his batting average rounded to the nearest hundredth?

Name ______________________________

Lesson 17

COMMON CORE STANDARD CC.5.NBT.5

Lesson Objective: Multiply by 1-digit numbers.

Multiply by 1-Digit Numbers

You can use place value to help you multiply by 1-digit numbers.

Estimate. Then find the product. 378 × 6

Estimate: 400 × 6 = 2,400

Step 1 Multiply the ones.

	Thousands	Hundreds	Tens	Ones
		3	[4] 7	**8**
×				**6**
				8

Step 2 Multiply the tens.

	Thousands	Hundreds	Tens	Ones
		[4] 3	[4] **7**	8
×				6
			6	8

Step 3 Multiply the hundreds.

	Thousands	Hundreds	Tens	Ones
		[4] **3**	[4] 7	8
×				6
	2,	**2**	6	8

So, 378 × 6 = 2,268.

Complete to find the product.

1. 7 × 472 Estimate: 7 × ________ = ________

Multiply the ones.

```
  472
×   7
-----
```

Multiply the tens.

```
    1
  472
×   7
-----
```

Multiply the hundreds.

```
   51
  472
×   7
-----
```

Estimate. Then find the product.

2. Estimate: ________

```
  863
×   8
-----
```

3. Estimate: ________

```
  809
×   8
-----
```

4. Estimate: ________

```
  932
×   7
-----
```

5. Estimate: ________

```
  2,767
×     7
-------
```

Name ______________________________

Lesson 17
CC.5.NBT.5

Multiply by 1-Digit Numbers

Estimate. Then find the product.

1. Estimate: 3,600

$$\begin{array}{r} {}^{1\,5} \\ 416 \\ \times\ \ 9 \\ \hline 3{,}744 \end{array}$$

2. Estimate: ________

$$\begin{array}{r} 1{,}374 \\ \times\ \ 6 \\ \hline \end{array}$$

3. Estimate: ________

$$\begin{array}{r} 726 \\ \times\ \ 5 \\ \hline \end{array}$$

4. Estimate: ________

$$\begin{array}{r} 872 \\ \times\ \ 3 \\ \hline \end{array}$$

5. Estimate: ________

$$\begin{array}{r} 2{,}308 \\ \times\ \ 9 \\ \hline \end{array}$$

6. Estimate: ________

$$\begin{array}{r} 1{,}564 \\ \times\ \ 5 \\ \hline \end{array}$$

Estimate. Then find the product.

7. 4×979

8. 503×7

9. $5 \times 4{,}257$

10. $6{,}018 \times 9$

11. 758×6

12. 3×697

13. $2{,}141 \times 8$

14. $7 \times 7{,}956$

Problem Solving REAL WORLD

15. Mr. and Mrs. Dorsey and their three children are flying to Springfield. The cost of each ticket is $179. Estimate how much the tickets will cost. Then find the exact cost of the tickets.

____

____

____

16. Ms. Tao flies roundtrip twice yearly between Jacksonville and Los Angeles on business. The distance between the two cities is 2,150 miles. Estimate the distance she flies for both trips. Then find the exact distance.

____

____

____

Name ______________________

COMMON CORE STANDARD CC.5.NBT.5
Lesson Objective: Multiply by 2-digit numbers.

Multiply by 2-Digit Numbers

You can use place value and regrouping to multiply.

Find 29 × 63.

Step 1 Write the problem vertically.
Multiply by the ones.

```
   2
  63
× 29
 567 ← 63 × 9 = (60 × 9) + (3 × 9)
              = 540 + 27, or 567
```

Step 2 Multiply by the tens.

```
   2̸
   63
 × 29
  567
1,260 ← 63 × 20 = (60 × 20) + (3 × 20)
                = 1,200 + 60, or 1,260
```

Step 3 Add the partial products.

```
     63
   × 29
    567
+ 1,260
  1,827
```

So, 63 × 29 = 1,827.

Complete to find the product.

1.

```
  57
× 14
     ← 57 × ____
+    ← 57 × ____
```

2.

```
  76
× 45
     ← 76 × ____
+    ← 76 × ____
```

3.

```
 139
× 12
     ← 139 × ____
+    ← 139 × ____
```

4. Find 26 × 69. Estimate first.

```
  69
× 26
```

Estimate: __________

Name

Multiply by 2-Digit Numbers

Estimate. Then find the product.

1. Estimate: 4,000

$$\begin{array}{r} 82 \\ \times\ 49 \\ \hline 738 \\ +\ 3280 \\ \hline 4{,}018 \end{array}$$

2. Estimate: ____

$$\begin{array}{r} 92 \\ \times\ 68 \\ \hline \end{array}$$

3. Estimate: ____

$$\begin{array}{r} 396 \\ \times\ 37 \\ \hline \end{array}$$

4. 23×67

5. 86×33

6. 78×71

7. 309×29

8. 612×87

9. 476×72

Problem Solving REAL WORLD

10. A company shipped 48 boxes of canned dog food. Each box contains 24 cans. How many cans of dog food did the company ship in all?

11. There were 135 cars in a rally. Each driver paid a $25 fee to participate in the rally. How much money did the drivers pay in all?

Name ____________________

Lesson 19

COMMON CORE STANDARD CC.5.NBT.6

Lesson Objective: Use properties of operations to solve problems.

Algebra • Properties

Properties of operations are characteristics of the operations that are always true.

Property	Examples
Commutative Property of Addition or Multiplication	Addition: $3 + 4 = 4 + 3$ Multiplication: $8 \times 2 = 2 \times 8$
Associative Property of Addition or Multiplication	Addition: $(1 + 2) + 3 = 1 + (2 + 3)$ Multiplication: $6 \times (7 \times 2) = (6 \times 7) \times 2$
Distributive Property	$8 \times (2 + 3) = (8 \times 2) + (8 \times 3)$
Identity Property of Addition	$9 + 0 = 9$ $0 + 3 = 3$
Identity Property of Multiplication	$54 \times 1 = 54$ $1 \times 16 = 16$

Use properties to find 37 + 24 + 43.

$37 + 24 + 43 = 24 + \underline{37} + 43$ Use the Commutative Property of Addition to reorder the addends.

$= 24 + (37 + 43)$ Use the Associative Property of Addition to group the addends.

$= 24 + \underline{80}$ Use mental math to add.

$= \underline{104}$

Grouping 37 and 43 makes the problem easier to solve because their sum, 80, is a multiple of 10.

Use properties to find the sum or product.

1. $31 + 27 + 29$ ________

2. $41 \times 0 \times 3$ ________

3. $4 + (6 + 21)$ ________

Complete the equation, and tell which property you used.

4. $(2 \times \_\_\_) + (2 \times 2) = 2 \times (5 + 2)$

____

____

5. $\_\_\_ \times 1 = 15$

____

____

Name ______________________

Properties

Use properties to find the sum or product.

1. 6×89
   $6 \times (90 - 1)$
   $(6 \times 90) - (6 \times 1)$
   $540 - 6$
   534

2. $93 + (68 + 7)$

   ______

3. $5 \times 23 \times 2$

   ______

4. 8×51

   ______

5. $34 + 0 + 18 + 26$

   ______

6. 6×107

   ______

Complete the equation, and tell which property you used.

7. $(3 \times 10) \times 8 =$ ______ $\times (10 \times 8)$

   ______

8. $16 + 31 = 31 +$ ______

   ______

9. $0 +$ ______ $= 91$

   ______

10. $21 \times$ ______ $= 9 \times 21$

   ______

Problem Solving REAL WORLD

11. The Metro Theater has 20 rows of seats with 18 seats in each row. Tickets cost $5. The theater's income in dollars if all seats are sold is $(20 \times 18) \times 5$. Use properties to find the total income.

   ______

12. The numbers of students in the four sixth-grade classes at Northside School are 26, 19, 34, and 21. Use properties to find the total number of students in the four classes.

   ______

Name ______________________________

COMMON CORE STANDARD CC.5.NBT.6

Lesson Objective: Use multiplication to solve division problems.

Relate Multiplication to Division

Use the Distributive Property to find the quotient of 56 ÷ 4.

Step 1
Write a related multiplication sentence for the division problem.

$56 \div 4 = \square$

$4 \times \square = 56$

Step 2
Use the Distributive Property to break apart the product into lesser numbers that are multiples of the divisor in the division problem. Use a multiple of 10 for one of the multiples.

$(40 + 16) = 56$

$(4 \times \mathbf{10}) + (4 \times \mathbf{4}) = 56$

$4 \times (\mathbf{10} + \mathbf{4}) = 56$

Step 3
To find the unknown factor, find the sum of the numbers inside the parentheses.

$10 + 4 = 14$

Step 4
Write the multiplication sentence with the unknown factor you found. Then, use the multiplication sentence to complete the division sentence.

$4 \times \mathbf{14} = 56$

$56 \div 4 = \mathbf{14}$

Use multiplication and the Distributive Property to find the quotient.

1. $68 \div 4 =$ ______

____

____

2. $75 \div 3 =$ ______

____

____

3. $96 \div 6 =$ ______

____

____

4. $80 \div 5 =$ ______

____

____

5. $54 \div 3 =$ ______

____

____

6. $105 \div 7 =$ ______

____

____

Name ______________________

Relate Multiplication to Division

Lesson **20**
CC.5.NBT.6

Use multiplication and the Distributive Property to find the quotient.

1. $70 \div 5 =$ **14**

$(5 \times 10) + (5 \times 4) = 70$

$5 \times 14 = 70$

2. $96 \div 6 =$ ______

3. $85 \div 5 =$ ______

4. $84 \div 6 =$ ______

5. $168 \div 7 =$ ______

6. $104 \div 4 =$ ______

7. $171 \div 9 =$ ______

8. $102 \div 6 =$ ______

9. $210 \div 5 =$ ______

Problem Solving REAL WORLD

10. Ken is making gift bags for a party. He has 64 colored pens and wants to put the same number in each bag. How many bags will Ken make if he puts 4 pens in each bag?

11. Maritza is buying wheels for her skateboard shop. She ordered a total of 92 wheels. If wheels come in packages of 4, how many packages will she receive?

Name ______________________________

COMMON CORE STANDARD CC.5.NBT.6

Lesson Objective: Use the strategy *solve a simpler problem* to solve problems.

Problem Solving • Multiplication and Division

In Brett's town, there are 128 baseball players on 8 different teams. Each team has an equal number of players. How many players are on each team?

Read the Problem	Solve the Problem
What do I need to find? I need to find **how many players are on each team in Brett's town**. **What information do I need to use?** There are **8 teams** with a total of **128 players**. **How will I use the information?** I can **divide** the total number of players by the number of teams. I can use a simpler problem to **divide**.	• First, I use the total number of players. **128 players** • To find the number of players on each team, I will need to solve this problem. 128 ÷ 8 = ___?___ • To find the quotient, I break 128 into two simpler numbers that are easier to divide. 128 ÷ 8 = (80 + **48**) ÷ 8 = (**80** ÷ 8) + (**48** ÷ 8) = **10** + 6 = **16** So, there are **16** players on each team.

1. Susan makes clay pots. She sells 125 pots per month to 5 stores. Each store buys the same number of pots. How many pots does each store buy?

125 ÷ 5 = (100 + ______) ÷ 5

= (100 ÷ 5) + (______ ÷ 5)

= ______ + 5

= ______

____

2. Lou grows 112 rosemary plants. He ships an equal number of plants to customers in 8 states. How many rosemary plants does he ship to each customer?

112 ÷ 8 = (80 + ______) ÷ 8

= (______ ÷ 8) + (______ ÷ 8)

= ______ + 4

= ______

____

Name ______________________

Lesson 21

CC.5.NBT.6

Problem Solving • Multiplication and Division

Solve the problems below. Show your work.

1. Dani is making punch for a family picnic. She adds 16 fluid ounces of orange juice, 16 fluid ounces of lemon juice, and 8 fluid ounces of lime juice to 64 fluid ounces of water. How many 8-ounce glasses of punch can she fill?

$$104 \div 8 = (40 + 64) \div 8$$
$$= (40 \div 8) + (64 \div 8)$$
$$= 5 + 8, \text{ or } 13$$

$16 + 16 + 8 + 64 = 104$ fluid ounces

13 glasses

2. Ryan has nine 14-ounce bags of popcorn to repackage and sell at the school fair. A small bag holds 3 ounces. How many small bags can he make?

____

3. Bianca is making scarves to sell. She has 33 pieces of blue fabric, 37 pieces of green fabric, and 41 pieces of red fabric. Suppose Bianca uses 3 pieces of fabric to make 1 scarf. How many scarves can she make?

____

4. Jasmine has 8 packs of candle wax to make scented candles. Each pack contains 14 ounces of wax. Jasmine uses 7 ounces of wax to make one candle. How many candles can she make?

____

5. Maurice puts 130 trading cards in protector sheets. He fills 7 sheets and puts the remaining 4 cards in an eighth sheet. Each of the filled sheets has the same number of cards. How many cards are in each filled sheet?

____

Name ______________________________

Lesson 22

COMMON CORE STANDARD CC.5.NBT.6

Lesson Objective: Place the first digit in the quotient by estimating or using place value.

Place the First Digit

When you divide, you can use estimation or place value to place the first digit of the quotient.

Divide.

6)1,266

- Estimate. 1,200 ÷ 6 = 200, so the first digit of the quotient is in the hundreds place.
- Divide the hundreds.
- Divide the tens.
- Divide the ones.

So, 1,266 ÷ 6 = 211.

Since 211 is close to the estimate, 200, the answer is reasonable.

```
    211
 6)1,266
  -12
    06
    -6
     06
     -6
      0
```

Divide.

8,895 ÷ 8

- Use place value to place the first digit.
- Look at the first digit.
  If the first digit is less than the divisor, then the first digit of the quotient will be in the hundreds place.
  If the first digit is greater than or equal to the divisor, then the first digit of the quotient will be in the thousands place.
- Since 8 thousands can be shared among 8 groups, the first digit of the quotient will be in the thousands place. Now divide.

So, 8,895 ÷ 8 is 1,111 r7.

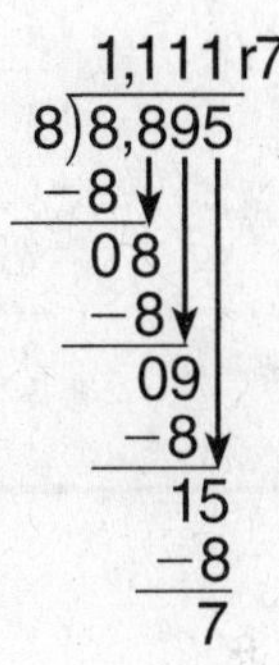

```
  1,111 r7
 8)8,895
  -8
   08
   -8
    09
    -8
     15
     -8
      7
```

Divide.

1. 3)627 **2.** 5)7,433 **3.** 4)5,367 **4.** 9)6,470

5. 8)2,869 **6.** 6)1,299 **7.** 4)893 **8.** 7)4,418

Name ______________________

Place the First Digit

Lesson 22
CC.5.NBT.6

Divide.

1. $4\overline{)388}$

$$\begin{array}{r} 97 \\ 4\overline{)\;388} \\ -36 \\ \hline 28 \\ -28 \\ \hline 0 \end{array}$$

97

2. $4\overline{)457}$

3. $8\overline{)712}$

4. $9\overline{)204}$

5. $2,117 \div 3$

6. $520 \div 8$

7. $1,812 \div 4$

8. $3,476 \div 6$

Problem Solving REAL WORLD

9. The school theater department made \$2,142 on ticket sales for the three nights of their play. The department sold the same number of tickets each night and each ticket cost \$7. How many tickets did the theater department sell each night?

10. Andreus made \$625 mowing yards. He worked for 5 consecutive days and earned the same amount of money each day. How much money did Andreus earn per day?

Name ______________________________

Lesson 23

COMMON CORE STANDARD CC.5.NBT.6

Lesson Objective: Divide 3- and 4-digit dividends by 1-digit divisors.

Divide by 1-Digit Divisors

You can use compatible numbers to help you place the first digit in the quotient. Then you can divide and check your answer.

Divide. $4\overline{)757}$

Step 1 Estimate with compatible numbers to decide where to place the first digit.

757 ÷ 4
↓
800 ÷ 4 = 200

The first digit of the quotient is in the hundreds place.

Step 2 Divide.

$$\begin{array}{r} 189 \text{ r1} \\ 4\overline{)757} \\ -4 \\ \hline 35 \\ -32 \\ \hline 37 \\ -36 \\ \hline 1 \end{array}$$

Step 3 Check your answer.

$$\begin{array}{rl} 189 & \leftarrow \text{quotient} \\ \times\ 4 & \leftarrow \text{divisor} \\ \hline 756 & \\ +\ \ 1 & \leftarrow \text{remainder} \\ \hline 757 & \leftarrow \text{dividend} \end{array}$$

Since 189 is close to the estimate of 200, the answer is reasonable.

So, 757 ÷ 4 is 189 r1.

Divide. Check your answer.

1. $8\overline{)136}$

2. $7\overline{)297}$

3. $5\overline{)8{,}126}$

4. $7\overline{)4{,}973}$

5. $3\overline{)741}$

6. $7\overline{)456}$

Name ______________________________

Divide by 1-Digit Divisors

Divide.

1. $4\overline{)724}$

$$\begin{array}{r} 181 \\ 4\overline{)724} \\ -4 \\ \hline 32 \\ -32 \\ \hline 04 \\ -4 \\ \hline 0 \end{array}$$

181

2. $5\overline{)312}$

3. $278 \div 2$

4. $336 \div 7$

Find the value of *n* in each equation. Write what *n* represents in the related division problem.

5. $n = 3 \times 45$

6. $643 = 4 \times 160 + n$

7. $n = 6 \times 35 + 4$

Problem Solving REAL WORLD

8. Randy has 128 ounces of dog food. He feeds his dog 8 ounces of food each day. How many days will the dog food last?

9. Angelina bought a 64-ounce can of lemonade mix. She uses 4 ounces of mix for each pitcher of lemonade. How many pitchers of lemonade can Angelina make from the can of mix?

Name ______________________

Lesson 24

COMMON CORE STANDARD CC.5.NBT.6

Lesson Objective: Model division with 2-digit divisors using base-ten blocks.

Division with 2-Digit Divisors

You can use base-ten blocks to model division with 2-digit divisors.

Divide. 154 ÷ 11

Step 1 Model 154 with base-ten blocks.

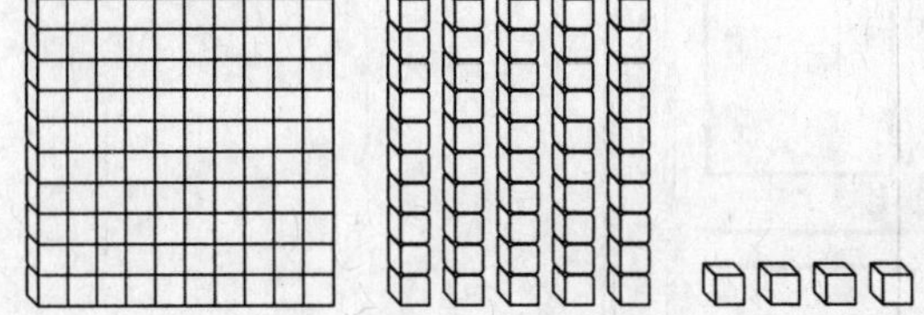

Step 2 Make equal groups of 11. Each group should contain __1__ ten and __1__ one.

You can make 4 groups of 11 without regrouping.

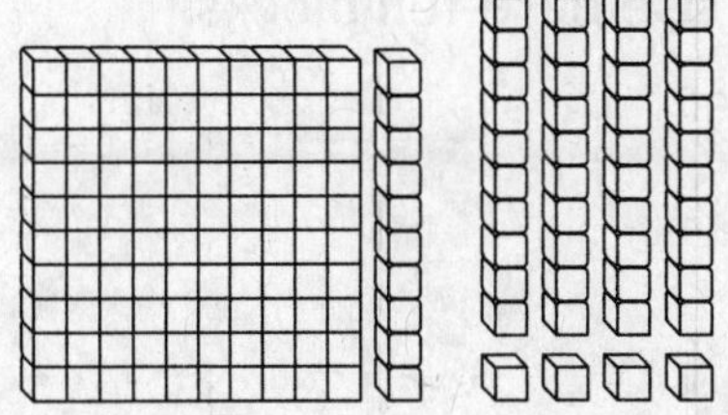

Step 3 Regroup 1 hundred as __10 tens__.

Regroup 1 ten as __10 ones__.

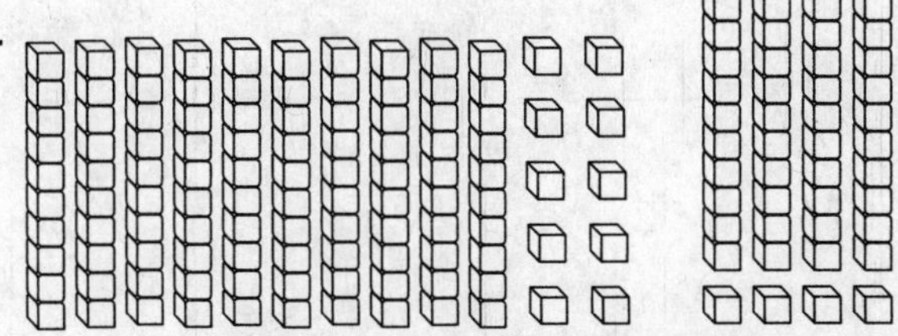

Step 4 Use the regrouped blocks to make as many groups of 11 as possible. Then count the total number of groups.

There are __14__ groups. So, 154 ÷ 11 = __14__.

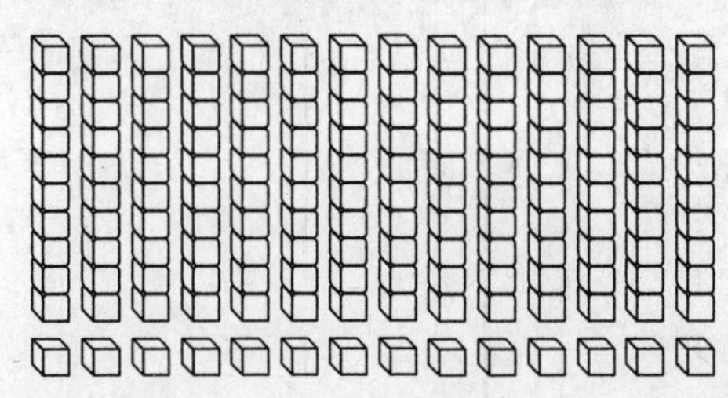

Divide. Use base-ten blocks.

1. 192 ÷ 12 ______

2. 182 ÷ 14 ______

Name ______

Division with 2-Digit Divisors

Use the quick picture to divide.

1. 132 ÷ 12 = 11

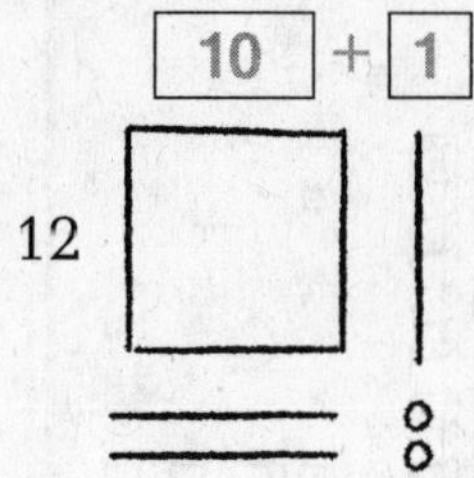

2. 168 ÷ 14 = ______

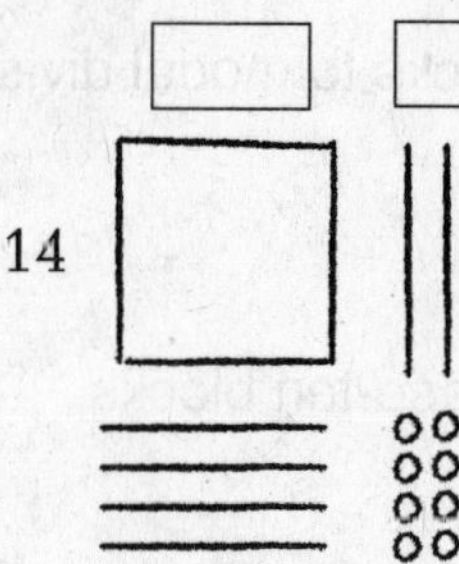

Divide. Use base-ten blocks.

3. 195 ÷ 13 = ______
4. 143 ÷ 11 = ______
5. 165 ÷ 15 = ______

Divide. Draw a quick picture.

6. 192 ÷ 16 = ______
7. 169 ÷ 13 = ______

Problem Solving REAL WORLD

8. There are 182 seats in a theater. The seats are evenly divided into 13 rows. How many seats are in each row?

9. There are 156 students at summer camp. The camp has 13 cabins. An equal number of students sleep in each cabin. How many students sleep in each cabin?

Name ______________________________

Lesson 25

COMMON CORE STANDARD CC.5.NBT.6

Lesson Objective: Use partial quotients to divide by 2-digit divisors.

Partial Quotients

Divide. Use partial quotients.

858 ÷ 57

		Quotient
Step 1 Estimate the number of groups of 57 that are in 858. You know 57 × 10 = 570. Since 570 < 858, at least 10 groups of 57 are in 858. Write 10 in the quotient column, because 10 groups of the divisor, 57, are in the dividend, 858.	858 −570 288	10
Step 2 Now estimate the number of groups of 57 that are in 288. You know 60 × 4 = 240. So at least 4 groups of 57 are in 288. Subtract 228 from 288, because 57 × 4 = 228. Write 4 in the quotient column, because 4 groups of the divisor, 57, are in 288.	288 −228 60	4
Step 3 Identify the number of groups of 57 that are in 60. 57 × 1 = 57, so there is 1 group of 57 in 60. Write 1 in the quotient column.	60 −57 remainder → 3	+ 1 15
Step 4 Find the total number of groups of the divisor, 57, that are in the dividend, 858, by adding the numbers in the quotient column. Include the remainder in your answer.		**Answer:** 15 r3

Divide. Use partial quotients.

1. $17\overline{)476}$

2. $14\overline{)365}$

3. $25\overline{)753}$

4. 462 ÷ 11

5. 1,913 ÷ 47

6. 1,085 ÷ 32

Name ________________________

Partial Quotients

Divide. Use partial quotients.

1. $18\overline{)236}$

$$\begin{array}{rll} 18\overline{)236} & & \\ -180 & \leftarrow 10 \times 18 & 10 \\ 56 & & \\ -36 & \leftarrow 2 \times 18 & 2 \\ 20 & & \\ -18 & \leftarrow 1 \times 18 & +1 \\ 2 & & 13 \end{array}$$

236 ÷ 18 is 13 r2.

2. $36\overline{)540}$

3. $27\overline{)624}$

4. 478 ÷ 16

5. 418 ÷ 22

6. 625 ÷ 25

7. 514 ÷ 28

8. 322 ÷ 14

9. 715 ÷ 25

Problem Solving REAL WORLD

10. A factory processes 1,560 ounces of olive oil per hour. The oil is packaged into 24-ounce bottles. How many bottles does the factory fill in one hour?

____

11. A pond at a hotel holds 4,290 gallons of water. The groundskeeper drains the pond at a rate of 78 gallons of water per hour. How long will it take to drain the pond?

____

Name ________________________

Lesson 26

COMMON CORE STANDARD CC.5.NBT.6

Lesson Objective: Estimate quotients using compatible numbers.

Estimate with 2-Digit Divisors

You can use *compatible numbers* to estimate quotients. Compatible numbers are numbers that are easy to compute with mentally.

To find two estimates with compatible numbers, first round the divisor. Then list multiples of the rounded divisor until you find the two multiples that are closest to the dividend. Use the one less than and the one greater than the dividend.

Use compatible numbers to find two estimates. 4,125 ÷ 49

Step 1 Round the divisor to the nearest ten.
49 rounds to 50.

Step 2 List multiples of 50 until you get the two closest to the dividend, 4,125.
Some multiples of 50 are:
500 1,000 1,500 2,000 2,500 3,000 3,500 4,000 4,500
4,000 and 4,500 are closest to the dividend.

Step 3 Divide the compatible numbers to estimate the quotient.
4,000 ÷ 50 = 80 4,500 ÷ 50 = 90

The more reasonable estimate is 4,000 ÷ 50 = 80, because 4,000 is closer to 4,125 than 4,500 is.

Use compatible numbers to find two estimates.

1. $42\overline{)1,578}$

2. $73\overline{)4,858}$

3. $54\overline{)343}$

4. 4,093 ÷ 63

5. 4,785 ÷ 79

6. 7,459 ÷ 94

Use compatible numbers to estimate the quotient.

7. 847 ÷ 37

8. 6,577 ÷ 89

9. 218 ÷ 29

Name ______________________________

Lesson 26

CC.5.NBT.6

Estimate with 2-Digit Divisors

Use compatible numbers to find two estimates.

1. $18\overline{)1,322}$

$1,200 \div 20 = 60$

$1,400 \div 20 = 70$

2. $17\overline{)1,569}$

3. $27\overline{)735}$

4. $12\overline{)478}$

5. $336 \div 12$

6. $1,418 \div 22$

7. $16\overline{)2,028}$

8. $2,242 \div 33$

Use compatible numbers to estimate the quotient.

9. $82\overline{)5,514}$

10. $61\overline{)5,320}$

11. $28\overline{)776}$

12. $23\overline{)1,624}$

Problem Solving REAL WORLD

13. A cubic yard of topsoil weighs 4,128 pounds. About how many 50-pound bags of topsoil can you fill with one cubic yard of topsoil?

____

14. An electronics store places an order for 2,665 USB flash drives. One shipping box holds 36 flash drives. About how many boxes will it take to hold all the flash drives?

____

Name ______________________

Divide by 2-Digit Divisors

When you divide by a 2-digit divisor, you can use estimation to help you place the first digit in the quotient. Then you can divide.

Divide. $53\overline{)2{,}369}$

Step 1 Use compatible numbers to estimate the quotient. Then use the estimate to place the first digit in the quotient.

$$\begin{array}{r} 40 \\ 50\overline{)2{,}000} \end{array}$$

The first digit will be in the tens place.

Step 2 Divide the tens.

$$\begin{array}{r} 4 \\ 53\overline{)2{,}369} \\ -\,212 \\ \hline 24 \end{array}$$

Think:

Divide: 236 tens ÷ 53

Multiply: 53 × 4 tens = 212 tens

Subtract: 236 tens − 212 tens

Compare: 24 < 53, so the first digit of the quotient is reasonable.

Step 3 Bring down the 9 ones. Then divide the ones.

$$\begin{array}{r} 44 \text{ r}37 \\ 53\overline{)2{,}369} \\ -\,212\downarrow \\ \hline 249 \\ -\,212 \\ \hline 37 \end{array}$$

Think:

Divide: 249 ones ÷ 53

Multiply: 53 × 4 ones = 212 ones

Subtract: 249 ones − 212 ones

Compare: 37 < 53, so the second digit of the quotient is reasonable.

Write the remainder to the right of the whole number part of the quotient.

So, 2,369 ÷ 53 is 44 r37.

Divide. Check your answer.

1. $52\overline{)612}$ **2.** $63\overline{)917}$ **3.** $89\overline{)1{,}597}$

4. $43\overline{)641}$ **5.** $27\overline{)4{,}684}$ **6.** $64\overline{)8{,}455}$

Name ______________________________

Divide by 2-Digit Divisors

Lesson 27
CC.5.NBT.6

Divide. Check your answer.

1. 385 ÷ 12

$$\begin{array}{r} 32 \text{ r1} \\ 12\overline{)385} \\ -36 \\ \hline 25 \\ -24 \\ \hline 1 \end{array}$$

2. 837 ÷ 36

3. 1,650 ÷ 55

4. 5,634 ÷ 18

5. 7,231 ÷ 24

6. 5,309 ÷ 43

7. $37\overline{)3,774}$

8. $54\overline{)1,099}$

9. $28\overline{)6,440}$

10. $52\overline{)5,256}$

11. $85\overline{)1,955}$

12. $46\overline{)5,624}$

Problem Solving REAL WORLD

13. The factory workers make 756 machine parts in 36 hours. Suppose the workers make the same number of machine parts each hour. How many machine parts do they make each hour?

____

14. One bag holds 12 bolts. Several bags filled with bolts are packed into a box and shipped to the factory. The box contains a total of 2,760 bolts. How many bags of bolts are in the box?

____

Name ______________________________

COMMON CORE STANDARD CC.5.NBT.6

Lesson Objective: Adjust the quotient if the estimate is too high or too low.

Adjust Quotients

When you divide, you can use the first digit of your estimate as the first digit of your quotient. Sometimes the first digit will be too high or too low. Then you have to adjust the quotient by increasing or decreasing the first digit.

Estimate Too High		**Estimate Too Low**	
Divide. 271 ÷ 48		**Divide.** 2,462 ÷ 27	
Estimate. 300 ÷ 50 = 6		**Estimate.** 2,400 ÷ 30 = 80	
Try 6 ones. $\begin{array}{r} 6 \\ 48\overline{)271} \\ -\ 288 \end{array}$ You cannot subtract 288 from 271. So, the estimate is too high.	Try 5 ones. $\begin{array}{r} 5\text{ r}31 \\ 48\overline{)271} \\ -\ 240 \\ \hline 31 \end{array}$ So, 271 ÷ 48 is 5 r31.	Try 8 tens. $\begin{array}{r} 8 \\ 27\overline{)2,462} \\ -\ 2\ 16 \\ \hline 30 \end{array}$ 30 is greater than the divisor. So, the estimate is too low.	Try 9 tens. $\begin{array}{r} 91\text{ r}5 \\ 27\overline{)2,462} \\ -\ 2\ 43 \\ \hline 32 \\ -\ 27 \\ \hline 5 \end{array}$ So, 2,462 ÷ 27 is 91 r5.

Adjust the estimated digit in the quotient, if needed. Then divide.

1. $\begin{array}{r} 2 \\ 58\overline{)1,325} \end{array}$

2. $\begin{array}{r} 6 \\ 37\overline{)241} \end{array}$

3. $\begin{array}{r} 8 \\ 29\overline{)2,276} \end{array}$

Divide.

4. $16\overline{)845}$

5. $24\overline{)217}$

6. $37\overline{)4,819}$

Name ____________________

Adjust Quotients

Lesson 28
CC.5.NBT.6

Adjust the estimated digit in the quotient, if needed. Then divide.

1. $16\overline{)976}$ (estimated digit 5)
   -80
   17

   $16\overline{)976}$ = 61
   -96
   16
   -16
   0

2. $24\overline{)689}$ (estimated digit 3)

3. $65\overline{)2,210}$ (estimated digit 3)

4. $38\overline{)7,035}$ (estimated digit 2)

Divide.

5. $2,961 \div 47$

6. $2,072 \div 86$

7. $1,280 \div 25$

8. $31\overline{)1,496}$

9. $86\overline{)6,290}$

10. $95\overline{)4,000}$

11. $44\overline{)2,910}$

12. $82\overline{)4,018}$

Problem Solving

13. A copier prints 89 copies in one minute. How long does it take the copier to print 1,958 copies?

____

14. Erica is saving her money to buy a dining room set that costs $580. If she saves $29 each month, how many months will she need to save to have enough money to buy the set?

____

Name ____________________

Lesson 29

COMMON CORE STANDARD CC.5.NBT.6

Lesson Objective: Solve problems by using the strategy *Draw a Diagram*.

Problem Solving • Division

Sara and Sam picked apples over the weekend. Sam picked nine times as many apples as Sara. Together, they picked 310 apples. How many apples did each person pick?

Read the Problem

What do I need to find?	What information do I need to use?	How will I use the information?
I need to find the number of apples each person picked.	I need to know that Sam and Sara picked a total of 310 apples. I need to know that Sam picked 9 times as many apples as Sara.	I can use the strategy draw a diagram to organize the information. I can draw and use a bar model to write the division problem that will help me find the number of apples Sam and Sara each picked.

Solve the Problem

My bar model needs to have one box for the number of apples Sara picked and nine boxes for the number of apples Sam picked. I can divide the total number of apples picked by the total number of boxes.

Sara: | 31 |

Sam: | 31 | 31 | 31 | 31 | 31 | 31 | 31 | 31 | 31 |

Total: 310

$$\begin{array}{r} 31 \\ 10\overline{)310} \\ -30 \\ \hline 10 \\ -10 \\ \hline 0 \end{array}$$

So, Sara picked 31 apples and Sam picked 279 apples.

Solve each problem. To help, draw a bar model on a separate sheet of paper.

1. Kai picked 11 times as many blueberries as Nico. Together, they picked 936 blueberries. How many blueberries did each boy pick?

____

2. Jen wrote 10 times as many pages of a school report as Tom. They wrote 396 pages altogether. How many pages did each student write?

____

Name ______________________

Problem Solving • Division

Show your work. Solve each problem.

1. Duane has 12 times as many baseball cards as Tony. Between them, they have 208 baseball cards. How many baseball cards does each boy have?

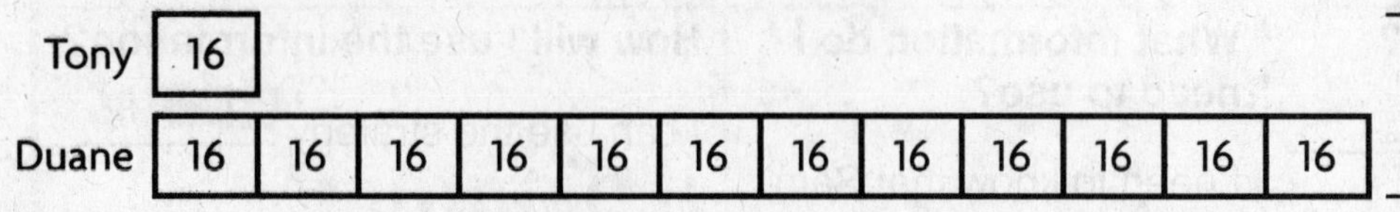

$208 \div 13 = 16$

Tony: 16 cards; Duane: 192 cards

2. Hallie has 10 times as many pages to read for her homework assignment as Janet. Altogether, they have to read 264 pages. How many pages does each girl have to read?

____

3. Hank has 48 fish in his aquarium. He has 11 times as many tetras as guppies. How many of each type of fish does Hank have?

____

4. Kelly has 4 times as many songs on her music player as Lou. Tiffany has 6 times as many songs on her music player as Lou. Altogether, they have 682 songs on their music players. How many songs does Kelly have?

____

Name ____________________

COMMON CORE STANDARD CC.5.NBT.7

Lesson Objective: Model decimal addition using base-ten blocks.

Decimal Addition

You can use decimal models to help you add decimals.

Add. 1.25 + 0.85

Step 1 Shade squares to represent 1.25.

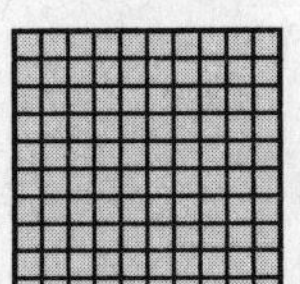
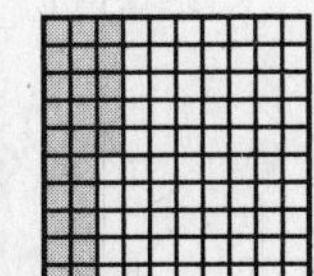

Remember:
Since there are only 75 squares left in the second model, you need to add another whole model for the remaining 10 squares.

Step 2 Shade additional squares to represent adding 0.85.

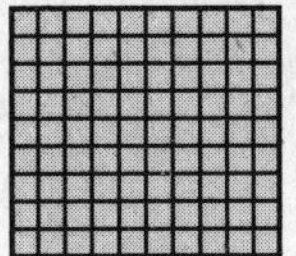

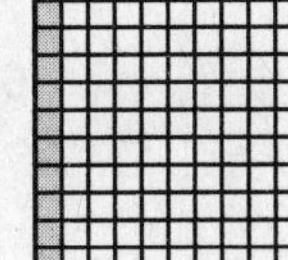

Step 3 Count the total number of shaded squares. There are 2 whole squares and 10 one-hundredths squares shaded. So, 2.10 wholes in all are shaded.

So, 1.25 + 0.85 = 2.10.

Add. Use decimal models. Draw a picture to show your work.

1. 2.1 + 0.59

____

2. 1.4 + 0.22

____

3. 1.27 + 1.15

____

4. 0.81 + 0.43

____

Name ______________________

Decimal Addition

Add. Draw a quick picture.

1. 0.5 + 0.6 = 1.1

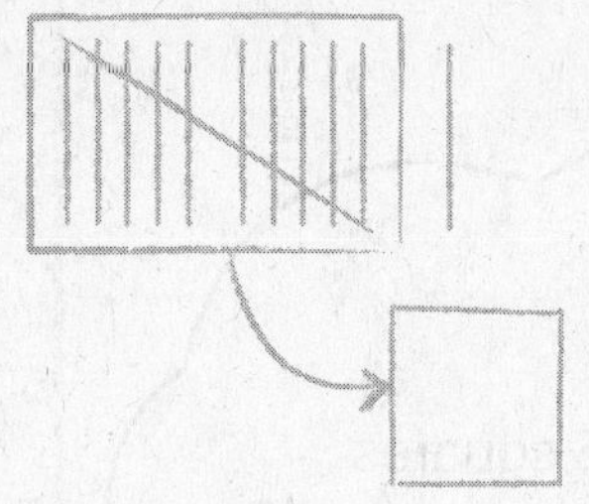

2. 0.15 + 0.36 = ________

3. 0.8 + 0.7 = ________

4. 0.35 + 0.64 = ________

5. 0.54 + 0.12 = ________

6. 0.51 + 0.28 = ________

7. 3.8 + 1.4 = ________

8. 2.71 + 2.15 = ________

9. 2.9 + 1.4 = ________

Problem Solving REAL WORLD

10. Draco bought 0.6 pound of bananas and 0.9 pound of grapes at the farmers' market. What is the total weight of the fruit?

____

11. Nancy biked 2.65 miles in the morning and 3.19 miles in the afternoon. What total distance did she bike?

____

Name ___________________________

COMMON CORE STANDARD CC.5.NBT.7

Lesson Objective: Model decimal subtraction using base-ten blocks.

Decimal Subtraction

You can use decimal models to help you subtract decimals.

Subtract. 1.85 − 0.65

Step 1 Shade squares to represent 1.85.

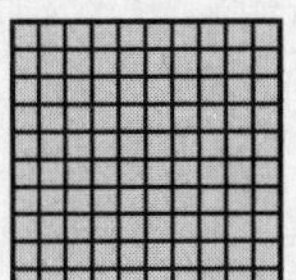
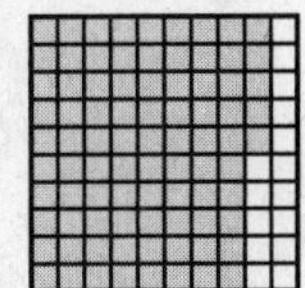

Step 2 Circle and cross out 65 of the shaded squares to represent subtracting 0.65.

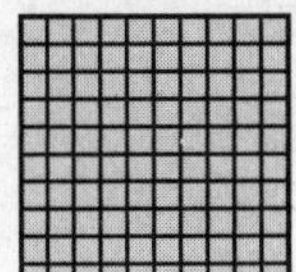
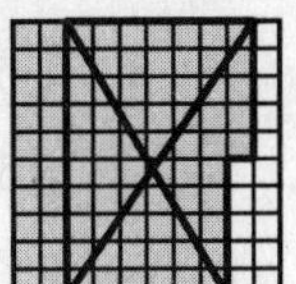

Remember:
By circling and crossing out shaded squares, you can see how many squares are taken away, or subtracted.

Step 3 Count the shaded squares that are not crossed out. Altogether, 1 whole square and 20 one-hundredths squares, or 1.20 wholes, are NOT crossed out.

So, 1.85 − 0.65 = 1.20.

Subtract. Use decimal models. Draw a picture to show your work.

1. 1.4 − 0.61

____

2. 1.6 − 1.08

____

3. 0.84 − 0.17

____

4. 1.39 − 1.14

____

Name ____________________

Lesson 31
CC.5.NBT.7

Decimal Subtraction

Subtract. Draw a quick picture.

1. 0.7 − 0.2 = 0.5

2. 0.45 − 0.24 = ________

3. 0.92 − 0.51 = ________

4. 0.67 − 0.42 = ________

5. 0.9 − 0.2 = ________

6. 3.25 − 1.67 = ________

7. 4.1 − 2.7 = ________

8. 3.12 − 2.52 = ________

9. 3.6 − 1.8 = ________

Problem Solving REAL WORLD

10. Yelina made a training plan to run 5.6 miles per day. So far, she has run 3.1 miles today. How much farther does she have to run to meet her goal for today?

____

11. Tim cut a 2.3-foot length of pipe from a pipe that was 4.1 feet long. How long is the remaining piece of pipe?

____

Name ______________________

Lesson 32

COMMON CORE STANDARD CC.5.NBT.7

Lesson Objective: Make reasonable estimates of decimal sums and differences.

Estimate Decimal Sums and Differences

You can use rounding to help you estimate sums and differences.

Use rounding to estimate 1.24 + 0.82 + 3.4.

Round to the nearest whole number. Then add.

1.24 → 1
0.82 → 1
+ 3.4 → + 3

5

So, the sum is about 5.

Remember:
If the digit to the right of the place you are rounding to is:

- less than 5, the digit in the rounding place stays the same.
- greater than or equal to 5, the digit in the rounding place increases by 1.

Use benchmarks to estimate 8.78 − 0.30.

8.78 → 8.75
− 0.30 → − 0.25

8.5

Think: 0.78 is between 0.75 and 1.
It is closer to 0.75.

Think: 0.30 is between 0.25 and 0.50.
It is closer to 0.25.

So, the difference is about 8.5.

Use rounding to estimate.

1. 51.23 −28.4 ______
2. $29.38 +$42.75 ______
3. 7.6 −2.15 ______
4. 0.74 +0.20 ______
5. 2.08 0.56 +0.41 ______

Use benchmarks to estimate.

6. 6.17 −3.5 ______
7. 1.73 1.4 +3.17 ______
8. 3.28 −0.86 ______
9. 15.27 +41.8 ______
10. $23.07 −$ 7.83 ______

11. 0.427 + 0.711 ______

12. 61.05 − 18.63 ______

13. 40.51 + 30.39 ______

Name ______________________

Lesson 32

CC.5.NBT.7

Estimate Decimal Sums and Differences

Use rounding to estimate.

1. 5.38 + 6.14

5
+6
11

2. 2.57 + 0.14

3. 9.65 − 3.12

4. 7.92 + 5.37

Use benchmarks to estimate.

5. 2.81 + 3.72

6. 12.54 + 7.98

7. 6.34 + 3.95

8. 16.18 − 5.94

9. 17.09 + 3.98

10. 14.01 − 4.51

11. 11.47 + 9.02

12. 19.97 − 11.02

Problem Solving

13. Elian bought 1.87 pounds of chicken and 2.46 pounds of turkey at the deli. About how much meat did he buy altogether?

14. Jenna bought a gallon of milk at the store for $3.58. About how much change did she receive from a $20 bill?

Name ________________________________

Lesson 33

COMMON CORE STANDARD CC.5.NBT.7

Lesson Objective: Add decimals using place value.

Add Decimals

Add. 4.37 + 9.8

Step 1 Estimate the sum.

4.37 + 9.8
↓ ↓
Estimate: 4 + 10 = 14

Step 2 Line up the place values for each number in a place-value chart. Then add.

	Ones		Tenths	Hundredths
	4	•	3	7
+	9	•	8	
	14	•	1	7

←sum

Step 3 Use your estimate to determine if your answer is reasonable.

Think: 14.17 is close to the estimate, 14. The answer is reasonable.

So, 4.37 + 9.8 = 14.17.

Estimate. Then find the sum.

1. Estimate: ____

  1.20
+ 0.34

2. Estimate: ____

  1.52
+ 1.21

3. Estimate: ____

  12.25
+ 11.25

4. Estimate: ____

  10.75
+ 1.11

5. Estimate: ____

  22.65
+ 18.01

6. Estimate: ____

  34.41
+ 15.37

Name ______________________

Add Decimals

Estimate. Then find the sum.

1. Estimate: ______

$$\begin{array}{r} 2.85 \\ +7.29 \\ \hline \end{array}$$

$$\begin{array}{r} ^{1\,1} \\ 2.85 \\ +7.29 \\ \hline 10.14 \end{array}$$

2. Estimate: ______

$$\begin{array}{r} 4.23 \\ +6.51 \\ \hline \end{array}$$

3. Estimate: ______

$$\begin{array}{r} 6.8 \\ +4.2 \\ \hline \end{array}$$

4. Estimate: ______

$$\begin{array}{r} 2.7 \\ +5.37 \\ \hline \end{array}$$

Find the sum.

5. 6.8 + 4.4

6. 6.87 + 5.18

7. 3.14 + 2.9

8. 16.18 + 5.94

9. 19.8 + 31.45

10. 25.47 + 7.24

11. 9.17 + 5.67

12. 19.7 + 5.46

Problem Solving REAL WORLD

13. Marcela's dog gained 4.1 kilograms in two months. Two months ago, the dog's mass was 5.6 kilograms. What is the dog's current mass?

____

14. During last week's storm, 2.15 inches of rain fell on Monday and 1.68 inches of rain fell on Tuesday. What was the total amount of rainfall on both days?

____

Name ______________________________

Lesson 34

COMMON CORE STANDARD CC.5.NBT.7

Lesson Objective: Subtract decimals using place value.

Subtract Decimals

Subtract. 12.56 − 4.33

Step 1 Estimate the difference.

12.56 − 4.33
↓ ↓
Estimate: 13 − 4 = 9

Step 2 Line up the place values for each number in a place-value chart. Then subtract.

	Ones	Tenths	Hundredths
	12	• 5	6
−	4	• 3	3
	8	• 2	3

← difference

Step 3 Use your estimate to determine if your answer is reasonable.

Think: 8.23 is close to the estimate, 9. The answer is reasonable.

So, 12.56 − 4.33 = 8.23.

Estimate. Then find the difference.

1. Estimate: ____

1.97
− 0.79

2. Estimate: ____

4.42
− 1.26

3. Estimate: ____

10.25
− 8.25

Find the difference. Check your answer.

4. 5.75
− 1.11

5. 25.21
− 19.05

6. 42.14
− 25.07

Name ______________________________

Lesson 34

CC.5.NBT.7

Subtract Decimals

Estimate. Then find the difference.

1. Estimate: 3

$$\begin{array}{r} 6.5 \\ -3.9 \\ \hline \end{array}$$

$$\begin{array}{r} \overset{5\ 15}{\not{6}.\not{5}} \\ -3.9 \\ \hline 2.6 \end{array}$$

2. Estimate: ______

$$\begin{array}{r} 4.23 \\ -2.51 \\ \hline \end{array}$$

3. Estimate: ______

$$\begin{array}{r} 8.6 \\ -5.1 \\ \hline \end{array}$$

4. Estimate: ______

$$\begin{array}{r} 2.71 \\ -1.34 \\ \hline \end{array}$$

Find the difference. Check your answer.

5. $$\begin{array}{r} 16.3 \\ -\ 4.4 \\ \hline \end{array}$$

6. $$\begin{array}{r} 12.56 \\ -\ 5.18 \\ \hline \end{array}$$

7. $$\begin{array}{r} 3.14 \\ -\ 2.9 \\ \hline \end{array}$$

8. $$\begin{array}{r} 34.9 \\ -\ 4.29 \\ \hline \end{array}$$

9. 2.54 − 1.67

10. 25.8 − 14.7

11. 11.63 − 6.7

12. 5.24 − 2.14

Problem Solving REAL WORLD

13. The width of a tree was 3.15 inches last year. This year, the width is 5.38 inches. How much did the width of the tree increase?

____

14. The temperature decreased from 71.5°F to 56.8°F overnight. How much did the temperature drop?

____

Name ______________________________

COMMON CORE STANDARD CC.5.NBT.7

Lesson Objective: Identify, describe, and create numeric patterns with decimals.

Algebra • Patterns with Decimals

Marla wants to download some songs from the Internet. The first song costs $1.50, and each additional song costs $1.20. How much will 2, 3, and 4 songs cost?

1 song
$1.50

2 songs
?

3 songs
?

4 songs
?

Step 1 Identify the first term in the sequence.
Think: The cost of 1 song is $1.50. The first term is $1.50.

Step 2 Identify whether the sequence is increasing or decreasing from one term to the next.
Think: Marla will pay $1.20 for each additional song.
The sequence is increasing.

Step 3 Write a rule that describes the sequence. Start with $1.50 and add $1.20.

Step 4 Use your rule to find the unknown terms in the sequence.

Number of Songs	**1**	**2**	**3**	**4**
Cost	**$1.50**	**1.50 + 1.20 = $2.70**	**2.70 + 1.20 = $3.90**	**3.90 + 1.20 = $5.10**

So, 2 songs cost $2.70, 3 songs cost $3.90, and 4 songs cost $5.10.

Write a rule for the sequence.

1. 0.4, 0.7, 1.0, 1.3, …

Rule: ______________________

2. 5.25, 5.00, 4.75, 4.50, …

Rule: ______________________

Write a rule for the sequence, then find the unknown term.

3. 26.1, 23.8, 21.5, _____, 16.9

____

4. 4.62, 5.03, _____, 5.85, 6.26

____

Name ___________________________

Lesson 35
CC.5.NBT.7

Patterns with Decimals

Write a rule for the sequence. Then find the unknown term.

1. 2.6, 3.92, 5.24, 6.56, 7.88

   Think: 2.6 + ? = 3.92; 3.92 + ? = 5.24

   2.6 + 1.32 = 3.92
   3.92 + 1.32 = 5.24

   Rule: add 1.32

2. 25.7, 24.1, ______, 20.9, 19.3

   Rule: ______________

3. 14.33, 13.22, 12.11, 11.00, ______

   Rule: ______________

4. 1.75, ______, 6.75, 9.25, 11.75

   Rule: ______________

Write the first four terms of the sequence.

5. **Rule:** start at 17.3, add 0.9

   ______, ______, ______, ______

6. **Rule:** start at 28.6, subtract 3.1

   ______, ______, ______, ______

Problem Solving

7. The Ride-It Store rents bicycles. The cost is \$8.50 for 1 hour, \$13.65 for 2 hours, \$18.80 for 3 hours, and \$23.95 for 4 hours. If the pattern continues, how much will it cost Nate to rent a bike for 6 hours?

   ____

8. Lynne walks dogs every day to earn money. The fees she charges per month are 1 dog, \$40; 2 dogs, \$37.25 each; 3 dogs, \$34.50 each; 4 dogs, \$31.75 each. A pet store wants her to walk 8 dogs. If the pattern continues, how much will Lynne charge to walk each of the 8 dogs?

   ____

Name ______________________________

COMMON CORE STANDARD CC.5.NBT.7

Lesson Objective: Solve problems using the strategy *make a table.*

Problem Solving • Add and Subtract Money

At the end of April, Mrs. Lei had a balance of $476.05. Since then she has written checks for $263.18 and $37.56, and made a deposit of $368.00. Her checkbook balance currently shows $498.09. Find Mrs. Lei's correct balance.

Read the Problem

What do I need to find?

I need to find Mrs. Lei's correct checkbook balance.

What information do I need to use?

I need to use the April balance, and the check and deposit amounts.

How will I use the information?

I need to make a table and use the information to subtract the checks and add the deposit to find the correct balance.

Solve the Problem

Balancing Mrs. Lei's Checkbook			
April balance			$476.05
Deposit		$368.00	+$368.00
			$844.05
Check	$263.18		−$263.18
			$580.87
Check	$37.56		−$37.56
			$543.31

Mrs. Lei's correct balance is $543.31.

1. At the end of June, Mr. Kent had a balance of $375.98. Since then he has written a check for $38.56 and made a deposit of $408.00. His checkbook shows a balance of $645.42. Find Mr. Kent's correct balance.

____

2. Jordan buys a notebook for himself and each of 4 friends. Each notebook costs $1.85. Make a table to find the cost of 5 notebooks.

____

Name ______________________________

Problem Solving • Add and Subtract Money

Lesson 36
CC.5.NBT.7

Solve. Use the table to solve 1–3.

Bowl-a-Rama		
	Regular Cost	Member's Cost
Lane Rental (up to 4 people)	$9.75	$7.50
Shoe Rental	$3.95	$2.95

1. Dorian and Jack decided to go bowling. They each need to rent shoes and 1 lane, and Jack is a member. If Jack pays for both of them with $20, what change should he receive?

   Calculate the cost: $7.50 + $3.95 + $2.95 = $14.40

   Calculate the change: $20 − $14.40 = $5.60

2. Natalie and her friends decided to rent 4 lanes at regular cost for a party. Ten people need to rent shoes, and 4 people are members. What is the total cost for the party?

   ____

3. Warren paid $23.85 and received no change. He is a member and rented 2 lanes. How many pairs of shoes did he rent?

   ____

Use the following information to solve 4–6.

At the concession stand, medium sodas cost $1.25 and hot dogs cost $2.50.

4. Natalie's group brought in pizzas, but is buying the drinks at the concession stand. How many medium sodas can Natalie's group buy with $20? Make a table to show your answer.

   ____

5. Jack bought 2 medium sodas and 2 hot dogs. He paid with $20. What was his change?

   ____

6. How much would it cost to buy 3 medium sodas and 2 hot dogs?

   ____

Name ______________________

Lesson 37

COMMON CORE STANDARD CC.5.NBT.7

Lesson Objective: Choose a method to find a decimal sum or difference.

Choose a Method

There is more than one way to find the sums and differences of whole numbers and decimals. You can use properties, mental math, place value, a calculator, or paper and pencil.

Choose a method. Find the sum or difference.

- Use mental math for problems with fewer digits or rounded numbers.

$$\begin{array}{r} 2.86 \\ -\ 1.2 \\ \hline 1.66 \end{array}$$

- Use place value for larger numbers.

$$\begin{array}{r} \scriptsize{1\ 1} \\ \$15.79 \\ +\ \$32.81 \\ \hline \$48.60 \end{array}$$

- Use a calculator for difficult numbers or very large numbers.

[3] [8] [.] [4] [4] [−] [2] [5] [.] [8] [6] [=] 12.58

Find the sum or difference.

1. $\begin{array}{r} 73.9 \\ +\ 4.37 \\ \hline \end{array}$

2. $\begin{array}{r} 127.35 \\ +\ 928.52 \\ \hline \end{array}$

3. $\begin{array}{r} 10 \\ +\ 2.25 \\ \hline \end{array}$

4. $\begin{array}{r} 0.36 \\ +\ 1.55 \\ \hline \end{array}$

5. $\begin{array}{r} 71.4 \\ +\ 11.5 \\ \hline \end{array}$

6. $\begin{array}{r} 90.4 \\ +\ 88.76 \\ \hline \end{array}$

7. $\begin{array}{r} 3.3 \\ +\ 5.6 \\ \hline \end{array}$

8. $\begin{array}{r} 14.21 \\ 1.79 \\ +\ 15.88 \\ \hline \end{array}$

9. 68.20 − 42.10 ____________

10. 2.25 − 1.15 ____________

11. 875.33 − 467.79 ____________

12. 97.26 − 54.90 ____________

Name ____________________

Lesson 37
CC.5.NBT.7

Choose a Method

Find the sum or difference.

1. 7.24 + 3.18

Example worked answer: 7.24 + 3.18 (carry 1) = 10.42

2. 5.2 + 6.47 + 12.16

3. 6.37 − 4.98

4. 0.64 + 9.68 + 1.47

5. 14.87 + 3.65

6. 60.12 − 14.05

7. 2.72 + 9.48

8. 16.85 + 83.4

9. \$13.60 − \$8.74 ____________

10. \$25.00 − \$16.32 ____________

11. 13.65 + 6.90 + 4.35 ____________

Problem Solving REAL WORLD

12. Jill bought 6.5 meters of blue lace and 4.12 meters of green lace. What was the total length of lace she bought?

13. Zack bought a coat for \$69.78. He paid with a \$100 bill and received \$26.73 in change. How much was the sales tax?

Name ________________________________

Lesson 38

COMMON CORE STANDARD CC.5.NBT.7

Lesson Objective: Model multiplication of whole numbers and decimals.

Multiply Decimals and Whole Numbers

You can draw a quick picture to help multiply a decimal and a whole number.

Find the product. 4 × 0.23

Draw a quick picture. Each bar represents one tenth, or 0.1. Each circle represents one hundredth, or 0.01.

Step 1

Draw __4__ groups of __2__ tenths and __3__ hundredths.

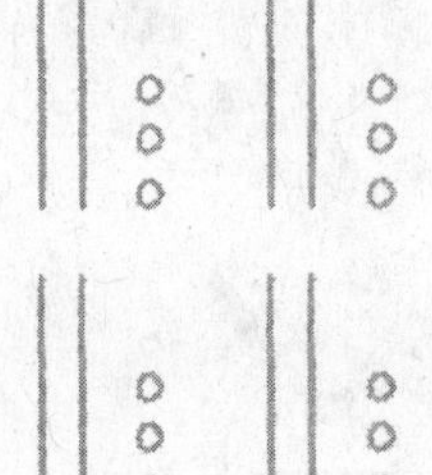

So, 4 × 0.23 = __0.92__.

Step 2

Combine the tenths. Then combine the hundredths.

Step 3

There are __12__ hundredths. Rename __10__ hundredths as __1__ tenth. Then you will have __9__ tenths and __2__ hundredths.

Find the product. Use a quick picture.

1. 2 × 0.19 = ________

2. 3 × 0.54 = ________

3. 4 × 0.07 = ________

4. 3 × 1.22 = ________

Name ______________________

Lesson 38
CC.5.NBT.7

Multiply Decimals and Whole Numbers

Use the decimal model to find the product.

1. $4 \times 0.07 =$ 0.28

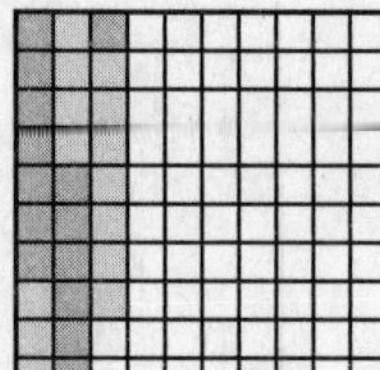

2. $3 \times 0.27 =$ ______

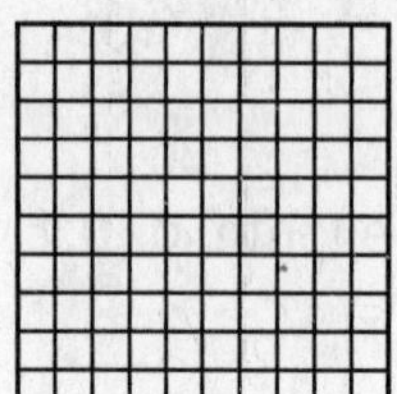

3. $2 \times 0.45 =$ ______

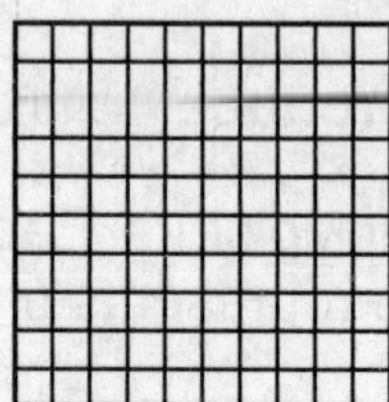

Find the product. Draw a quick picture.

4. $2 \times 0.8 =$ ______

5. $3 \times 0.33 =$ ______

6. $5 \times 0.71 =$ ______

7. $4 \times 0.23 =$ ______

Problem Solving REAL WORLD

8. In physical education class, Sonia walks a distance of 0.12 mile in 1 minute. At that rate, how far can she walk in 9 minutes?

______

9. A certain tree can grow 0.45 meter in one year. At that rate, how much can the tree grow in 3 years?

______

Name ________________________________

Lesson Objective: Multiply a decimal and a whole number using drawings and place value.

Multiplication with Decimals and Whole Numbers

To find the product of a one-digit whole number and a decimal, multiply as you would multiply whole numbers. To find the number of decimal places in the product, add the number of decimal places in the factors.

To multiply 6 × 4.25, multiply as you would multiply 6 × 425.

Step 1
Multiply the ones.

$$\begin{array}{r} {}^{3}\\ 425 \\ \times\quad 6 \\ \hline 0 \end{array}$$

Step 2
Multiply the tens.

$$\begin{array}{r} {}^{1\,3}\\ 425 \\ \times\quad 6 \\ \hline 50 \end{array}$$

Step 3
Multiply the hundreds. Then place the decimal point in the product.

$$\begin{array}{r} {}^{1\,3}\\ 4.25 \\ \times\quad 6 \\ \hline 25.50 \end{array}$$

4.25 ← **2 decimal places**
× 6 ← + **0 decimal places**
25.50 ← **2 decimal places**

So, 6 × 4.25 = **25.50**.

Place the decimal point in the product.

1. 8.23 × 6 = 4 9.3 8

Think: The place value of the decimal factor is hundredths.

2. 6.3 × 4 = 2 5 2

3. 16.82 × 5 = 8 4 1 0

Find the product.

4. 5.19 × 3

5. 7.2 × 8

6. 37.46 × 7

Name ______________________________

Lesson 39
CC.5.NBT.7

Multiplication with Decimals and Whole Numbers

Find the product.

1. 2.7 × 4

10.8

Think: The place value of the decimal factor is tenths.

2. 7.6 × 8

3. 0.35 × 6

4. 8.42 × 9

5. 14.05 × 7

6. 23.82 × 5

7. 4 × 9.3

8. 3 × 7.9

9. 5 × 42.89

10. 8 × 2.6

11. 6 × 0.92

12. 9 × 1.04

13. 7 × 2.18

14. 3 × 19.54

Problem Solving

15. A half-dollar coin issued by the United States Mint measures 30.61 millimeters across. Mikk has 9 half dollars. He lines them up end to end in a row. What is the total length of the row of half dollars?

____

16. One pound of grapes costs $3.49. Linda buys exactly 3 pounds of grapes. How much will the grapes cost?

____

Name ______________________

Lesson 40

COMMON CORE STANDARD CC.5.NBT.7

Lesson Objective: Use expanded form and place value to multiply a decimal and a whole number.

Multiply Using Expanded Form

You can use a model and partial products to help you find the product of a two-digit whole number and a decimal.

Find the product. 13×6.8

Step 1 Draw a large rectangle. Label its longer side 13 and its shorter side 6.8. The area of the large rectangle represents the product, 13 × 6.8.

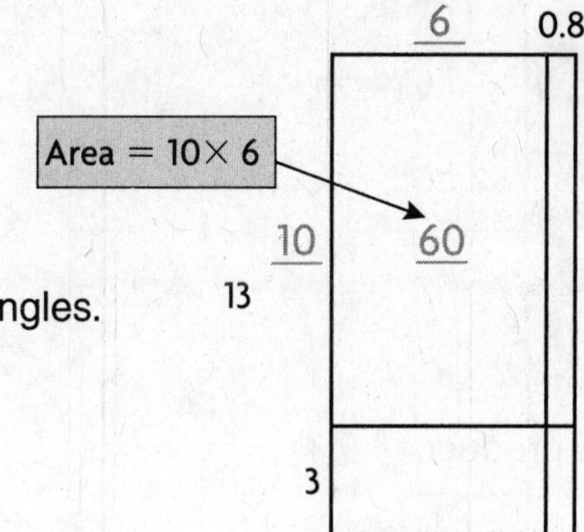

Step 2 Rewrite the factors in expanded form. Divide the large rectangle into four smaller rectangles. Use the expanded forms to label the smaller rectangles.

13 = 10 + 3   6.8 = 6 + 0.8

Step 3 Multiply to find the area of each small rectangle.

$10 \times 6 =$ 60 $10 \times 0.8 =$ 8 $3 \times 6 =$ 18 $3 \times 0.8 =$ 2.4

Step 4 Add to find the total area.

60 + 8 + 18 + 2.4 = 88.4

So, $13 \times 6.8 =$ 88.4.

Draw a model to find the product.

1. $18 \times 0.25 =$ ________

2. $26 \times 7.2 =$ ________

Find the product.

3. $17 \times 9.3 =$ ________

4. $21 \times 43.5 =$ ________

5. $48 \times 4.74 =$ ________

Name ____________________

Multiply Using Expanded Form

Draw a model to find the product.

1. $37 \times 9.5 =$ 351.5

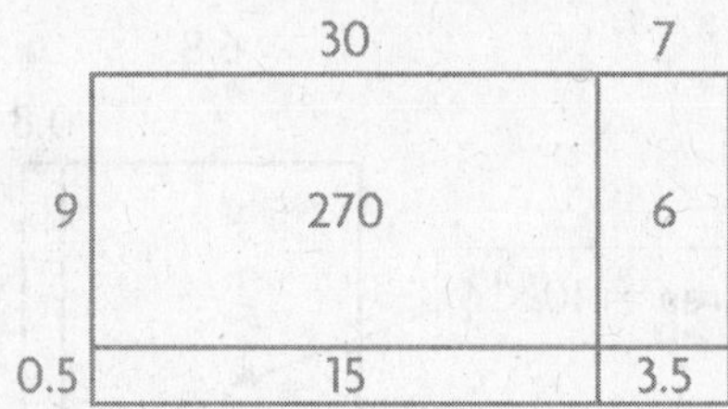

2. $84 \times 0.24 =$ ________

Find the product.

3. $13 \times 0.53 =$ ________

4. $27 \times 89.5 =$ ________

5. $32 \times 12.71 =$ ________

6. $17 \times 0.52 =$ ________

7. $23 \times 59.8 =$ ________

8. $61 \times 15.98 =$ ________

Problem Solving REAL WORLD

9. An object that weighs one pound on the moon will weigh about 6.02 pounds on Earth. Suppose a moon rock weighs 11 pounds on the moon. How much will the same rock weigh on Earth?

____

10. Tessa is on the track team. For practice and exercise, she runs 2.25 miles each day. At the end of 14 days, how many total miles will Tessa have run?

____

Name ______________________________

Lesson 41

COMMON CORE STANDARD CC.5.NBT.7

Lesson Objective: Solve problems using the strategy *draw a diagram* to multiply money.

Problem Solving • Multiply Money

Three students in the garden club enter a pumpkin-growing contest. Jessie's pumpkin is worth $12.75. Mara's pumpkin is worth 4 times as much as Jessie's. Hayden's pumpkin is worth $22.25 more than Mara's. How much is Hayden's pumpkin worth?

Read the Problem	Solve the Problem
What do I need to find? I need to find how much Hayden's pumpkin is worth.	The amount that Hayden's and Mara's pumpkins are worth depends on how much Jessie's pumpkin is worth. Draw a diagram to compare the amounts without calculating. Then use the diagram to find how much each person's pumpkin is worth.
What information do I need to use? I need to use the worth of Jessie's pumpkin to find how much Mara's and Hayden's pumpkins are worth.	Jessie: [$12.75] Mara: [$12.75][$12.75][$12.75][$12.75] Hayden: [$12.75][$12.75][$12.75][$12.75][$22.25]
How will I use the information: I can draw a diagram to show how much Jessie's and Mara's pumpkins are worth to find how much Hayden's pumpkin is worth.	**Jessie:** $12.75 **Mara:** 4 × $12.75 = $51.00 **Hayden:** $51.00 + $22.25 = $73.25
So Hayden's pumpkin is worth $73.25.	

1. Three friends go to the local farmers' market. Latasha spends $3.35. Helen spends 4 times as much as Latasha. Dee spends $7.50 more than Helen. How much does Dee spend?

   ____

2. Alexia raises $75.23 for a charity. Sue raises 3 times as much as Alexia. Manuel raises $85.89. How much money do the three friends raise for the charity in all?

   ____

Name ______________________________

Problem Solving • Multiply Money

Solve each problem.

1. Three friends go to the local farmers' market. Ashlee spends $8.25. Natalie spends 4 times as much as Ashlee. Patrick spends $9.50 more than Natalie. How much does Patrick spend?

Ashlee	$8.25				
Natalie	$8.25	$8.25	$8.25	$8.25	
Patrick	$8.25	$8.25	$8.25	$8.25	$9.50

$4 \times \$8.25 = \$33.00$

$\$33.00 + \$9.50 = \$42.50$

$42.50

2. Kimmy's savings account has a balance of $76.23 in June. By September, her balance is 5 times as much as her June balance. Between September and December, Kimmy deposits a total of $87.83 into her account. If she does not withdraw any money from her account, what should Kimmy's balance be in December?

____

3. Amy raises $58.75 to participate in a walk-a-thon. Jeremy raises $23.25 more than Amy. Oscar raises 3 times as much as Jeremy. How much money does Oscar raise?

____

4. It costs $5.50 per hour to rent a pair of ice skates, for up to 2 hours. After 2 hours, the rental cost per hour decreases to $2.50. How much does it cost to rent a pair of ice skates for 4 hours?

____

Name ____________________

COMMON CORE STANDARD CC.5.NBT.7

Lesson Objective: Model multiplication by decimals.

Decimal Multiplication

You can use decimal squares to multiply decimals.

Multiply. 0.2 × 0.9

Step 1 Draw a square with 10 equal rows and 10 equal columns.

Step 2 Shade 9 columns to represent 0.9.

Step 3 Shade 2 rows to represent 0.2.

Step 4 Count the number of small squares where the shadings overlap: 18 squares, or 0.18.

So, 0.2 × 0.9 = 0.18.

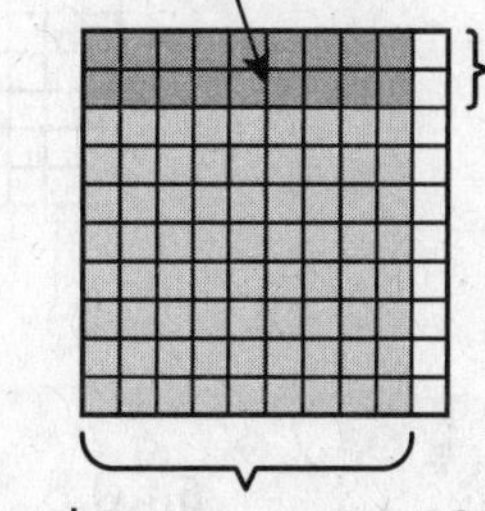

Multiply. Use the decimal model.

1. 0.3 × 0.2 = ________

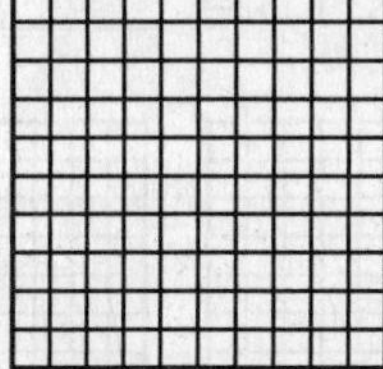

2. 0.9 × 0.5 = ________

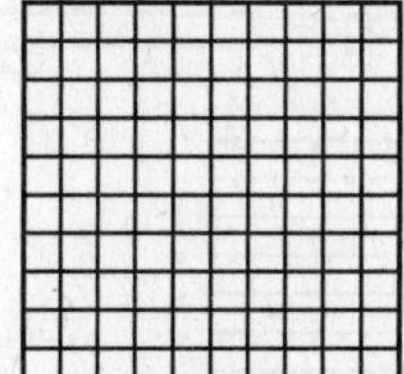

3. 0.1 × 1.8 = ________

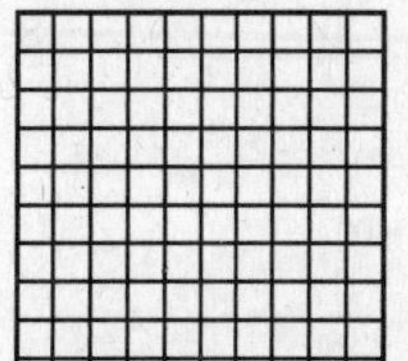
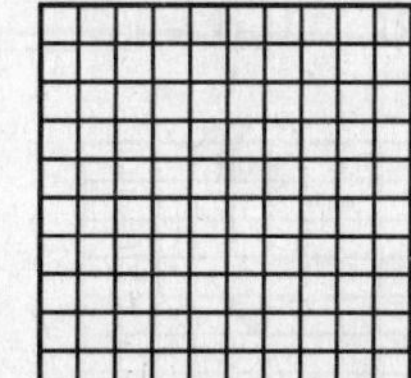

4. 0.4 × 0.4 = ________

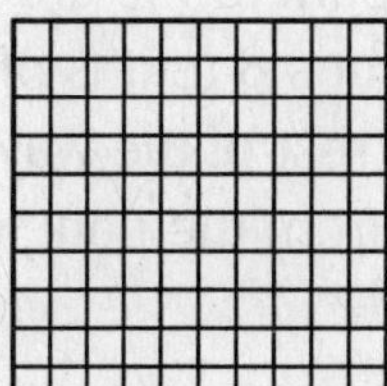

5. 0.6 × 0.5 = ________

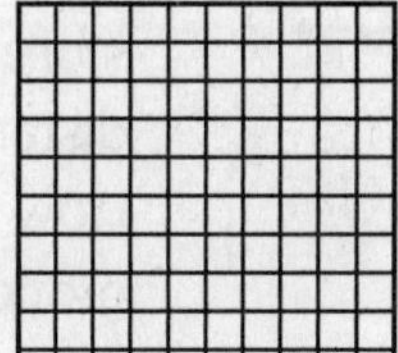

6. 0.4 × 1.2 = ________

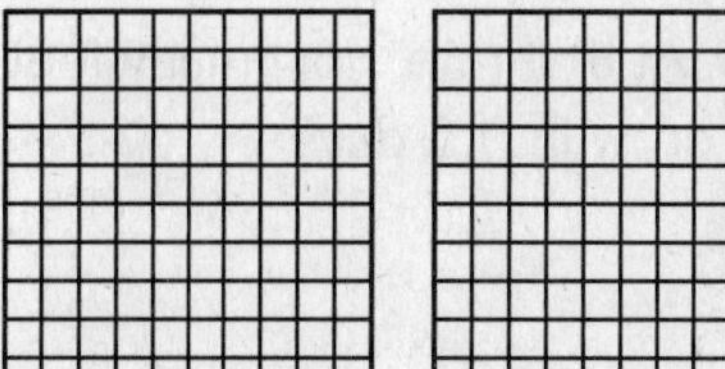

Name ______________________

Decimal Multiplication

Lesson 42
CC.5.NBT.7

Multiply. Use the decimal model.

1. 0.3 × 0.6 = 0.18

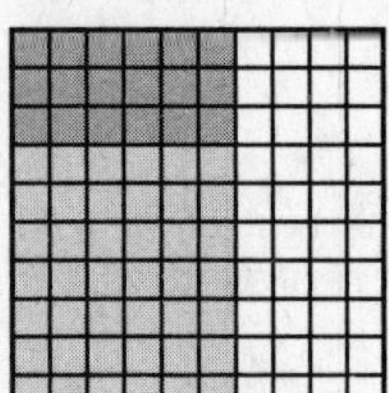

2. 0.2 × 0.8 = __________

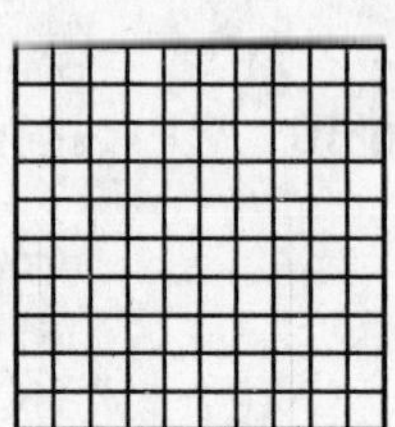

3. 0.5 × 1.7 = __________

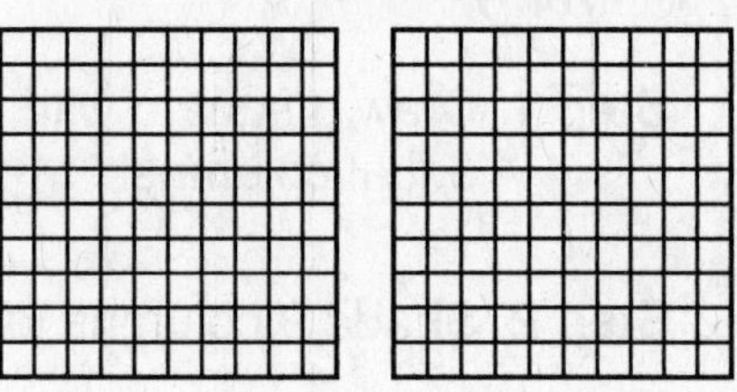

4. 0.6 × 0.7 = __________

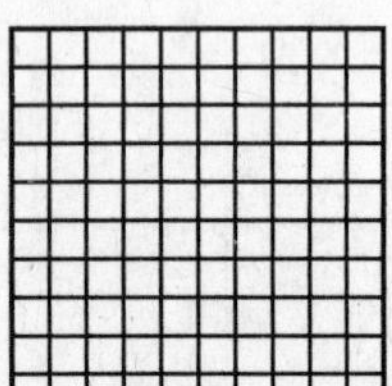

5. 0.8 × 0.5 = __________

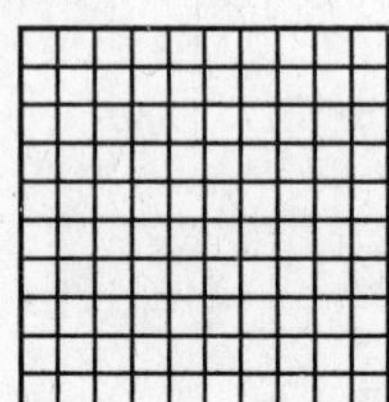

6. 0.4 × 1.9 = __________

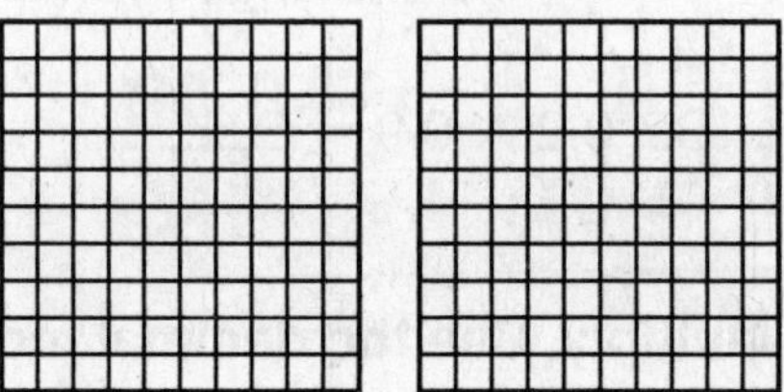

7. 0.8 × 0.8 = __________

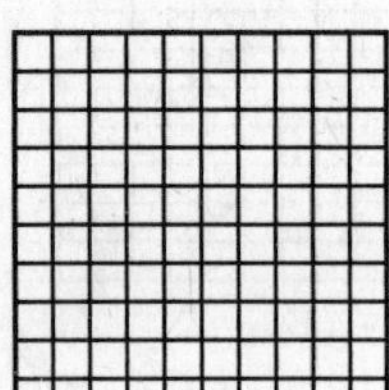

8. 0.2 × 0.5 = __________

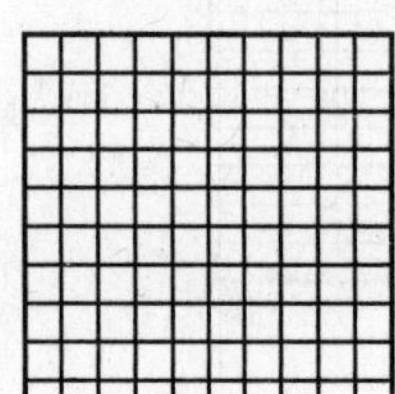

9. 0.8 × 1.3 = __________

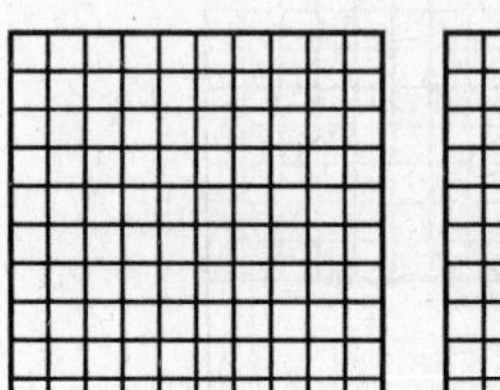
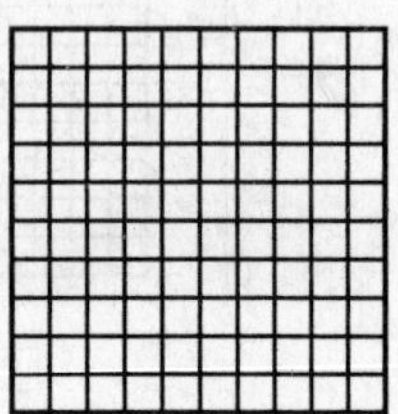

Problem Solving

10. A certain bamboo plants grow 1.2 feet in 1 day. At that rate, how many feet could the plant grow in 0.5 day?

____

11. The distance from the park to the grocery store is 0.9 mile. Ezra runs 8 tenths of that distance and walks the rest of the way. How far does Ezra run from the park to the grocery store?

____

Name ______________________

Lesson 43

COMMON CORE STANDARD CC.5.NBT.7

Lesson Objective: Place the decimal point in decimal multiplication.

Multiply Decimals

Multiply. 9.3 × 5.27

Step 1 Multiply as with whole numbers.

```
    2 6
      2
    527
  ×  93
  1,581
+ 47,430
  49,011
```

Step 2 Add the number of decimal places in the factors to place the decimal point in the product.

```
    5.27 ←     2 decimal places
  ×  9.3 ← + 1 decimal place
   1,581
+ 47,430
  49.011 ←     3 decimal places
```

So, 9.3 × 5.27 = **49.011**.

Place the decimal point in the product.

1. 1.6 × 0.7 = 1 1 2

2. 14.2 × 7.6 = 1 0 7 9 2

3. 3.59 × 4.8 = 1 7 2 3 2

Find the product.

4. 5.7 × 0.8

5. 35.1 × 8.4

6. 2.19 × 6.3

Name ______________________

Multiply Decimals

Find the product.

1.
```
   5.8        58
 × 2.4      × 24
 13.92       232
         + 1,160
           1,392
```

2.
```
  7.3
× 9.6
```

3.
```
 46.3
× 0.8
```

4.
```
 29.5
× 1.3
```

5.
```
 3.76
× 4.8
```

6.
```
 9.07
× 6.5
```

7. 0.42 × 75.3

8. 5.6 × 61.84

9. 7.5 × 18.74

10. 0.9 × 53.8

Problem Solving

11. Aretha runs a marathon in 3.25 hours. Neal takes 1.6 times as long to run the same marathon. How many hours does it take Neal to run the marathon?

____

12. Tiffany catches a fish that weighs 12.3 pounds. Frank catches a fish that weighs 2.5 times as much as Tiffany's fish. How many pounds does Frank's fish weigh?

____

Name ______________________________

COMMON CORE STANDARD CC.5.NBT.7

Lesson Objective: Multiply decimals with zeros in the product.

Zeros in the Product

Sometimes when you multiply two decimals, there are not enough digits in the product to place the decimal point.

Multiply. 0.9 × 0.03

Step 1 Multiply as with whole numbers.

$$\begin{array}{r} 3 \\ \times\ 9 \\ \hline 27 \end{array}$$

Step 2 Find the number of decimal places in the product by adding the number of decimal places in the factors.

0.03 ← 2 decimal places

× 0.9 ← + 1 decimal place

← 3 decimal places

Step 3 Place the decimal point.

0.027 — There are not enough digits in the product to place the decimal point. Write zeros as needed to the left of the product to place the decimal point.

So, 0.9 × 0.03 = 0.027.

Write zeros in the product.

1. $\begin{array}{r} 0.8 \\ \times\ 0.1 \\ \hline \square 8 \end{array}$

2. $\begin{array}{r} 0.04 \\ \times\ 0.7 \\ \hline \square 28 \end{array}$

3. $\begin{array}{r} 0.03 \\ \times\ 0.3 \\ \hline \square 9 \end{array}$

Find the product.

4. $\begin{array}{r} \$0.06 \\ \times\ 0.5 \\ \hline \end{array}$

5. $\begin{array}{r} 0.09 \\ \times\ 0.8 \\ \hline \end{array}$

6. $\begin{array}{r} 0.05 \\ \times\ 0.7 \\ \hline \end{array}$

Name ______________________

Lesson 44

CC.5.NBT.7

Zeros in the Product

Find the product.

1. $\begin{array}{r} 0.07 \\ \times\ 0.2 \\ \hline 0.014 \end{array}$ $\begin{array}{r} 7 \\ \times 2 \\ \hline 14 \end{array}$

2. $\begin{array}{r} 0.3 \\ \times\ 0.1 \\ \hline \end{array}$

3. $\begin{array}{r} 0.05 \\ \times\ 0.8 \\ \hline \end{array}$

4. $\begin{array}{r} 0.08 \\ \times\ 0.3 \\ \hline \end{array}$

5. $\begin{array}{r} 0.06 \\ \times\ 0.7 \\ \hline \end{array}$

6. $\begin{array}{r} 0.2 \\ \times\ 0.4 \\ \hline \end{array}$

7. $\begin{array}{r} 0.05 \\ \times\ 0.4 \\ \hline \end{array}$

8. $\begin{array}{r} 0.08 \\ \times\ 0.8 \\ \hline \end{array}$

9. $\begin{array}{r} \$0.90 \\ \times\ 0.1 \\ \hline \end{array}$

10. $\begin{array}{r} 0.02 \\ \times\ 0.3 \\ \hline \end{array}$

11. $\begin{array}{r} 0.09 \\ \times\ 0.5 \\ \hline \end{array}$

12. $\begin{array}{r} \$0.05 \\ \times\ 0.2 \\ \hline \end{array}$

Problem Solving

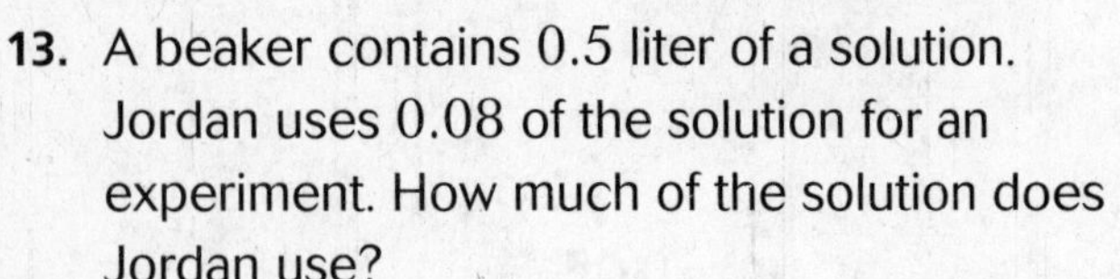

13. A beaker contains 0.5 liter of a solution. Jordan uses 0.08 of the solution for an experiment. How much of the solution does Jordan use?

____

14. A certain type of nuts are on sale at \$0.35 per pound. Tamara buys 0.2 pound of nuts. How much will the nuts cost?

____

Name ____________________

Lesson 45

COMMON CORE STANDARD CC.5.NBT.7

Lesson Objective: Model division of decimals by whole numbers.

Divide Decimals by Whole Numbers

You can draw a quick picture to help you divide a decimal by a whole number.

In a decimal model, each large square represents one, or 1. Each bar represents one-tenth, or 0.1.

Divide. 1.2 ÷ 3

Step 1 Draw a quick picture to represent the dividend, 1.2.

Step 2 Draw 3 circles to represent the divisor, 3.

Step 3 You cannot evenly divide 1 into 3 groups. Regroup 1 as 10 tenths. There are 12 tenths in 1.2.

Step 4 Share the tenths equally among 3 groups.

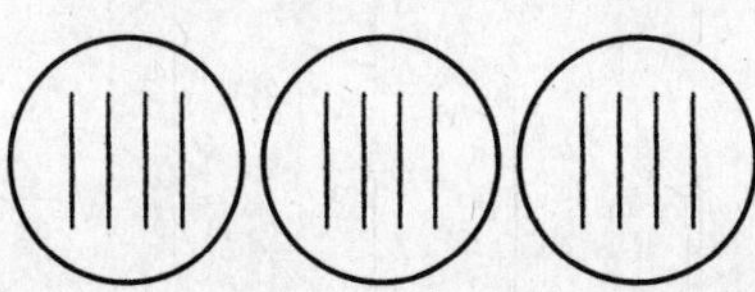

Each group contains 0 ones and 4 tenths.

So, 1.2 ÷ 3 = 0.4.

Divide. Draw a quick picture.

1. 2.7 ÷ 9 = ________

2. 4.8 ÷ 8 = ________

3. 2.8 ÷ 7 = ________

4. 7.25 ÷ 5 = ________

5. 3.78 ÷ 3 = ________

6. 8.52 ÷ 4 = ________

Name ______________________________

Lesson 45
CC.5.NBT.7

Divide Decimals by Whole Numbers

Use the model to complete the number sentence.

1. 1.2 ÷ 4 = 0.3

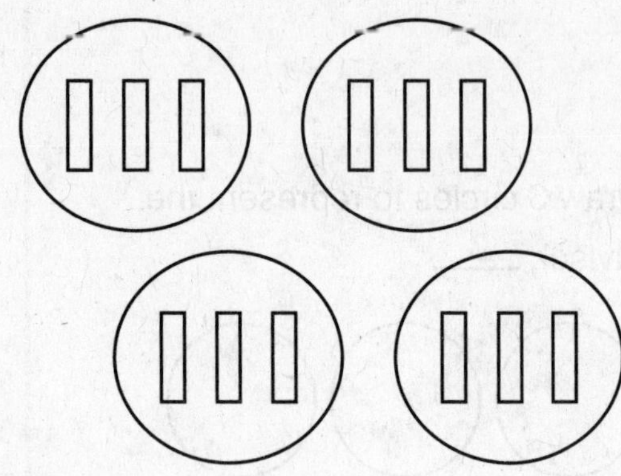

2. 3.69 ÷ 3 = ________

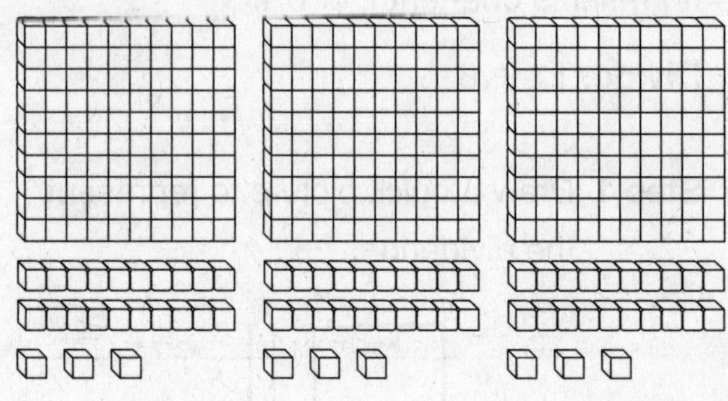

Divide. Use base-ten blocks.

3. 4.9 ÷ 7 = ________

4. 3.6 ÷ 9 = ________

5. 2.4 ÷ 8 = ________

6. 6.48 ÷ 4 = ________

7. 3.01 ÷ 7 = ________

8. 4.26 ÷ 3 = ________

Problem Solving REAL WORLD

9. In PE class, Carl runs a distance of 1.17 miles in 9 minutes. At that rate, how far does Carl run in one minute?

____

10. Marianne spends $9.45 on 5 greeting cards. Each card costs the same amount. What is the cost of one greeting card?

____

Name ___________________________

Lesson 46

COMMON CORE STANDARD CC.5.NBT.7

Lesson Objective: Estimate decimal quotients.

Estimate Quotients

You can use multiples and compatible numbers to estimate decimal quotients.

Estimate. 249.7 ÷ 31

Step 1 Round the divisor, 31, to the nearest 10.

31 rounded to the nearest 10 is 30.

Step 2 Find the multiples of 30 that the dividend, 249.7, is between.

249.7 is between 240 and 270.

Step 3 Divide each multiple by the rounded divisor, 30.

240 ÷ 30 = 8 270 ÷ 30 = 9

So, two possible estimates are 8 and 9.

Use compatible numbers to estimate the quotient.

1. 23.6 ÷ 7

_____ ÷ _____ = _____

2. 469.4 ÷ 62

_____ ÷ _____ = _____

Estimate the quotient.

3. 338.7 ÷ 49

4. 75.1 ÷ 9

5. 674.8 ÷ 23

6. 61.9 ÷ 7

7. 96.5 ÷ 19

8. 57.2 ÷ 8

Name ______________________

Estimate Quotients

Use compatible numbers to estimate the quotient.

1. $19.7 \div 3$

$18 \div 3 = 6$

2. $394.6 \div 9$

3. $308.3 \div 15$

Estimate the quotient.

4. $63.5 \div 5$

5. $57.8 \div 81$

6. $172.6 \div 39$

7. $43.6 \div 8$

8. $2.8 \div 6$

9. $467.6 \div 8$

10. $209.3 \div 48$

11. $737.5 \div 9$

12. $256.1 \div 82$

Problem Solving REAL WORLD

13. Taylor uses 645.6 gallons of water in 7 days. Suppose he uses the same amount of water each day. About how much water does Taylor use each day?

____

14. On a road trip, Sandy drives 368.7 miles. Her car uses a total of 18 gallons of gas. About how many miles per gallon does Sandy's car get?

____

Name ___________________________

Lesson 47

COMMON CORE STANDARD CC.5.NBT.7

Lesson Objective: Divide decimals by whole numbers.

Division of Decimals by Whole Numbers

Divide. 19.61 ÷ 37

Step 1 Estimate the quotient.
2,000 hundredths ÷ 40 = 50 hundredths, or 0.50.
So, the quotient will have a zero in the ones place.

$$37\overline{)19.61}$$ quotient: 0

Step 2 Divide the tenths.
Use the estimate. Try 5 in the tenths place.

Multiply. 5 × 37 = 185

Subtract. 196 − 185 = 11

Check. 11 < 37

$$\begin{array}{r} 0\,5 \\ 37\overline{)19.61} \\ -18\,5 \\ \hline 1\,1 \end{array}$$

Step 3 Divide the hundredths.
Estimate: 120 hundredths ÷ 40 = 3 hundredths.

Multiply. 3 × 37 = 111

Subtract. 111 − 111 = 0

Check. 0 < 37

Place the decimal point in the quotient.

So, 19.61 ÷ 37 = 0.53.

$$\begin{array}{r} 0.53 \\ 37\overline{)19.61} \\ -18\,5 \\ \hline 1\,11 \\ -1\,11 \\ \hline 0 \end{array}$$

Write the quotient with the decimal point placed correctly.

1. 5.94 ÷ 3 = 198 ________

2. 48.3 ÷ 23 = 21 ________

Divide.

3. $9\overline{)61.2}$

4. $17\overline{)83.3}$

5. $9\overline{)7.38}$

Name ______________________________

Lesson 47
CC.5.NBT.7

Division of Decimals by Whole Numbers

Divide.

1. $7\overline{)9.24}$ = 1.32
   −7
   22
   −21
   14
   −14
   0

2. $6\overline{)5.04}$

3. $23\overline{)85.1}$

4. $36\overline{)86.4}$

5. $6\overline{)\$6.48}$

6. $8\overline{)59.2}$

7. $5\overline{)2.35}$

8. $41\overline{)278.8}$

9. $19\overline{)\$70.49}$

10. $4\overline{)\$9.48}$

11. $18\overline{)82.8}$

12. $37\overline{)32.93}$

Problem Solving

13. On Saturday, 12 friends go ice skating. Altogether, they pay $83.40 for admission. They share the cost equally. How much does each person pay?

____

14. A team of 4 people participates in a 400-yard relay race. Each team member runs the same distance. The team completes the race in a total of 53.2 seconds. What is the average running time for each person?

____

Name ______________________________

Lesson 48

COMMON CORE STANDARD CC.5.NBT.7

Lesson Objective: Model division by decimals.

Decimal Division

You can use decimal models to divide tenths.

Divide. 1.8 ÷ 0.3.

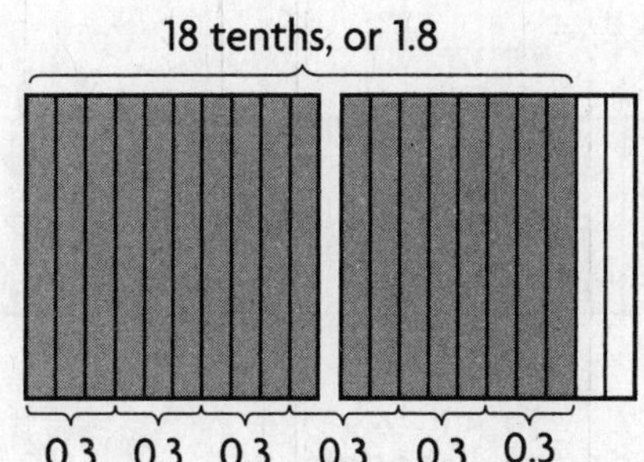

Step 1 Shade 18 tenths to represent the dividend, __1.8__.

Step 2 Divide the 18 tenths into groups of __3__ tenths to represent the divisor, __0.3__.

Step 3 Count the groups.

There are __6__ groups of 0.3 in 1.8. So, 1.8 ÷ 0.3 = __6__.

You can use decimal models to divide hundredths.

Divide. 0.42 ÷ 0.06

There are 42 shaded squares, or __0.42__.

There are __7__ groups of __6__ hundredths.

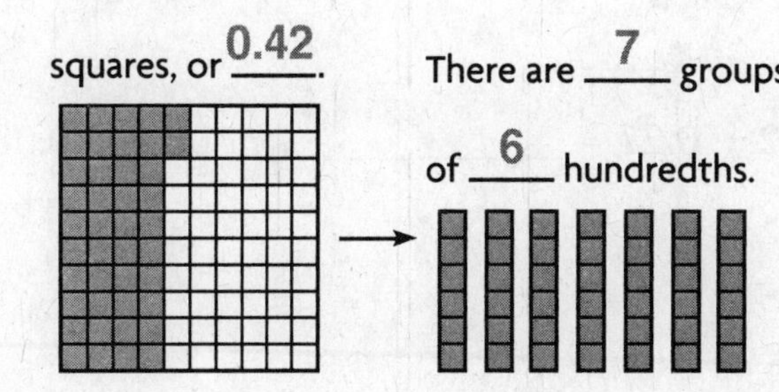

Step 1 Shade 42 squares to represent the dividend, __0.42__.

Step 2 Divide the 42 small squares into groups of __6__ hundredths to represent the divisor, __0.06__.

Step 3 Count the groups.

There are __7__ groups of 0.06 in 0.42. So, 0.42 ÷ 0.06 = __7__.

Use the model to complete the number sentence.

1. 1.4 ÷ 0.7 = __________

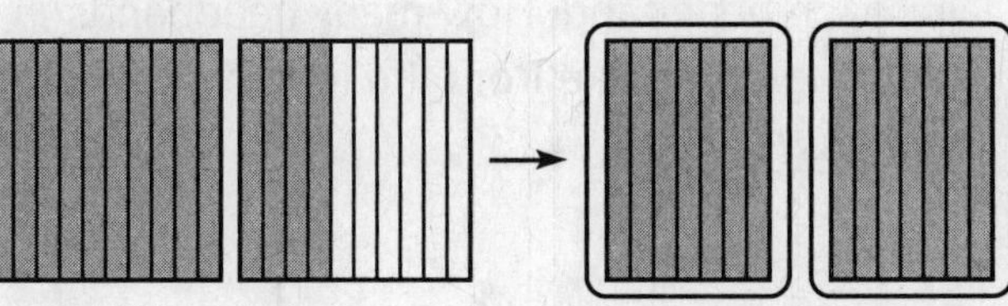

2. 0.15 ÷ 0.03 = __________

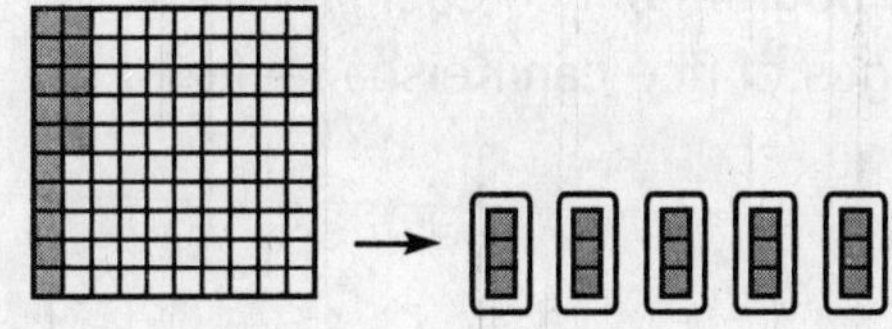

Divide. Use decimal models.

3. 2.7 ÷ 0.3 = __________

4. 0.52 ÷ 0.26 = __________

5. 0.96 ÷ 0.16 = __________

Name ________________________________

Lesson 48
CC.5.NBT.7

Decimal Division

Use the model to complete the number sentence.

1. $1.6 \div 0.4 =$ 4

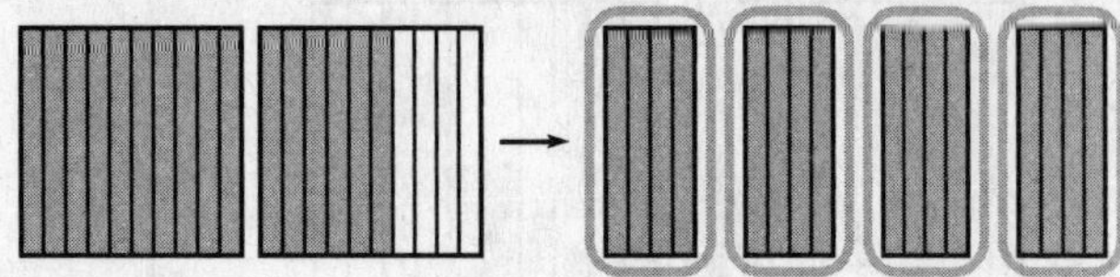

2. $0.36 \div 0.06 =$ ________

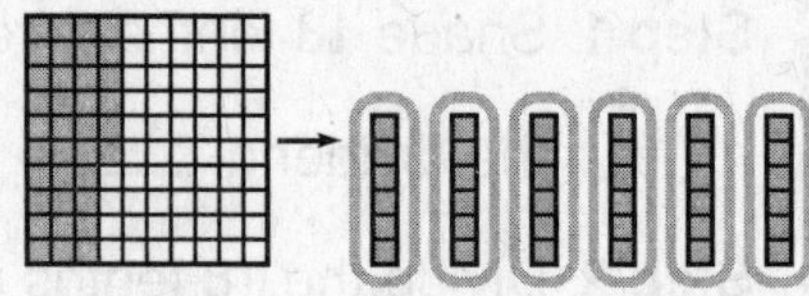

Divide. Use decimal models.

3. $2.8 \div 0.7 =$ ________

4. $0.40 \div 0.05 =$ ________

5. $0.45 \div 0.05 =$ ________

6. $1.62 \div 0.27 =$ ________

7. $0.56 \div 0.08 =$ ________

8. $1.8 \div 0.9 =$ ________

Problem Solving REAL WORLD

9. Keisha buys 2.4 kilograms of rice. She separates the rice into packages that contain 0.4 kilogram of rice each. How many packages of rice can Keisha make?

____

10. Leighton is making cloth headbands. She has 4.2 yards of cloth. She uses 0.2 yard of cloth for each headband. How many headbands can Leighton make from the length of cloth she has?

____

Name ______________________________

Lesson 49

COMMON CORE STANDARD CC.5.NBT.7

Lesson Objective: Place the decimal point in decimal division.

Divide Decimals

You can multiply the dividend and the divisor by the same power of 10 to make the divisor a whole number. As long as you multiply both the dividend and the divisor by the same power of 10, the quotient stays the same.

Example 1: Divide. 0.84 ÷ 0.07

Multiply the dividend, 0.84, and the divisor, 0.07, by the power of 10 that makes the divisor a whole number.

0.84 ÷ 0.07 = ?

× 100 × 100

84 ÷ 7 = 12

Since 84 ÷ 7 = 12, you know that 0.84 ÷ 0.07 = 12.

Example 2: Divide. 4.42 ÷ 3.4

Multiply both the dividend and the divisor by 10 to make the divisor a whole number.

3.4)4.42 — Multiply 3.4 and 4.42 both by 10 → 34)44.2

Divide as you would whole numbers. Place the decimal point in the quotient, above the decimal point in the dividend.

```
    1.3
34)44.2
  - 34
   102
 - 102
     0
```

So, 4.42 ÷ 3.4 = 1.3.

Copy and complete the pattern.

1. 54 ÷ 6 = ______
5.4 ÷ ______ = 9
______ ÷ 0.06 = 9

2. 184 ÷ 23 = ______
18.4 ÷ ______ = 8
______ ÷ 0.23 = 8

3. 138 ÷ 2 = ______
13.8 ÷ ______ = 69
______ ÷ 0.02 = 69

Divide.

4. 1.4)9.8

5. 0.3)0.6

6. 3.64 ÷ 1.3

Name ___________________________

Divide Decimals

Divide.

1. $0.4\overline{)8.4}$

   Multiply both 0.4 and 8.4 by 10 to make the divisor a whole number. Then divide.

   $$\begin{array}{r} 21 \\ 4\overline{)84} \\ -8 \\ \hline 04 \\ -4 \\ \hline 0 \end{array}$$

2. $0.2\overline{)0.4}$

3. $0.07\overline{)1.68}$

4. $0.37\overline{)5.18}$

5. $0.4\overline{)10.4}$

6. $6.3 \div 0.7$

7. $1.52 \div 1.9$

8. $12.24 \div 0.34$

9. $10.81 \div 2.3$

Problem Solving REAL WORLD

10. At the market, grapes cost $0.85 per pound. Clarissa buys grapes and pays a total of $2.55. How many pounds of grapes does she buy?

    ____

11. Damon kayaks on a river near his home. He plans to kayak a total of 6.4 miles. Damon kayaks at an average speed of 1.6 miles per hour. How many hours will it take Damon to kayak the 6.4 miles?

    ____

Name ______________________________

Lesson 50

COMMON CORE STANDARD CC.5.NBT.7

Lesson Objective: Write a zero in the dividend to find a quotient.

Write Zeros in the Dividend

When there are not enough digits in the dividend to complete the division, you can write zeros to the right of the last digit in the dividend. Writing zeros will not change the value of the dividend or the quotient.

Divide. 5.2 ÷ 8

Step 1 Divide as you would whole numbers. Place the decimal point in the quotient above the decimal point in the dividend.

$$\begin{array}{r} 0.6 \\ 8\overline{)5.2} \\ -4\,8 \\ \hline 4 \end{array}$$

The decimal point in the quotient is directly above the decimal point in the dividend.

Step 2 The difference is less than the divisor. Write a 0 in the dividend and continue to divide.

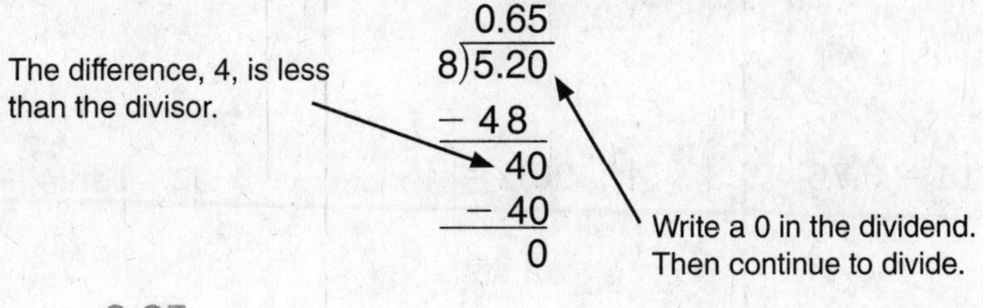

$$\begin{array}{r} 0.65 \\ 8\overline{)5.20} \\ -4\,8 \\ \hline 40 \\ -40 \\ \hline 0 \end{array}$$

The difference, 4, is less than the divisor.

Write a 0 in the dividend. Then continue to divide.

So, 5.2 ÷ 8 = 0.65.

Write the quotient with the decimal point placed correctly.

1. 3 ÷ 0.4 = 75

2. 25.2 ÷ 8 = 315

3. 60 ÷ 25 = 24

4. 8.28 ÷ 0.72 = 115

Divide.

5. $6\overline{)43.5}$

6. $1.4\overline{)7.7}$

7. $30\overline{)72}$

8. $0.18\overline{)0.63}$

Name ______________________________

Write Zeros in the Dividend

Lesson 50
CC.5.NBT.7

Divide.

1. $6\overline{)23.70}$ = 3.95
   −18
   57
   −54
   30
   −30
   0

2. $25\overline{)405}$

3. $0.6\overline{)12.9}$

4. $0.8\overline{)30}$

5. $4\overline{)36.2}$

6. $35\overline{)97.3}$

7. $7.8 \div 15$

8. $49 \div 14$

9. $52.2 \div 12$

10. $1.14 \div 0.76$

11. $20.2 \div 4$

12. $138.4 \div 16$

Problem Solving

13. Mark has a board that is 12 feet long. He cuts the board into 8 pieces that are the same length. How long is each piece?

____

14. Josh pays $7.59 for 2.2 pounds of ground turkey. What is the price per pound of the ground turkey?

____

Name ______________________

Lesson 51

COMMON CORE STANDARD CC.5.NBT.7

Lesson Objective: Solve multistep decimal problems using the strategy *work backward.*

Problem Solving • Decimal Operations

Rebecca spent $32.55 for a photo album and three identical candles. The photo album cost $17.50 and the sales tax was $1.55. How much did each candle cost?

Read the Problem		
What do I need to find?	**What information do I need to use?**	**How will I use the information?**
I need to find the cost of each candle.	Rebecca spent $32.55 for a photo album and 3 candles. The photo album cost $17.50. The sales tax was $1.55.	I can use a flowchart and work backward from the total amount Rebecca spent to find the cost of each candle.

Solve the Problem

- Make a flowchart to show the information. Then work backward to solve.

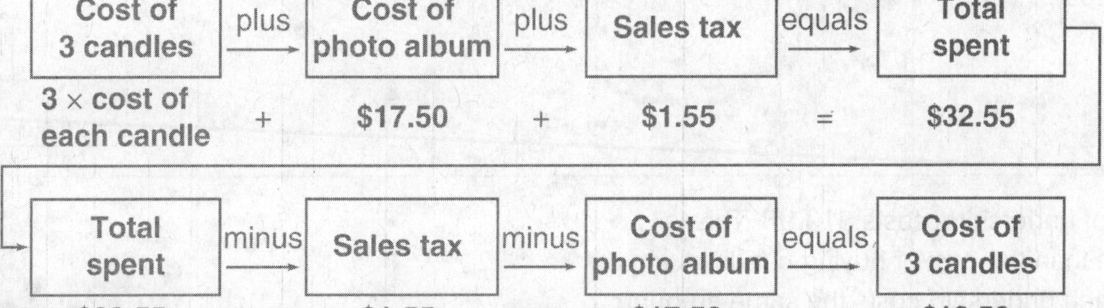

- Divide the cost of 3 candles by 3 to find the cost of each candle.

  $13.50 ÷ 3 = $4.50

  So, each candle cost $4.50.

Use a flowchart to help you solve the problem.

1. Maria spent $28.69 on one pair of jeans and two T-shirts. The jeans cost $16.49. Each T-shirt cost the same amount. The sales tax was $1.62. How much did each T-shirt cost?

____

2. At the skating rink, Sean and Patrick spent $17.45 on admission and snacks. They used one coupon for $2 off the admission cost. The snacks cost $5.95. What is the admission cost for one?

____

Name ______________________________

Lesson 51

CC.5.NBT.7

Problem Solving • Decimal Operations

1. Lily spent $30.00 on a T-shirt, a sandwich, and 2 books. The T-shirt cost $8.95, and the sandwich cost $7.25. The books each cost the same amount. How much did each book cost?

(2 × cost of each book) + $8.95 + $7.25 = $30.00
$30.00 − $8.95 − $7.25 = (2 × cost of each book)
(2 × cost of each book) = $13.80
$13.80 ÷ 2 = $6.90

$6.90

2. Meryl spends a total of $68.82 for 2 pairs of sneakers with the same cost. The sales tax is $5.32. Meryl also uses a coupon for $3.00 off her purchase. How much does each pair of sneakers cost?

____

3. A 6-pack of undershirts costs $13.98. This is $3.96 less than the cost of buying 6 individual shirts. If each undershirt costs the same amount, how much does each undershirt cost when purchased individually?

____

4. Mason spent $15.85 for 3 notebooks and 2 boxes of markers. The boxes of markers cost $3.95 each, and the sales tax was $1.23. Mason also used a coupon for $0.75 off his purchase. If each notebook had the same cost, how much did each notebook cost?

____

Name ______________________________

Lesson 52

COMMON CORE STANDARD CC.5.NF.1

Lesson Objective: Find a common denominator or a least common denominator to write equivalent fractions.

Common Denominators and Equivalent Fractions

You can find a common denominator of two fractions.

A **common denominator** of two fractions is a common multiple of their denominators.

Find a common denominator of $\frac{1}{6}$ and $\frac{7}{10}$. Rewrite the pair of fractions using a common denominator.

Step 1 Identify the denominators.
The denominators are 6 and 10.

Step 2 List the multiples of the greater denominator, 10.
Multiples of 10: 10, 20, 30, 40, 50, 60, ...

Step 3 Check if any of the multiples of the greater denominator are evenly divisible by the other denominator.

Both 30 and 60 are evenly divisible by 6.
Common denominators of $\frac{1}{6}$ and $\frac{7}{10}$ are 30 and 60.

Step 4 Rewrite the fractions with a denominator of 30.
Multiply the numerator and the denominator of each fraction by the same number so that the denominator results in 30.

$$\frac{1}{6} = \frac{1 \times 5}{6 \times 5} = \frac{5}{30} \qquad \frac{7}{10} = \frac{7 \times 3}{10 \times 3} = \frac{21}{30}$$

Use a common denominator to write an equivalent fraction for each fraction.

1. $\frac{5}{12}, \frac{2}{9}$

common denominator: ____________

____

2. $\frac{3}{8}, \frac{5}{6}$

common denominator: ____________

____

3. $\frac{2}{9}, \frac{1}{6}$

common denominator: ____________

____

4. $\frac{3}{4}, \frac{9}{10}$

common denominator: ____________

____

Name ___________________________

Common Denominators and Equivalent Fractions

Use a common denominator to write an equivalent fraction for each fraction.

1. $\frac{1}{5}, \frac{1}{2}$ common denominator: **10**

   Think: 10 is a multiple of 5 and 2. Find equivalent fractions with a denominator of 10.

   ____

2. $\frac{1}{4}, \frac{2}{3}$ common denominator: ______

   ____

3. $\frac{5}{6}, \frac{1}{3}$ common denominator: ______

   ____

4. $\frac{3}{5}, \frac{1}{3}$ common denominator: ______

   ____

5. $\frac{1}{2}, \frac{3}{8}$ common denominator: ______

   ____

6. $\frac{1}{6}, \frac{1}{4}$ common denominator: ______

   ____

Use the least common denominator to write an equivalent fraction for each fraction.

7. $\frac{5}{6}, \frac{2}{9}$

   ____

8. $\frac{1}{12}, \frac{3}{8}$

   ____

9. $\frac{5}{9}, \frac{2}{15}$

   ____

Problem Solving REAL WORLD

10. Ella spends $\frac{2}{3}$ hour practicing the piano each day. She also spends $\frac{1}{2}$ hour jogging. What is the least common denominator of the fractions?

    ____

11. In a science experiment, a plant grew $\frac{3}{4}$ inch one week and $\frac{1}{2}$ inch the next week. Use a common denominator to write an equivalent fraction for each fraction.

    ____

Name ______________________

Lesson 53

COMMON CORE STANDARD CC.5.NF.1

Lesson Objective: Use equivalent fractions to add and subtract fractions.

Add and Subtract Fractions

To add or subtract fractions with unlike denominators, you need to rename them as fractions with like denominators. You can do this by making a list of equivalent fractions.

Add. $\frac{5}{12} + \frac{1}{8}$

Step 1 Write equivalent fractions for $\frac{5}{12}$. $\frac{5}{12}, \frac{10}{24}, \frac{15}{36}, \frac{20}{48}$

Step 2 Write equivalent fractions for $\frac{1}{8}$. $\frac{1}{8}, \frac{2}{16}, \frac{3}{24}$

Step 3 Rewrite the problem using the equivalent fractions. Then add.

$\frac{5}{12} + \frac{1}{8}$ becomes $\frac{10}{24} + \frac{3}{24} = \frac{13}{24}$.

Stop when you find two fractions with the same denominator.

Subtract. $\frac{9}{10} - \frac{1}{2}$

Step 1 Write equivalent fractions for $\frac{9}{10}$. $\frac{9}{10}, \frac{18}{20}, \frac{27}{30}, \frac{36}{40}$

Step 2 Write equivalent fractions for $\frac{1}{2}$. $\frac{1}{2}, \frac{2}{4}, \frac{3}{6}, \frac{4}{8}, \frac{5}{10}$

Step 3 Rewrite the problem using the equivalent fractions. Then subtract.

$\frac{9}{10} - \frac{1}{2}$ becomes $\frac{9}{10} - \frac{5}{10} = \frac{4}{10}$. Written in simplest form, $\frac{4}{10} = \frac{2}{5}$.

Find the sum or difference. Write your answer in simplest form.

1. $\frac{2}{9} + \frac{1}{3}$ ________

2. $\frac{1}{2} + \frac{2}{5}$ ________

3. $\frac{1}{4} + \frac{1}{6}$ ________

4. $\frac{1}{5} + \frac{3}{4}$ ________

5. $\frac{7}{8} - \frac{1}{4}$ ________

6. $\frac{3}{4} - \frac{2}{3}$ ________

7. $\frac{9}{10} - \frac{4}{5}$ ________

8. $\frac{8}{9} - \frac{5}{6}$ ________

Name ______________________________

Lesson 53
CC.5.NF.1

Add and Subtract Fractions

Find the sum or difference. Write your answer in simplest form.

1. $\frac{1}{2} - \frac{1}{7}$

$\frac{1}{2} \rightarrow \frac{7}{14}$

$2\frac{1}{7} \rightarrow 2\frac{2}{14}$

$\frac{5}{14}$

2. $\frac{7}{10} - \frac{1}{2}$ ______

3. $\frac{1}{6} + \frac{1}{2}$ ______

4. $\frac{5}{8} + \frac{2}{5}$ ______

5. $\frac{9}{10} - \frac{1}{3}$ ______

6. $\frac{3}{4} - \frac{2}{5}$ ______

7. $\frac{5}{7} - \frac{1}{4}$ ______

8. $\frac{7}{8} + \frac{1}{3}$ ______

9. $\frac{5}{6} + \frac{2}{5}$ ______

10. $\frac{1}{6} - \frac{1}{10}$ ______

11. $\frac{6}{11} - \frac{1}{2}$ ______

12. $\frac{5}{6} + \frac{3}{7}$ ______

Problem Solving

13. Kaylin mixed two liquids for a science experiment. One container held $\frac{7}{8}$ cup and the other held $\frac{9}{10}$ cup. What is the total amount of the mixture?

____

14. Henry bought $\frac{1}{4}$ pound of screws and $\frac{2}{5}$ pound of nails to build a skateboard ramp. What is the total weight of the screws and nails?

____

Name ______________________________

Lesson 54

COMMON CORE STANDARD CC.5.NF.1

Lesson Objective: Add and subtract mixed numbers with unlike denominators.

Add and Subtract Mixed Numbers

When you add or subtract mixed numbers, you may need to rename the fractions as fractions with a common denominator.

Find the sum. Write the answer in simplest form. $5\frac{3}{4} + 2\frac{1}{3}$

Step 1 Model $5\frac{3}{4}$ and $2\frac{1}{3}$.

Step 2 A common denominator for $\frac{3}{4}$ and $\frac{1}{3}$ is 12, so rename $5\frac{3}{4}$ as $5\frac{9}{12}$ and $2\frac{1}{3}$ as $2\frac{4}{12}$.

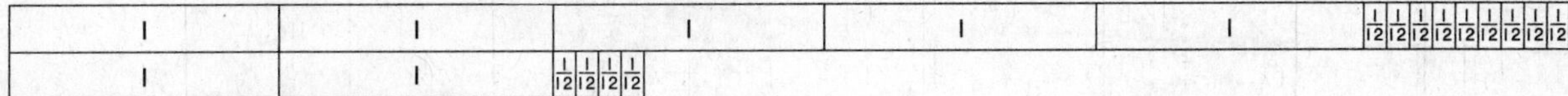

Step 3 Add the fractions.

$$\frac{9}{12} + \frac{4}{12} = \frac{13}{12}$$

Step 4 Add the whole numbers

$5 + 2 = 7$

Add the sums. Write the answer in simplest form.

$$\frac{13}{12} + 7 = 7\frac{13}{12}, \text{ or } 8\frac{1}{12}$$

So, $5\frac{3}{4} + 2\frac{1}{3} = 8\frac{1}{12}$.

Find the sum or difference. Write your answer in simplest form.

1. $2\frac{2}{9} + 4\frac{1}{6}$ ______

2. $10\frac{5}{6} + 5\frac{3}{4}$ ______

3. $11\frac{7}{8} - 9\frac{5}{6}$ ______

4. $18\frac{3}{5} - 14\frac{1}{2}$ ______

Name ____________________________

Lesson 54

CC.5.NF.1

Add and Subtract Mixed Numbers

Find the sum or difference. Write your answer in simplest form.

1. $3\frac{1}{2} - 1\frac{1}{5}$

$$\begin{array}{rcr} 3\frac{1}{2} & \rightarrow & 3\frac{5}{10} \\ -1\frac{1}{5} & \rightarrow & -1\frac{2}{10} \\ \hline & & 2\frac{3}{10} \end{array}$$

2. $2\frac{1}{3} + 1\frac{3}{4}$

3. $4\frac{1}{8} + 2\frac{1}{3}$

4. $5\frac{1}{3} + 6\frac{1}{6}$

5. $2\frac{1}{4} + 1\frac{2}{5}$

6. $5\frac{17}{18} - 2\frac{2}{3}$

7. $6\frac{3}{4} - 1\frac{5}{8}$

8. $5\frac{3}{7} - 2\frac{1}{5}$

9. $4\frac{1}{8} + 2\frac{5}{12}$

10. $6\frac{6}{7} - 2\frac{3}{4}$

11. $5\frac{5}{6} - 2\frac{3}{4}$

12. $2\frac{6}{25} - 1\frac{1}{10}$

Problem Solving REAL WORLD

13. Jacobi bought $7\frac{1}{2}$ pounds of meatballs. He decided to cook $1\frac{1}{4}$ pounds and freeze the rest. How many pounds did he freeze?

14. Jill walked $8\frac{1}{8}$ miles to a park and then $7\frac{2}{5}$ miles home. How many miles did she walk in all?

Name ______________________________

Lesson 55

COMMON CORE STANDARD CC.5.NF.1

Lesson Objective: Rename to find the difference of two mixed numbers.

Subtraction with Renaming

You can use a common denominator to find the difference of two mixed numbers.

Estimate. $9\frac{1}{6} - 2\frac{3}{4}$

Step 1 Estimate by using 0, $\frac{1}{2}$, and 1 as benchmarks.

$9\frac{1}{6} - 2\frac{3}{4} \rightarrow 9 - 3 = 6$

So, the difference should be close to 6.

Step 2 Identify a common denominator.

$9\frac{1}{6} - 2\frac{3}{4}$ A common denominator of 6 and 4 is 12.

Step 3 Write equivalent fractions using the common denominator.

$9\frac{1}{6} = 9 + \frac{1 \times 2}{6 \times 2} = 9\frac{2}{12}$

$2\frac{3}{4} = 2 + \frac{3 \times 3}{4 \times 3} = 2\frac{9}{12}$

Step 4 Rename if needed. Then subtract.

Since $\frac{2}{12} < \frac{9}{12}$, rename $9\frac{2}{12}$ as $8\frac{14}{12}$.

Subtract. $8\frac{14}{12} - 2\frac{9}{12} = 6\frac{5}{12}$

So, $9\frac{1}{6} - 2\frac{3}{4} = 6\frac{5}{12}$.

Since the difference of $6\frac{5}{12}$ is close to 6, the answer is reasonable.

Estimate. Then find the difference and write it in simplest form.

1. Estimate: ____________

$5\frac{1}{3} - 3\frac{5}{6}$ ______

2. Estimate: ____________

$7\frac{1}{4} - 2\frac{5}{12}$ ______

3. Estimate: ____________

$8\frac{2}{3} - 2\frac{7}{9}$ ______

4. Estimate: ____________

$9\frac{2}{5} - 3\frac{3}{4}$ ______

5. Estimate: ____________

$7\frac{3}{16} - 1\frac{5}{8}$ ______

6. Estimate: ____________

$2\frac{4}{9} - 1\frac{11}{18}$ ______

Name ____________________

Lesson 55

CC.5.NF.1

Subtraction with Renaming

Estimate. Then find the difference and write it in simplest form.

1. Estimate: ________

$6\frac{1}{3} - 1\frac{2}{5}$

$$\begin{array}{r} 6\frac{1}{3} \rightarrow \overset{5}{\cancel{6}}\,\frac{\overset{20}{\cancel{5}}}{15} \\ -1\frac{2}{5} \rightarrow -1\frac{6}{15} \\ \hline 4\frac{14}{15} \end{array}$$

2. Estimate: ________

$4\frac{1}{2} - 3\frac{5}{6}$

3. Estimate: ________

$9 - 3\frac{7}{8}$

4. Estimate: ________

$2\frac{1}{6} - 1\frac{2}{7}$

5. Estimate: ________

$8 - 6\frac{1}{9}$

6. Estimate: ________

$9\frac{1}{4} - 3\frac{2}{3}$

7. Estimate: ________

$2\frac{1}{8} - 1\frac{2}{7}$

8. Estimate: ________

$8\frac{1}{5} - 3\frac{5}{9}$

9. Estimate: ________

$10\frac{2}{3} - 5\frac{9}{10}$

Problem Solving REAL WORLD

10. Carlene bought $8\frac{1}{16}$ yards of ribbon to decorate a shirt. She only used $5\frac{1}{2}$ yards. How much ribbon does she have left over?

____

11. During his first vet visit, Pedro's puppy weighed $6\frac{1}{8}$ pounds. On his second visit, he weighed $9\frac{1}{16}$ pounds. How much weight did he gain between visits?

____

Name ______________________________

Lesson 56

COMMON CORE STANDARD CC.5.NF.1

Lesson Objective: Identify, describe, and create numeric patterns with fractions.

Algebra • Patterns with Fractions

You can find an unknown term in a sequence by finding a rule for the sequence.

Find the unknown term in the sequence.

$1\frac{2}{5}, 1\frac{7}{10}, 2, \_\_\_, 2\frac{3}{5}$

Step 1 Find equivalent fractions with a common denominator for all of the terms.

The denominators are 5 and 10. A common denominator is 10.

$1\frac{2}{5} = 1\frac{4}{10}$ and $2\frac{3}{5} = 2\frac{6}{10}$

Step 2 Write the terms in the sequence using the common denominator.

$1\frac{4}{10}, 1\frac{7}{10}, 2, \_\_\_, 2\frac{6}{10}$

Step 3 Write a rule that describes the pattern.

The sequence increases. To find the difference between terms, subtract at least two pairs of consecutive terms.

$1\frac{7}{10} - 1\frac{4}{10} = \frac{3}{10}$ $\quad$ $2 - 1\frac{7}{10} = \frac{3}{10}$

So, a rule is to add $\frac{3}{10}$.

Step 4 Use the rule to find the unknown term.

Add $\frac{3}{10}$ to the third term to find the unknown term.

$2 + \frac{3}{10} = 2\frac{3}{10}$

Write a rule for the sequence. Then, find the unknown term.

1. $2\frac{2}{3}, 3\frac{1}{2}, \_\_\_, 5\frac{1}{6}, 6$

Rule: ______________________

2. $4\frac{1}{2}, 3\frac{7}{8}, 3\frac{1}{4}, \_\_\_, 2$

Rule: ______________________

Name ___________________________

Lesson 56

CC.5.NF.1

Patterns with Fractions

Write a rule for the sequence. Then, find the unknown term.

1. $\frac{1}{2}, \frac{2}{3}, \underline{\frac{5}{6}}, 1, 1\frac{1}{6}$

Think: The pattern is increasing. Add $\frac{1}{6}$ to find the next term.

Rule: ___________________________

2. $1\frac{3}{8}, 1\frac{3}{4}, 2\frac{1}{8}$, ______, $2\frac{7}{8}$

Rule: ___________________________

3. $1\frac{9}{10}, 1\frac{7}{10}$, ______, $1\frac{3}{10}, 1\frac{1}{10}$

Rule: ___________________________

4. $2\frac{5}{12}, 2\frac{1}{6}, 1\frac{11}{12}$, ______, $1\frac{5}{12}$

Rule: ___________________________

Write the first four terms of the sequence.

5. Rule: start at $\frac{1}{2}$, add $\frac{1}{3}$

____

6. Rule: start at $3\frac{1}{8}$, subtract $\frac{3}{4}$

____

7. Rule: start at $5\frac{1}{2}$, add $1\frac{1}{5}$

____

8. Rule: start at $6\frac{2}{3}$, subtract $1\frac{1}{4}$

____

9. Jarett's puppy weighed $3\frac{3}{4}$ ounces at birth. At one week old, the puppy weighed $5\frac{1}{8}$ ounces. At two weeks old, the puppy weighed $6\frac{1}{2}$ ounces. If the weight gain continues in this pattern, how much will the puppy weigh at three weeks old?

____

10. A baker started out with 12 cups of flour. She had $9\frac{1}{4}$ cups of flour left after the first batch of batter she made. She had $6\frac{1}{2}$ cups of flour left after the second batch of batter she made. If she makes two more batches of batter, how many cups of flour will be left?

____

Name ______________________

Lesson 57

COMMON CORE STANDARD CC.5.NF.1

Lesson Objective: Add fractions and mixed numbers with unlike denominators using the properties.

Algebra • Use Properties of Addition

You can use the properties of addition to help you add fractions with unlike denominators.

Use the Commutative Property and the Associative Property.

Add. $\left(3\frac{2}{5} + 1\frac{7}{15}\right) + 2\frac{1}{5}$

$\left(3\frac{2}{5} + 1\frac{7}{15}\right) + 2\frac{1}{5} = \left(1\frac{7}{15} + 3\frac{2}{5}\right) + 2\frac{1}{5}$ ← Use the Commutative Property to order fractions with like denominators.

$= 1\frac{7}{15} + \left(3\frac{2}{5} + 2\frac{1}{5}\right)$ ← Use the Associative Property to group fractions with like denominators.

$= 1\frac{7}{15} + 5\frac{3}{5}$ ← Use mental math to add the fractions with like denominators.

$= 1\frac{7}{15} + 5\frac{9}{15}$ ← Write equivalent fractions with like denominators. Then add.

$= 6\frac{16}{15} = 7\frac{1}{15}$ ← Rename and simplify.

Use the properties and mental math to solve. Write your answer in simplest form.

1. $\left(\frac{5}{7} + \frac{3}{14}\right) + \frac{4}{7}$ ______

2. $\left(\frac{2}{5} + \frac{5}{9}\right) + \frac{7}{9}$ ______

3. $\left(3\frac{7}{10} + 5\frac{3}{4}\right) + \frac{3}{4}$ ______

4. $2\frac{5}{12} + \left(4\frac{2}{3} + 3\frac{7}{12}\right)$ ______

5. $3\frac{3}{8} + \left(2\frac{1}{5} + 5\frac{1}{8}\right)$ ______

6. $\left(4\frac{3}{7} + 2\frac{1}{6}\right) + 3\frac{5}{7}$ ______

Name ______________________

Lesson 57

CC.5.NF.1

Use Properties of Addition

Use the properties and mental math to solve. Write your answer in simplest form.

1. $\left(2\frac{1}{3} + 1\frac{2}{5}\right) + 3\frac{2}{3}$

$= \left(1\frac{2}{5} + 2\frac{1}{3}\right) + 3\frac{2}{3}$

$= 1\frac{2}{5} + \left(2\frac{1}{3} + 3\frac{2}{3}\right)$

$= 1\frac{2}{5} + 6$

$= 7\frac{2}{5}$

2. $8\frac{1}{5} + \left(4\frac{2}{5} + 3\frac{3}{10}\right)$

3. $\left(1\frac{3}{4} + 2\frac{3}{8}\right) + 5\frac{7}{8}$

4. $2\frac{1}{10} + \left(1\frac{2}{7} + 4\frac{9}{10}\right)$

5. $\left(4\frac{3}{5} + 6\frac{1}{3}\right) + 2\frac{3}{5}$

6. $1\frac{1}{4} + \left(3\frac{2}{3} + 5\frac{3}{4}\right)$

7. $\left(7\frac{1}{8} + 1\frac{2}{7}\right) + 4\frac{3}{7}$

8. $3\frac{1}{4} + \left(3\frac{1}{4} + 5\frac{1}{5}\right)$

9. $6\frac{2}{3} + \left(5\frac{7}{8} + 2\frac{1}{3}\right)$

Problem Solving REAL WORLD

10. Elizabeth rode her bike $6\frac{1}{2}$ miles from her house to the library and then another $2\frac{2}{5}$ miles to her friend Milo's house. If Carson's house is $2\frac{1}{2}$ miles beyond Milo's house, how far would she travel from her house to Carson's house?

____

11. Hassan made a vegetable salad with $2\frac{3}{8}$ pounds of tomatoes, $1\frac{1}{4}$ pounds of asparagus, and $2\frac{7}{8}$ pounds of potatoes. How many pounds of vegetables did he use altogether?

____

Name ____________________

COMMON CORE STANDARD CC.5.NF.2

Lesson Objective: Use models to add fractions with unlike denominators.

Addition with Unlike Denominators

Karen is stringing a necklace with beads. She puts green beads on $\frac{1}{2}$ of the string and purple beads on $\frac{3}{10}$ of the string. How much of the string does Karen cover with beads?

You can use fraction strips to help you add fractions with unlike denominators. Trade fraction strips of fractions with unlike denominators for equivalent strips of fractions with like denominators.

Use fraction strips to find the sum. Write your answer in simplest form.

$\frac{1}{2} + \frac{3}{10}$

Step 1 Use a $\frac{1}{2}$ strip and three $\frac{1}{10}$ strips to model fractions with unlike denominators.

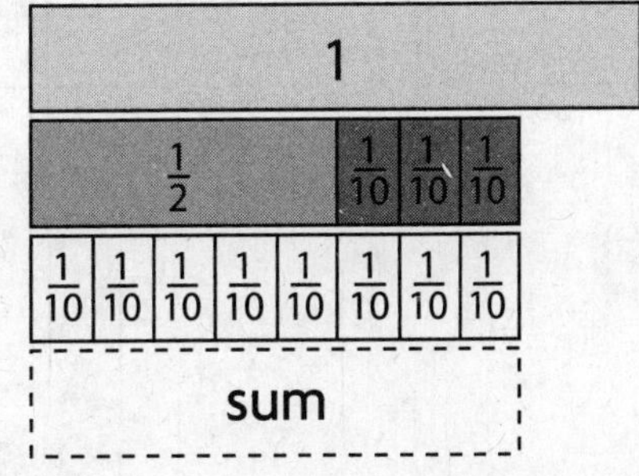

Step 2 Trade the $\frac{1}{2}$ strip for five $\frac{1}{10}$ strips.

$\frac{1}{2} + \frac{3}{10} = \frac{5}{10} + \frac{3}{10}$

Step 3 Add the fractions with like denominators.

$\frac{5}{10} + \frac{3}{10} = \frac{8}{10}$

Step 4 Write the answer in simplest form.

$\frac{8}{10} = \frac{4}{5}$

So, Karen covers $\frac{4}{5}$ of the string with beads.

Use fraction strips to find the sum. Write your answer in simplest form.

1. $\frac{3}{8} + \frac{3}{4}$ ____________

2. $\frac{2}{3} + \frac{1}{4}$ ____________

3. $\frac{5}{6} + \frac{7}{12}$ ____________

Name ______________________

Lesson 58
CC.5.NF.2

Addition with Unlike Denominators

Use fraction strips to find the sum. Write your answer in simplest form.

1. $\frac{1}{2} + \frac{3}{4}$

$\frac{1}{2} + \frac{3}{4} = \frac{2}{4} + \frac{3}{4} = \frac{5}{4}$, or $1\frac{1}{4}$

$1\frac{1}{4}$

2. $\frac{1}{3} + \frac{1}{4}$

3. $\frac{3}{5} + \frac{1}{2}$

4. $\frac{3}{8} + \frac{1}{2}$

5. $\frac{1}{4} + \frac{5}{8}$

6. $\frac{2}{3} + \frac{3}{4}$

7. $\frac{1}{2} + \frac{2}{5}$

8. $\frac{2}{3} + \frac{1}{2}$

9. $\frac{7}{8} + \frac{1}{2}$

10. $\frac{5}{6} + \frac{1}{3}$

11. $\frac{1}{5} + \frac{1}{2}$

12. $\frac{3}{4} + \frac{3}{8}$

Problem Solving REAL WORLD

13. Brandus bought $\frac{1}{3}$ pound of ground turkey and $\frac{3}{4}$ pound of ground beef to make sausages. How many pounds of meat did he buy?

14. To make a ribbon and bow for a hat, Stacey needs $\frac{5}{6}$ yard of black ribbon and $\frac{2}{3}$ yard of red ribbon. How much total ribbon does she need?

Name ______________________________

Lesson 59

COMMON CORE STANDARD CC.5.NF.2

Lesson Objective: Use models to subtract fractions with unlike denominators.

Subtraction with Unlike Denominators

You can use fraction strips to help you subtract fractions with unlike denominators. Trade fraction strips of fractions with unlike denominators for equivalent strips of fractions with like denominators.

Use fraction strips to find the difference. Write your answer in simplest form.

$\frac{1}{2} - \frac{1}{10}$

Step 1 Use a $\frac{1}{2}$ fraction strip to model the first fraction.

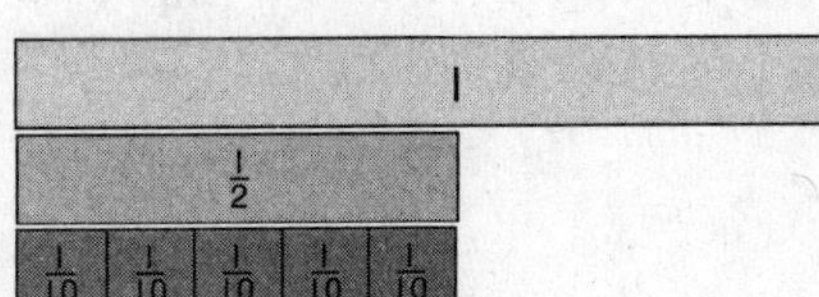

Step 2 Trade the $\frac{1}{2}$ strip for five $\frac{1}{10}$ strips.

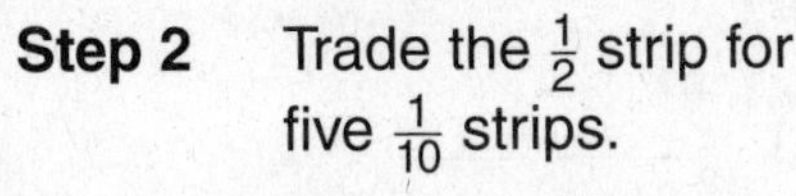

$\frac{1}{2} - \frac{1}{10} = \frac{5}{10} - \frac{1}{10}$

Step 3 Subtract by taking away $\frac{1}{10}$.

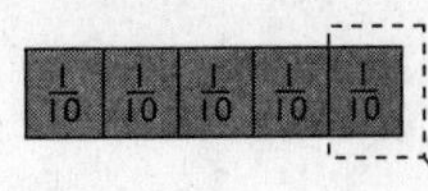

$\frac{5}{10} - \frac{1}{10} = \frac{4}{10}$

So, $\frac{1}{2} - \frac{1}{10} = \frac{4}{10}$. Written in simplest form, $\frac{4}{10} = \frac{2}{5}$.

Use fraction strips to find the difference. Write your answer in simplest form.

1. $\frac{7}{8} - \frac{1}{2}$ ____________

2. $\frac{2}{3} - \frac{1}{4}$ ____________

3. $\frac{5}{6} - \frac{1}{3}$ ____________

4. $\frac{1}{2} - \frac{1}{3}$ ____________

5. $\frac{9}{10} - \frac{4}{5}$ ____________

6. $\frac{2}{3} - \frac{5}{12}$ ____________

Name ______________________

Subtraction with Unlike Denominators

Use fraction strips to find the difference. Write your answer in simplest form.

1. $\frac{1}{2} - \frac{1}{3}$

   $\frac{1}{2} - \frac{1}{3} = \frac{3}{6} - \frac{2}{6} = \frac{1}{6}$

   $\frac{1}{6}$

2. $\frac{3}{4} - \frac{3}{8}$ ________

3. $\frac{7}{8} - \frac{1}{2}$ ________

4. $\frac{1}{2} - \frac{1}{5}$ ________

5. $\frac{2}{3} - \frac{1}{4}$ ________

6. $\frac{4}{5} - \frac{1}{2}$ ________

7. $\frac{3}{4} - \frac{1}{3}$ ________

8. $\frac{5}{8} - \frac{1}{2}$ ________

9. $\frac{7}{10} - \frac{1}{2}$ ________

10. $\frac{9}{10} - \frac{2}{5}$ ________

11. $\frac{5}{8} - \frac{1}{4}$ ________

12. $\frac{2}{3} - \frac{1}{2}$ ________

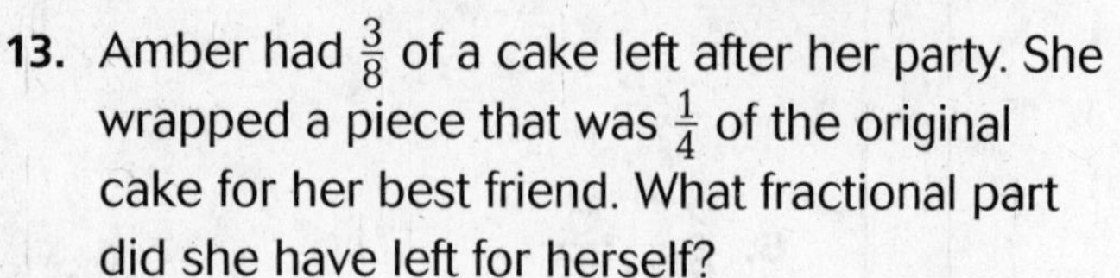

13. Amber had $\frac{3}{8}$ of a cake left after her party. She wrapped a piece that was $\frac{1}{4}$ of the original cake for her best friend. What fractional part did she have left for herself?

    ____

14. Wesley bought $\frac{1}{2}$ pound of nails for a project. When he finished the project, he had $\frac{1}{4}$ pound of the nails left. How many pounds of nails did he use?

    ____

COMMON CORE STANDARD CC.5.NF.2

Lesson Objective: Make reasonable estimates of fraction sums and differences.

Name ______________________

Estimate Fraction Sums and Differences

You can round fractions to 0, to $\frac{1}{2}$, or to 1 to estimate sums and differences.

Estimate the sum. $\frac{4}{6} + \frac{1}{9}$

Step 1 Find $\frac{4}{6}$ on the number line.
Is it closest to 0, $\frac{1}{2}$, or 1?
The fraction $\frac{4}{6}$ is closest to $\frac{1}{2}$.

$\frac{0}{6}$ $\frac{1}{6}$ $\frac{2}{6}$ $\frac{3}{6}$ $\frac{4}{6}$ $\frac{5}{6}$ $\frac{6}{6}$

0 $\frac{1}{2}$ 1

Step 2 Find $\frac{1}{9}$ on the number line.
Is it closest to 0, $\frac{1}{2}$, or 1?
The fraction $\frac{1}{9}$ is closest to 0.

$\frac{0}{9}$ $\frac{1}{9}$ $\frac{2}{9}$ $\frac{3}{9}$ $\frac{4}{9}$ $\frac{5}{9}$ $\frac{6}{9}$ $\frac{7}{9}$ $\frac{8}{9}$ $\frac{9}{9}$

0 $\frac{1}{2}$ 1

Step 3 To estimate the sum $\frac{4}{6} + \frac{1}{9}$, add the two rounded numbers.

$\frac{1}{2} + 0 = \frac{1}{2}$

So, $\frac{4}{6} + \frac{1}{9}$ is about $\frac{1}{2}$.

Estimate the sum or difference.

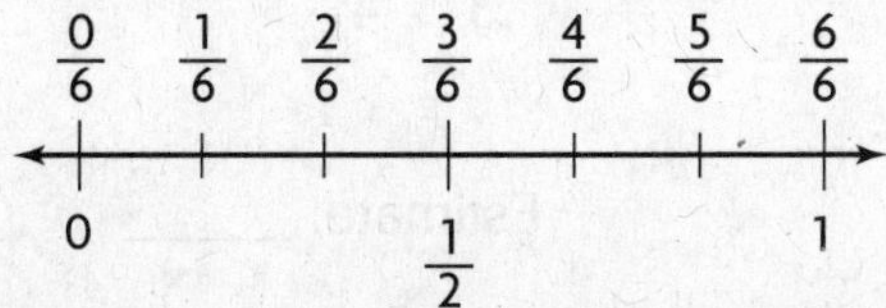

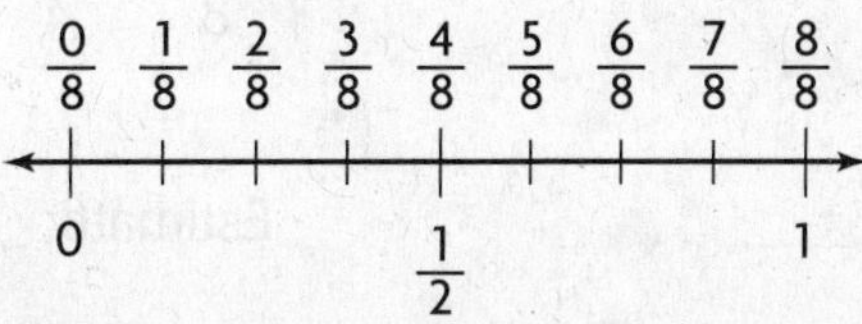

1. $\frac{4}{6} + \frac{1}{8}$ ________

2. $\frac{2}{6} + \frac{7}{8}$ ________

3. $\frac{5}{6} - \frac{3}{8}$ ________

4. $\frac{4}{6} + \frac{3}{8}$ ________

5. $\frac{7}{8} - \frac{5}{6}$ ________

6. $\frac{1}{6} + \frac{7}{8}$ ________

Name ______________________________

Lesson 60

CC.5.NF.2

Estimate Fraction Sums and Differences

Estimate the sum or difference.

1. $\frac{1}{2} - \frac{1}{3}$

   Think: $\frac{1}{3}$ is closer to $\frac{1}{2}$ than to 0.

   Estimate: 0

2. $\frac{1}{8} + \frac{1}{4}$

   Estimate: ______

3. $\frac{4}{5} - \frac{1}{2}$

   Estimate: ______

4. $2\frac{3}{5} - 1\frac{3}{8}$

   Estimate: ______

5. $\frac{1}{5} + \frac{3}{7}$

   Estimate: ______

6. $\frac{2}{5} + \frac{2}{3}$

   Estimate: ______

7. $2\frac{2}{3} + \frac{3}{4}$

   Estimate: ______

8. $1\frac{7}{8} - 1\frac{1}{2}$

   Estimate: ______

9. $4\frac{1}{8} - \frac{3}{4}$

   Estimate: ______

10. $3\frac{9}{10} - 1\frac{2}{5}$

    Estimate: ______

11. $2\frac{5}{8} + 1\frac{1}{4}$

    Estimate: ______

12. $1\frac{1}{3} - \frac{1}{4}$

    Estimate: ______

Problem Solving REAL WORLD

13. For a fruit salad recipe, Jenna combined $\frac{3}{8}$ cup of raisins, $\frac{7}{8}$ cup of oranges, and $\frac{3}{4}$ cup of apples. About how many cups of fruit are in the salad?

    ____

14. Tyler had $2\frac{7}{16}$ yards of fabric. He used $\frac{3}{4}$ yard to make a vest. About how much fabric did he have left?

    ____

Name ___________________________

Lesson 61

COMMON CORE STANDARD CC.5.NF.2

Lesson Objective: Solve problems using the strategy *work backward.*

Problem Solving • Practice Addition and Subtraction

Makayla walks for exercise. She wants to walk a total of 6 miles. On Monday, she walked $2\frac{5}{6}$ miles. On Tuesday, she walked $1\frac{1}{3}$ miles. How many more miles does Makayla need to walk to reach her goal?

Read the Problem	Solve the Problem
What do I need to find? I need to find the distance that Makayla needs to walk.	• Start with the equation. $6 = 2\frac{5}{6} + 1\frac{1}{3} + x$ Subtraction is the inverse operation of addition.
What information do I need to use? I need to use the distance she wants to walk and the distance she has already walked.	• Use subtraction to work backward and rewrite the equation. $6 - 2\frac{5}{6} - 1\frac{1}{3} = x$ • Subtract to find the value of *x*. $6 = 5\frac{6}{6}$, $-2\frac{5}{6} = -2\frac{5}{6}$, result $3\frac{1}{6}$ → $3\frac{1}{6} = 2\frac{7}{6}$, $-1\frac{1}{3} = -1\frac{2}{6}$, result $1\frac{5}{6}$
How will I use the information? First I can write an equation $6 = 2\frac{5}{6} + 1\frac{1}{3} + x$. Then I can work backward to solve the problem.	Estimate to show that your answer is reasonable. $3 + 1 + 2 = 6$ So, Makayla has to walk $1\frac{5}{6}$ more miles to reach her goal.

1. Ben has $5\frac{3}{4}$ cups of sugar. He uses $\frac{2}{3}$ cup of sugar to make cookies. Then he uses $2\frac{1}{2}$ cups of sugar to make fresh lemonade. How many cups of sugar does Ben have left?

   ____

2. Cheryl has 5 ft of ribbon. She cuts a $3\frac{3}{4}$-ft strip to make a hair bow. Then she cuts a $\frac{5}{6}$-ft strip for a border on a scrapbook page. Is there enough ribbon for Cheryl to cut two $\frac{1}{3}$-ft pieces to put on a picture frame? **Explain.**

   ____

   ____

Name ______________________

Problem Solving • Practice Addition and Subtraction

Read each problem and solve.

1. From a board 8 feet in length, Emmet cut two $2\frac{1}{3}$-foot bookshelves. How much of the board remained?

   Write an equation: $8 = 2\frac{1}{3} + 2\frac{1}{3} + x$

   Rewrite the equation to work backward:

   $8 - 2\frac{1}{3} - 2\frac{1}{3} = x$

   Subtract twice to find the length remaining: $3\frac{1}{3}$ **feet**

2. Lynne bought a bag of grapefruit, $1\frac{5}{8}$ pounds of apples, and $2\frac{3}{16}$ pounds of bananas. The total weight of her purchases was $7\frac{1}{2}$ pounds. How much did the bag of grapefruit weigh? ______________

3. Mattie's house consists of two stories and an attic. The first floor is $8\frac{5}{6}$ feet tall, the second floor is $8\frac{1}{2}$ feet tall, and the entire house is $24\frac{1}{3}$ feet tall. How tall is the attic? ______________

4. It is $10\frac{3}{5}$ miles from Alston to Barton and $12\frac{1}{2}$ miles from Barton to Chester. The distance from Alston to Durbin, via Barton and Chester, is 35 miles. How far is it from Chester to Durbin? ______________

5. Marcie bought a 50-foot roll of packing tape. She used two $8\frac{5}{6}$-foot lengths. How much tape is left on the roll? ______________

6. Meg started her trip with $11\frac{1}{2}$ gallons of gas in her car's gas tank. She bought an additional $6\frac{4}{5}$ gallons on her trip and arrived back home with $3\frac{3}{10}$ gallons left. How much gas did she use on the trip? ______________

Name ______________________

Lesson 62

COMMON CORE STANDARD CC.5.NF.3

Lesson Objective: Solve division problems and decide when to write a remainder as a fraction.

Interpret the Remainder

Erin has 87 ounces of trail mix. She puts an equal number of ounces in each of 12 bags. How many ounces does she put in each bag?

$$\begin{array}{r} 7 \text{ r3} \\ 12\overline{)87} \\ \underline{-84} \\ 3 \end{array}$$

First, divide to find the quotient and remainder. Then, decide how to use the quotient and the remainder to answer the question.

- The dividend, 87, represents the total number of ounces of trail mix.
- The divisor, 12, represents the total number of bags.
- The quotient, 7, represents the whole-number part of the number of ounces in each bag.
- The remainder, 3, represents the number of ounces left over.

Divide the 3 ounces in the remainder by the divisor, 12, to write the remainder as a fraction: $\frac{3}{12}$

Write the fraction part in simplest form in your answer.

So, Erin puts $7\frac{1}{4}$ ounces of trail mix in each bag.

Interpret the remainder to solve.

1. Harry goes on a canoe trip with his scout troop. They will canoe a total of 75 miles and want to travel 8 miles each day. How many days will they need to travel the entire distance?

____

2. Hannah and her family want to hike 8 miles per day along a 125-mile-long trail. How many days will Hannah and her family hike exactly 8 miles?

____

3. There are 103 students eating lunch in the cafeteria. Each table seats 4 students. All the tables are full, except for one table. How many students are sitting at the table that is not full?

____

4. Emily buys 240 square feet of carpet. She can convert square feet to square yards by dividing the number of square feet by 9. How many square yards of carpet did Emily buy? (Hint: Write the remainder as a fraction.)

____

Name ______________________

Interpret the Remainder

Interpret the remainder to solve.

1. Warren spent 140 hours making 16 wooden toy trucks for a craft fair. If he spent the same amount of time making each truck, how many hours did he spend making each truck?

$$\begin{array}{r} 8 \\ 16\overline{)140} \\ -128 \\ \hline 12 \end{array}$$

$8\frac{3}{4}$ hours

2. Marcia has 412 bouquets of flowers for centerpieces. She uses 8 flowers for each centerpiece. How many centerpieces can she make?

3. On the 5th grade class picnic, 50 students share 75 sandwiches equally. How many sandwiches does each student get?

4. One plant container holds 14 tomato seedlings. If you have 1,113 seedlings, how many containers do you need to hold all the seedlings?

Problem Solving REAL WORLD

5. Fiona bought 212 stickers to make a sticker book. If she places 18 stickers on each page, how many pages will her sticker book have?

6. Jenny has 220 ounces of cleaning solution that she wants to divide equally among 12 large containers. How much cleaning solution should she put in each container?

Name ______________________

Lesson 63

COMMON CORE STANDARD CC.5.NF.3

Lesson Objective: Interpret a fraction as division and solve whole-number division problems that result in a fraction or mixed number.

Connect Fractions to Division

You can write a fraction as a division expression.

$\frac{4}{5} = 4 \div 5$ $\frac{15}{3} = 15 \div 3$

There are 8 students in a wood-working class and 5 sheets of plywood for them to share equally. What fraction of a sheet of plywood will each student get?

Divide. 5 ÷ 8 **Use a drawing.**

Step 1 Draw __5__ rectangles to represent 5 sheets of plywood. Since there are 8 students, draw lines to divide each piece of plywood into __eighths__.

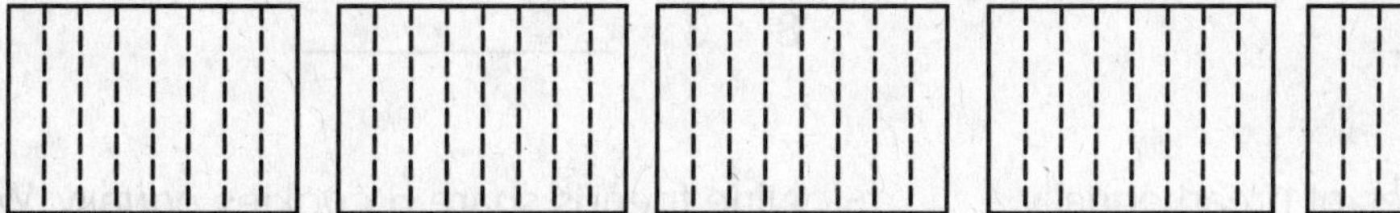

Each student's share of 1 sheet of plywood is $\frac{1}{8}$.

Step 2 Count the total number of eighths each student gets.

Since there are 5 sheets of plywood, each student will get 5 of the __eighths__, or $\frac{5}{8}$.

Step 3 Complete the number sentence.

$5 \div 8 = \frac{5}{8}$

Step 4 Check your answer.

Since $\frac{5}{8} \times 8 = 5$, the quotient is correct.

So, each student will get $\frac{5}{8}$ of a sheet of plywood.

Complete the number sentence to solve.

1. Ten friends share 6 pizzas equally. What fraction of a pizza does each friend get?

$6 \div 10 =$ ______

2. Four students share 7 sandwiches equally. How much of a sandwich does each student get?

$7 \div 4 =$ ______

Name ______________________________

Lesson 63
CC.5.NF.3

Connect Fractions to Division

Complete the number sentence to solve.

1. Six students share 8 apples equally. How many apples does each student get?

   $8 \div 6 = \underline{\frac{8}{6}, \text{ or } 1\frac{1}{3}}$

2. Ten boys share 7 cereal bars equally. What fraction of a cereal bar does each boy get?

   $7 \div 10 =$ ____________

3. Eight friends share 12 pies equally. How many pies does each friend get?

   $12 \div 8 =$ ____________

4. Three girls share 8 yards of fabric equally. How many yards of fabric does each girl get?

   $8 \div 3 =$ ____________

5. Five bakers share 2 loaves of bread equally. What fraction of a loaf of bread does each baker get?

   $2 \div 5 =$ ____________

6. Nine friends share 6 cookies equally. What fraction of a cookie does each friend get?

   $6 \div 9 =$ ____________

7. Twelve students share 3 pizzas equally. What fraction of a pizza does each student get?

   $3 \div 12 =$ ____________

8. Three sisters share 5 sandwiches equally. How many sandwiches does each sister get?

   $5 \div 3 =$ ____________

Problem Solving REAL WORLD

9. There are 12 students in a jewelry-making class and 8 sets of charms. What fraction of a set of charms will each student get?

   ____

   ____

10. Five friends share 6 cheesecakes equally. How many cheesecakes will each friend get?

    ____

    ____

Name ______________________________

Lesson 64

COMMON CORE STANDARD CC.5.NF.4a

Lesson Objective: Model to find the fractional part of a group.

Find Part of a Group

Lauren bought 12 stamps for postcards. She gave Brianna $\frac{1}{6}$ of them. How many stamps did Lauren give to Brianna?

Find $\frac{1}{6}$ of 12.

Step 1 What is the denominator in the fraction of the stamps Lauren gave to Brianna? 6
So, divide the 12 stamps into 6 equal groups. Circle the groups.

Step 2 Each group represents $\frac{1}{6}$ of the stamps.

How many stamps are in 1 group? 2

So, $\frac{1}{6}$ of 12 is __2__, or $\frac{1}{6} \times 12$ is __2__.
So, Lauren gave Brianna __2__ stamps.

Use a model to solve.

1. $\frac{3}{4} \times 12 =$ ______

2. $\frac{1}{3} \times 9 =$ ______

3. $\frac{3}{5} \times 20 =$ ______

4. $\frac{4}{6} \times 18 =$ ______

Name ____________________

Lesson 64
CC.5.NF.4a

Find Part of a Group

Use a model to solve.

1. $\frac{3}{4} \times 12 =$ 9

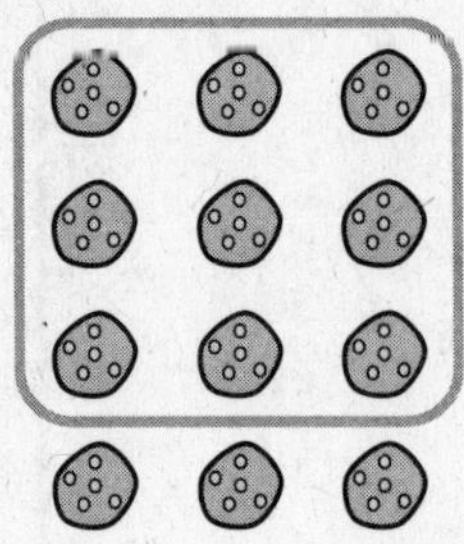

2. $\frac{7}{8} \times 16 =$ ______

3. $\frac{6}{10} \times 10 =$ ______

4. $\frac{2}{3} \times 9 =$ ______

5. $\frac{1}{6} \times 18 =$ ______

6. $\frac{4}{5} \times 10 =$ ______

Problem Solving REAL WORLD

7. Marco drew 20 pictures. He drew $\frac{3}{4}$ of them in art class. How many pictures did Marco draw in art class?

______

8. Caroline has 10 marbles. One half of them are blue. How many of Caroline's marbles are blue?

______

Name ____________________

Lesson 65

COMMON CORE STANDARD CC.5.NF.4a

Lesson Objective: Model the product of a fraction and a whole number.

Multiply Fractions and Whole Numbers

Find the product. $\frac{3}{8} \times 4$

Step 1 Draw 4 rectangles to represent the factor 4.

   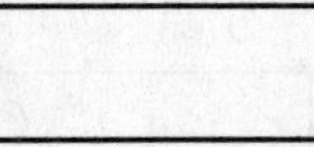

Step 2 The denominator of the factor $\frac{3}{8}$ is 8. So, divide the 4 rectangles into 8 equal parts.

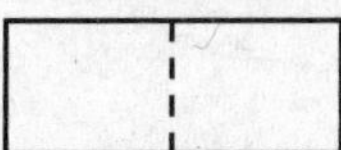 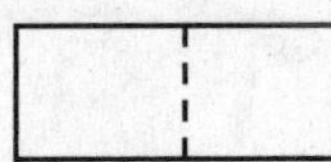 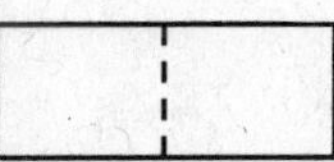 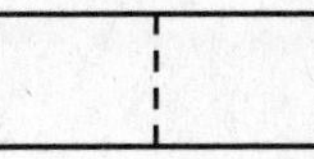

Step 3 The numerator of the factor $\frac{3}{8}$ is 3. So, shade 3 of the parts.

  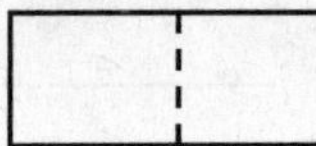 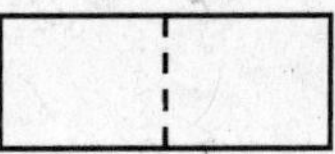

Step 4 The 4 rectangles have 3 shaded parts. Each rectangle is divided into 2 equal parts. So, $\frac{3}{2}$ of the rectangles are shaded.

So, $\frac{3}{8} \times 4$ is $\frac{3}{2}$, or $1\frac{1}{2}$.

Find the product.

1. $\frac{5}{12} \times 4 =$ ____________ **2.** $8 \times \frac{3}{4} =$ ____________ **3.** $\frac{7}{9} \times 3 =$ ____________

4. $5 \times \frac{4}{7} =$ ____________ **5.** $\frac{9}{10} \times 5 =$ ____________ **6.** $3 \times \frac{3}{4} =$ ____________

7. $\frac{7}{12} \times 6 =$ ____________ **8.** $12 \times \frac{2}{9} =$ ____________ **9.** $\frac{2}{9} \times 3 =$ ____________

Name ____________________

Lesson 65
CC.5.NF.4a

Multiply Fractions and Whole Numbers

Use the model to find the product.

1. $\frac{5}{12} \times 3 =$ $\frac{5}{4}$, or $1\frac{1}{4}$

1				1				1			
$\frac{1}{4}$	$\frac{1}{4}$	$\frac{1}{4}$	$\frac{1}{4}$	$\frac{1}{4}$	$\frac{1}{4}$	$\frac{1}{4}$	$\frac{1}{4}$	$\frac{1}{4}$	$\frac{1}{4}$	$\frac{1}{4}$	$\frac{1}{4}$

2. $3 \times \frac{3}{4} =$ ____________

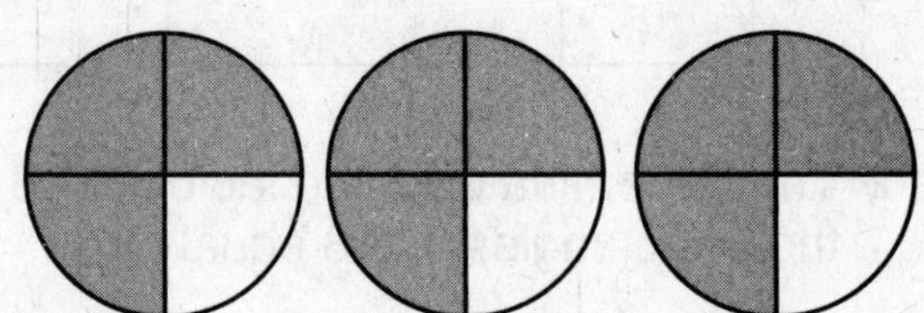

Find the product.

3. $\frac{2}{5} \times 5 =$ ____________

4. $7 \times \frac{2}{3} =$ ____________

5. $\frac{3}{8} \times 4 =$ ____________

6. $7 \times \frac{5}{6} =$ ____________

7. $\frac{5}{12} \times 6 =$ ____________

8. $9 \times \frac{2}{3} =$ ____________

Problem Solving

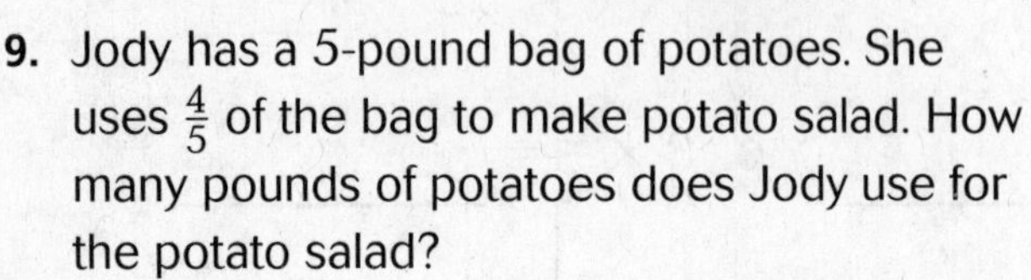

9. Jody has a 5-pound bag of potatoes. She uses $\frac{4}{5}$ of the bag to make potato salad. How many pounds of potatoes does Jody use for the potato salad?

____

10. Lucas lives $\frac{5}{8}$ mile from school. Kenny lives twice as far as Lucas from school. How many miles does Kenny live from school?

____

Name ____________________

Lesson 66

COMMON CORE STANDARD CC.5.NF.4a

Lesson Objective: Multiply fractions and whole numbers.

Fraction and Whole Number Multiplication

Find the product. $3 \times \frac{5}{6}$

$3 \times \frac{5}{6} = \frac{3}{\boxed{1}} \times \frac{5}{6}$ Write the whole-number factor, 3, as $\frac{3}{1}$.

$= \frac{3 \times \boxed{5}}{1 \times 6}$ Multiply the numerators. Then multiply the denominators.

$= \frac{\boxed{15}}{6}$

$= \boxed{2}\,\frac{3}{6}$, or $2\,\frac{\boxed{1}}{\boxed{2}}$ Write the product as a mixed number in simplest form.

So, $3 \times \frac{5}{6}$ is $\underline{2\frac{1}{2}}$.

Find the product. Write the product in simplest form.

1. $\frac{2}{3} \times 8 = \frac{2}{3} \times \frac{8}{\square}$

$= \frac{\square \times \square}{\square \times \square}$

$= \frac{\square}{\square}$, or ______

2. $4 \times \frac{2}{9} =$ ______

3. $6 \times \frac{3}{4} =$ ______

4. $\frac{4}{9} \times 3 =$ ______

5. $5 \times \frac{3}{8} =$ ______

6. $9 \times \frac{2}{3} =$ ______

7. $2 \times \frac{5}{6} =$ ______

8. $7 \times \frac{4}{10} =$ ______

Name ____________________

Lesson 66
CC.5.NF.4a

Fraction and Whole Number Multiplication

Find the product. Write the product in simplest form.

1. $4 \times \frac{5}{8} =$ $2\frac{1}{2}$

$4 \times \frac{5}{8} = \frac{20}{8}$

$\frac{20}{8} = 2\frac{4}{8}$, or $2\frac{1}{2}$

2. $\frac{2}{9} \times 3 =$ ____________

3. $\frac{4}{5} \times 10 =$ ____________

4. $\frac{3}{4} \times 9 =$ ____________

5. $8 \times \frac{5}{6} =$ ____________

6. $7 \times \frac{1}{2} =$ ____________

7. $\frac{2}{5} \times 6 =$ ____________

8. $9 \times \frac{2}{3} =$ ____________

9. $\frac{3}{10} \times 9 =$ ____________

10. $4 \times \frac{3}{8} =$ ____________

11. $\frac{3}{5} \times 7 =$ ____________

12. $\frac{1}{8} \times 6 =$ ____________

Problem Solving REAL WORLD

13. Leah makes aprons to sell at a craft fair. She needs $\frac{3}{4}$ yard of material to make each apron. How much material does Leah need to make 6 aprons?

____

14. The gas tank of Mr. Tanaka's car holds 15 gallons of gas. He used $\frac{2}{3}$ of a tank of gas last week. How many gallons of gas did Mr. Tanaka use?

____

Name ____________________

Lesson 67

COMMON CORE STANDARD CC.5.NF.4a

Lesson Objective: Multiply fractions.

Fraction Multiplication

To multiply fractions, you can multiply the numerators, then multiply the denominators. Write the product in simplest form.

Multiply. $\frac{3}{10} \times \frac{4}{5}$

Step 1 Multiply the numerators. Multiply the denominators.

$$\frac{3}{10} \times \frac{4}{5} = \frac{3 \times 4}{10 \times 5}$$

$$= \frac{12}{50}$$

Step 2 Write the product in simplest form.

$$\frac{12}{50} = \frac{12 \div 2}{50 \div 2}$$

$$= \frac{6}{25}$$

So, $\frac{3}{10} \times \frac{4}{5}$ is $\underline{\frac{6}{25}}$.

Find the product. Write the product in simplest form.

1. $\frac{3}{4} \times \frac{1}{5}$ ____________

2. $\frac{4}{7} \times \frac{5}{12}$ ____________

3. $\frac{3}{8} \times \frac{2}{9}$ ____________

4. $\frac{4}{5} \times \frac{5}{8}$ ____________

5. $\frac{1}{3} \times 4$ ____________

6. $\frac{3}{4} \times 8$ ____________

7. $\frac{5}{8} \times \frac{2}{3}$ ____________

8. $\frac{5}{6} \times \frac{3}{8}$ ____________

Name ______________________

Lesson 67
CC.5.NF.4a

Fraction Multiplication

Find the product. Write the product in simplest form.

1. $\frac{4}{5} \times \frac{7}{8} = \frac{4 \times 7}{5 \times 8}$
$= \frac{28}{40}$
$= \frac{7}{10}$

2. $3 \times \frac{1}{6}$ ______

3. $\frac{5}{9} \times \frac{3}{4}$ ______

4. $\frac{4}{7} \times \frac{1}{2}$ ______

5. $\frac{1}{8} \times 20$ ______

6. $\frac{4}{5} \times \frac{3}{8}$ ______

7. $\frac{6}{7} \times \frac{7}{9}$ ______

8. $8 \times \frac{1}{9}$ ______

9. $\frac{1}{14} \times 28$ ______

10. $\frac{3}{4} \times \frac{1}{3}$ ______

11. Karen raked $\frac{3}{5}$ of the yard. Minni raked $\frac{1}{3}$ of the amount Karen raked. How much of the yard did Minni rake?

______

12. In the pet show, $\frac{3}{8}$ of the pets are dogs. Of the dogs, $\frac{2}{3}$ have long hair. What fraction of the pets are dogs with long hair?

______

Algebra **Evaluate for the given value of the variable.**

13. $\frac{7}{8} \times c$ for $c = 8$ ______

14. $t \times \frac{3}{4}$ for $t = \frac{8}{9}$ ______

15. $\frac{1}{2} \times s$ for $s = \frac{3}{10}$ ______

16. $y \times 6$ for $y = \frac{2}{3}$ ______

Problem Solving

17. Jason ran $\frac{5}{7}$ of the distance around the school track. Sara ran $\frac{4}{5}$ of Jason's distance. What fraction of the total distance around the track did Sara run?

______

18. A group of students attend a math club. Half of the students are boys and $\frac{4}{9}$ of the boys have brown eyes. What fraction of the group are boys with brown eyes?

______

Name ______________________________

Lesson 68

COMMON CORE STANDARD CC.5.NF.4b

Lesson Objective: Multiply fractions using models.

Multiply Fractions

You can use a model to help you multiply two fractions.

Multiply. $\frac{1}{3} \times \frac{4}{5}$

Step 1 Draw a rectangle. Divide it into 5 equal columns. To represent the factor $\frac{4}{5}$, shade **4** of the 5 columns.

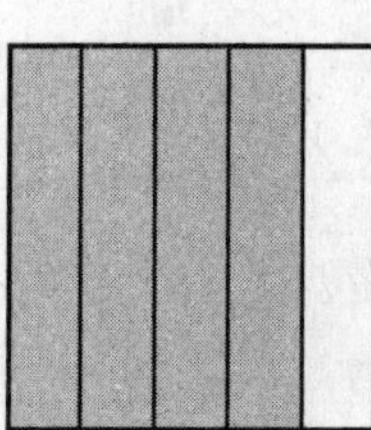

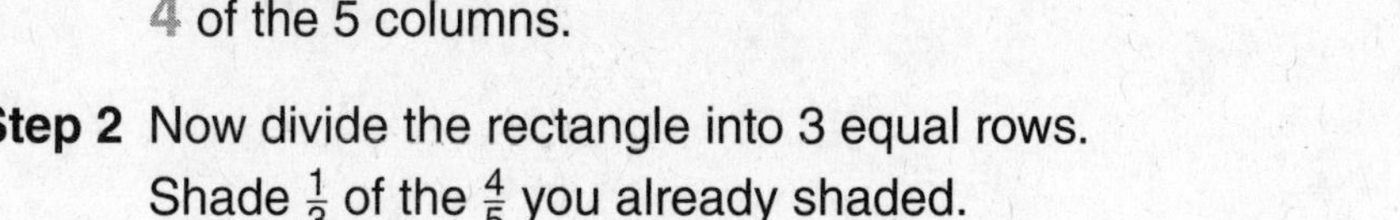

Step 2 Now divide the rectangle into 3 equal rows. Shade $\frac{1}{3}$ of the $\frac{4}{5}$ you already shaded.

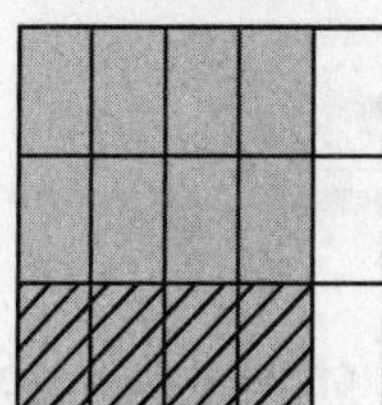

The rectangle is divided into **15** smaller rectangles. This is the denominator of the product.

There are 4 smaller rectangles that contain both types of shading. So, **4** is the numerator of the product.

So $\frac{4}{15}$ of the rectangles contain both types of shading.

Think: What is $\frac{1}{3}$ of $\frac{4}{5}$?

$\frac{1}{3} \times \frac{4}{5} =$ $\underline{\frac{4}{15}}$.

Find the product. Draw a model.

1.

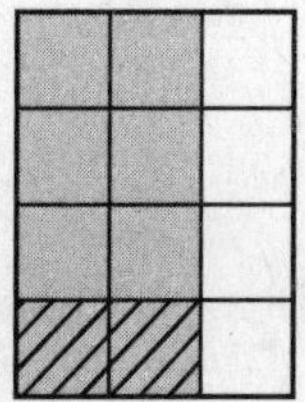

$\frac{1}{4} \times \frac{2}{3} =$ ________

2.

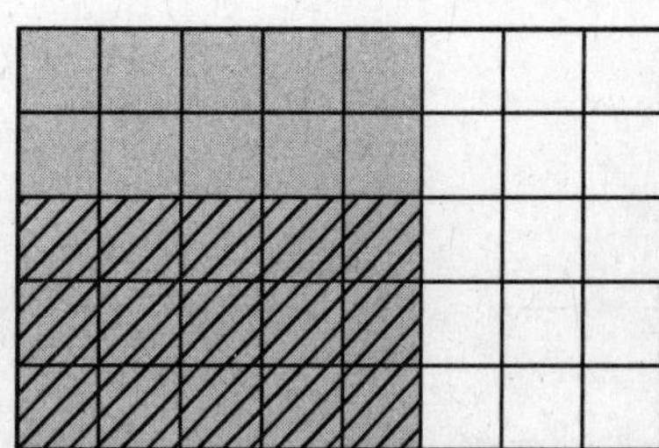

$\frac{3}{5} \times \frac{5}{8} =$ ________

3.

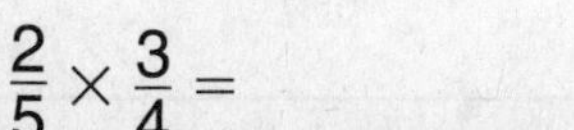

$\frac{2}{5} \times \frac{3}{4} =$ ________

4.

$\frac{2}{3} \times \frac{3}{8} =$ ________

Name ____________________

Lesson 68

CC.5.NF.4b

Multiply Fractions

Find the product.

1. 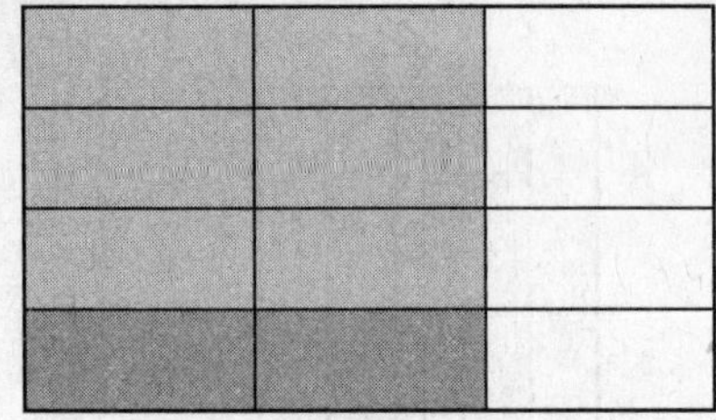

$\frac{1}{4} \times \frac{2}{3} =$ $\frac{2}{12}$, or $\frac{1}{6}$

2. 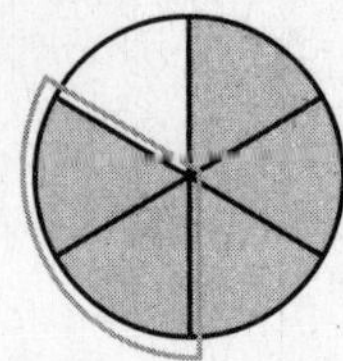

$\frac{2}{5} \times \frac{5}{6} =$ ____________

Find the product. Draw a model.

3. $\frac{4}{5} \times \frac{1}{2} =$ ____________

4. $\frac{3}{4} \times \frac{1}{3} =$ ____________

5. $\frac{3}{8} \times \frac{2}{3} =$ ____________

6. $\frac{3}{5} \times \frac{3}{5} =$ ____________

Problem Solving REAL WORLD

7. Nora has a piece of ribbon that is $\frac{3}{4}$ yard long. She will use $\frac{1}{2}$ of it to make a bow. What length of the ribbon will she use for the bow?

____

8. Marlon bought $\frac{7}{8}$ pound of turkey at the deli. He used $\frac{2}{3}$ of it to make sandwiches for lunch. How much of the turkey did Marlon use for sandwiches?

____

Name ______________________________

Lesson 69

COMMON CORE STANDARD CC.5.NF.4b

Lesson Objective: Use a model to multiply two mixed numbers and find the area of a rectangle.

Area and Mixed Numbers

You can use an area model to help you multiply mixed numbers.

Find the area. $1\frac{4}{5} \times 2\frac{1}{3}$

Step 1 Rewrite each mixed-number factor as the sum of a whole number and a fraction.

$1\frac{4}{5} = 1 + \frac{4}{5}$ and $2\frac{1}{3} = 2 + \frac{1}{3}$

Step 2 Draw an area model to show the original multiplication problem.

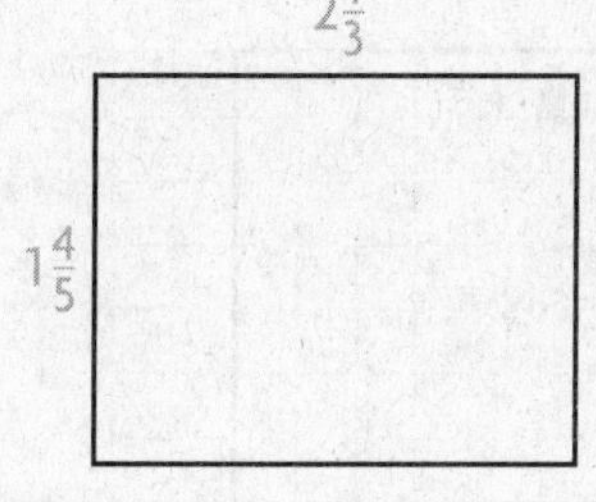

Step 3 Draw dashed lines, and label each section to show how you broke apart the mixed numbers in Step 1.

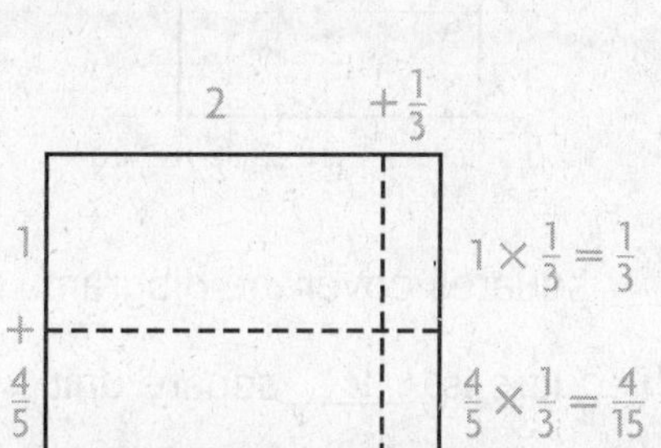

Step 4 Find the area of each section.

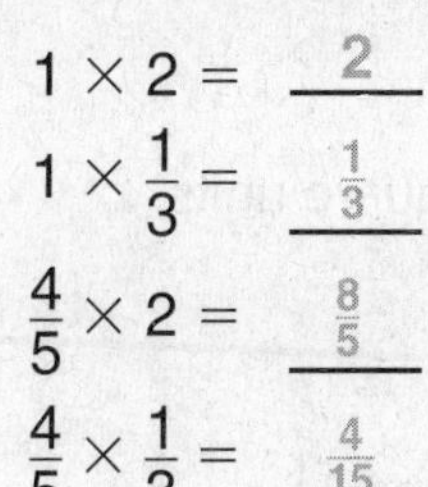
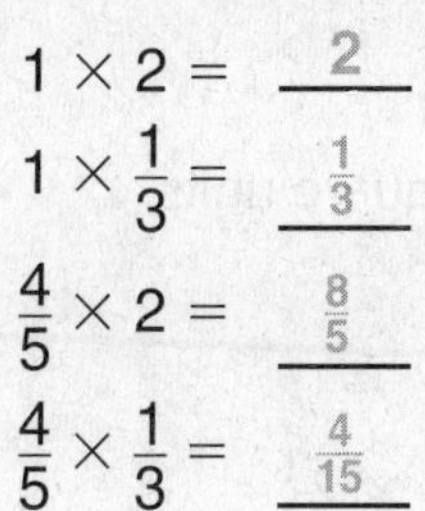

$1 \times 2 =$ __2__

$1 \times \frac{1}{3} =$ __$\frac{1}{3}$__

$\frac{4}{5} \times 2 =$ __$\frac{8}{5}$__

$\frac{4}{5} \times \frac{1}{3} =$ __$\frac{4}{15}$__

Step 5 Add the areas of each of the sections to find the total area of the rectangle.

$2 + \frac{1}{3} + \frac{8}{5} + \frac{4}{15} = \frac{\boxed{30}}{15} + \frac{\boxed{5}}{15} + \frac{\boxed{24}}{15} + \frac{4}{15}$

$= \frac{\boxed{63}}{15}$, or __$4\frac{1}{5}$__

So, $1\frac{4}{5} \times 2\frac{1}{3}$ is __$4\frac{1}{5}$__.

Use an area model to solve.

1. $1\frac{2}{3} \times 2\frac{1}{4}$

2. $1\frac{3}{4} \times 2\frac{3}{5}$

3. $2\frac{1}{2} \times 1\frac{1}{3}$

______________ ______________ ______________

Name ______________________

Lesson 69

CC.5.NF.4b

Area and Mixed Numbers

Use the grid to find the area.

1. Let each square represent $\frac{1}{4}$ unit by $\frac{1}{4}$ unit.

$2\frac{1}{4} \times 1\frac{1}{2} = \underline{3\frac{3}{8}}$

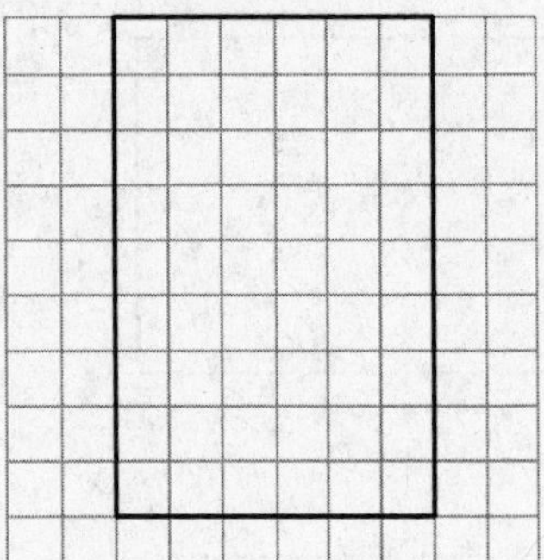

54 squares cover the diagram.

Each square is $\frac{1}{16}$ square unit.

The area of the diagram is

$54 \times \frac{1}{16} = \frac{54}{16} = 3\frac{3}{8}$ square units.

2. Let each square represent $\frac{1}{3}$ unit by $\frac{1}{3}$ unit.

$1\frac{2}{3} \times 2\frac{1}{3} =$ ______

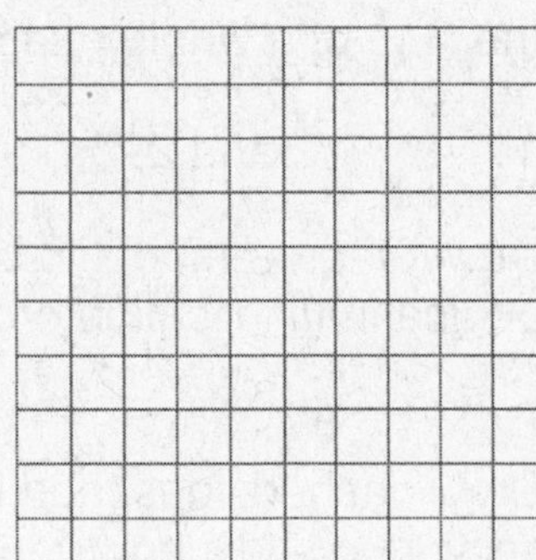

The area is ______ square units.

Use an area model to solve.

3. $1\frac{1}{8} \times 2\frac{1}{2}$

4. $2\frac{2}{3} \times 1\frac{1}{3}$

5. $1\frac{3}{4} \times 2\frac{1}{2}$

______ ______ ______

Problem Solving REAL WORLD

6. Ava's bedroom rug is $2\frac{3}{4}$ feet long and $2\frac{1}{2}$ feet wide. What is the area of the rug?

______

7. A painting is $2\frac{2}{3}$ feet long and $1\frac{1}{2}$ feet high. What is the area of the painting?

______

Name ______________________________

Lesson 70

COMMON CORE STANDARD CC.5.NF.5a

Lesson Objective: Relate the size of the product compared to the size of one factor when multiplying fractions.

Compare Fraction Factors and Products

You can use a model to determine how the size of the product compares to the size of one factor when multiplying fractions.

The factor is 1: $\frac{2}{3} \times 1$

- Draw a model to represent the factor 1. Divide it into 3 equal sections.
- Shade 2 of the 3 sections to represent the factor $\frac{2}{3}$.

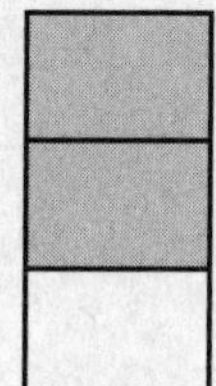

$\frac{2}{3}$ of the rectangle is shaded. So, $\frac{2}{3} \times 1$ is **equal to** $\frac{2}{3}$.

The factor is greater than 1: $\frac{2}{3} \times 2$

- Draw two rectangles to represent the factor 2. Divide each rectangle into 3 equal sections.
- Shade 2 of 3 sections in each to represent the factor $\frac{2}{3}$.

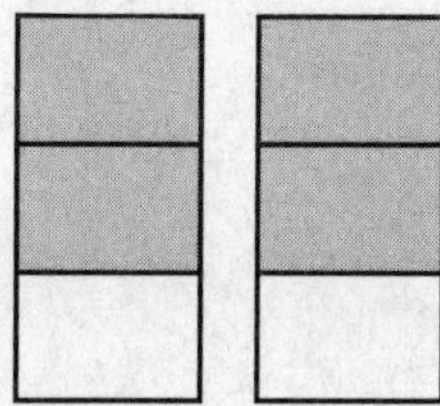

In all, 4 sections are shaded, which is greater than the number of sections in one rectangle. So, $\frac{2}{3} \times 2$ is **greater than** $\frac{2}{3}$.

The factor is less than 1: $\frac{2}{3} \times \frac{1}{6}$

- Draw a rectangle. Divide it into 6 equal columns. Shade 1 of the 6 columns to represent the factor $\frac{1}{6}$.
- Now divide the rectangle into 3 equal rows. Shade 2 of the 3 rows of the section already shaded to represent the factor $\frac{2}{3}$.

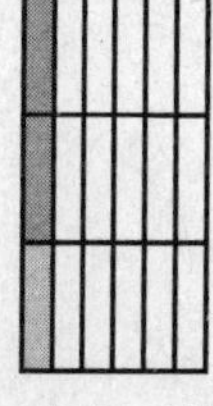

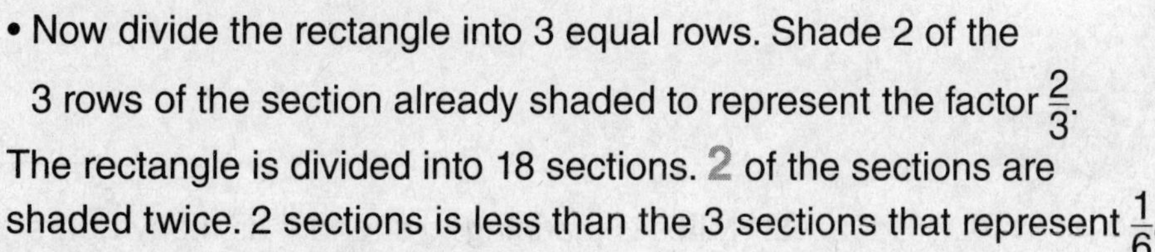

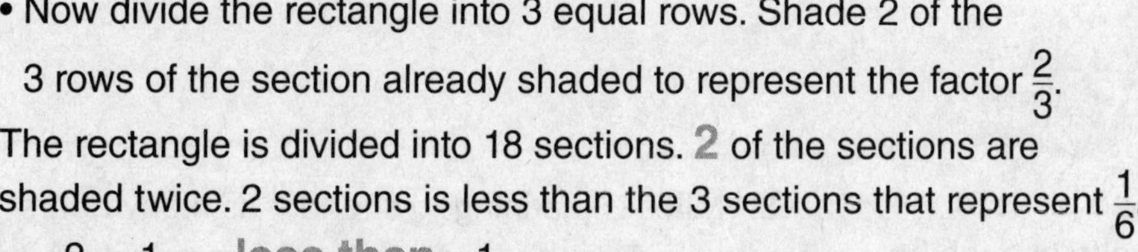

The rectangle is divided into 18 sections. **2** of the sections are shaded twice. 2 sections is less than the 3 sections that represent $\frac{1}{6}$.

So, $\frac{2}{3} \times \frac{1}{6}$ is **less than** $\frac{1}{6}$.

Complete the statement with *equal to*, *greater than*, or *less than*.

1. $\frac{3}{7} \times \frac{2}{5}$ will be ______________ $\frac{3}{7}$.

2. $\frac{7}{8} \times 3$ will be ______________ $\frac{7}{8}$.

3. $\frac{1}{6} \times \frac{5}{5}$ will be ______________ $\frac{1}{6}$.

4. $5 \times \frac{6}{7}$ will be ______________ 5.

Name ______________________

Compare Fraction Factors and Products

Lesson 70
CC.5.NF.5a

Complete the statement with *equal to, greater than,* or *less than.*

1. $\frac{3}{5} \times \frac{4}{7}$ will be **less than** $\frac{4}{7}$.

   Think: $\frac{4}{7}$ is multiplied by a number less than 1; so, $\frac{3}{5} \times \frac{4}{7}$ will be less than $\frac{4}{7}$.

2. $5 \times \frac{7}{8}$ will be ______________ $\frac{7}{8}$.

3. $6 \times \frac{2}{5}$ will be ______________ $\frac{2}{5}$.

4. $\frac{1}{9} \times 1$ will be ______________ $\frac{1}{9}$.

5. $\frac{7}{8} \times \frac{3}{5}$ will be ______________ $\frac{3}{5}$.

6. $\frac{4}{5} \times \frac{7}{7}$ will be ______________ $\frac{4}{5}$.

Problem Solving REAL WORLD

7. Starla is making hot cocoa. She plans to multiply the recipe by 4 to make enough hot cocoa for the whole class. If the recipe calls for $\frac{1}{2}$ teaspoon vanilla extract, will she need more than $\frac{1}{2}$ teaspoon or less than $\frac{1}{2}$ teaspoon of vanilla extract to make all the hot cocoa?

   ____

8. Miles is planning to spend $\frac{2}{3}$ as many hours bicycling this week as he did last week. Is Miles going to spend more hours or fewer hours bicycling this week than last week?

   ____

Name ______________________________

Lesson 71

COMMON CORE STANDARD CC.5.NF.5a

Lesson Objective: Relate the size of the product to the factors when multiplying fractions greater than one.

Compare Mixed Number Factors and Products

Complete each statement with *equal to*, *greater than*, or *less than*.

$1 \times 1\frac{3}{4}$ is ___?___ $1\frac{3}{4}$.

The Identity Property of Multiplication states that the product of

1 and any number is that number. So, $1 \times 1\frac{3}{4}$ is ___equal to___ $1\frac{3}{4}$.

$\frac{1}{2} \times 2\frac{1}{4}$ is ___?___ $2\frac{1}{4}$.

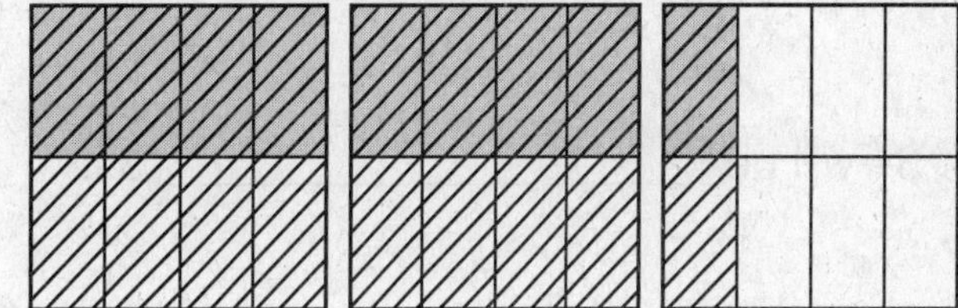

Draw three rectangles. Divide each rectangle into 4 equal columns.

Shade completely the first two rectangles and one column of the last rectangle to represent $\frac{1}{4}$.

Divide the rectangles into 2 rows. Shade one row to represent the factor $\frac{1}{2}$.

18 small rectangles are shaded. 9 rectangles have both types of shading. 9 rectangles is less than the 18 rectangles that represent $2\frac{1}{4}$.

So, $\frac{1}{2} \times 2\frac{1}{4}$ is ___less than___ $2\frac{1}{4}$.

When you multiply a mixed number by a fraction less than 1,

the product will be ___less than___ the mixed number.

$1\frac{1}{4} \times 1\frac{3}{4}$ is ___?___ $1\frac{1}{4}$.

Use what you know about the product of two whole numbers greater than 1 to determine the size of the product of two mixed numbers.

So, $1\frac{1}{4} \times 1\frac{3}{4}$ is ___greater than___ $1\frac{1}{4}$ and ___greater than___ $1\frac{3}{4}$.

When you multiply two mixed numbers, their product is ___greater than___ either factor.

Complete the statement with *equal to*, *greater than*, or *less than*.

1. $\frac{3}{5} \times 1\frac{2}{7}$ is ______________ $1\frac{2}{7}$.

2. $\frac{6}{6} \times 3\frac{1}{3}$ is ______________ $3\frac{1}{3}$.

3. $2\frac{1}{5} \times 1\frac{1}{4}$ is ______________ $1\frac{1}{4}$.

4. $\frac{8}{9} \times 4\frac{3}{4}$ is ______________ $4\frac{3}{4}$.

Name ______________________

Lesson 71
CC.5.NF.5a

Compare Mixed Number Factors and Products

Complete the statement with *equal to, greater than,* or *less than.*

1. $\frac{2}{3} \times 1\frac{5}{8}$ will be **less than** $1\frac{5}{8}$.

   Think: $1 \times 1\frac{5}{8}$ is $1\frac{5}{8}$.
   Since $\frac{2}{3}$ is less than 1,
   $\frac{2}{3} \times 1\frac{5}{8}$ will be less than $1\frac{5}{8}$.

2. $\frac{5}{5} \times 2\frac{3}{4}$ will be ______________ $2\frac{3}{4}$.

3. $3 \times 3\frac{2}{7}$ will be ______________ $3\frac{2}{7}$.

4. $9 \times 1\frac{4}{5}$ will be ______________ $1\frac{4}{5}$.

5. $1\frac{7}{8} \times 2\frac{3}{8}$ will be ______________ $2\frac{3}{8}$.

6. $3\frac{4}{9} \times \frac{5}{9}$ will be ______________ $3\frac{4}{9}$.

Problem Solving REAL WORLD

7. Fraser is making a scale drawing of a dog house. The dimensions of the drawing will be $\frac{1}{8}$ of the dimensions of the actual doghouse. The height of the actual doghouse is $36\frac{3}{4}$ inches. Will the dimensions of Fraser's drawing be equal to, greater than, or less than the dimensions of the actual dog house?

   ____

8. Jorge has a recipe that calls for $2\frac{1}{3}$ cups of flour. He plans to make $1\frac{1}{2}$ times the recipe. Will the amount of flour Jorge needs be equal to, greater than, or less than the amount of flour his recipe calls for?

   ____

Name ___________________________

Lesson 72

COMMON CORE STANDARD CC.5.NF.5b

Lesson Objective: Solve problems using the strategy *guess, check, and revise.*

Problem Solving • Find Unknown Lengths

Zach built a rectangular deck in his backyard. The area of the deck is 300 square feet. The length of the deck is $1\frac{1}{3}$ times as long as the width. What are the dimensions of the deck?

Read the Problem		
What do I need to find? I need to find the dimensions of the deck.	**What information do I need to use?** The deck has an area of 300 square feet, and the length is $1\frac{1}{3}$ as long as the width.	**How will I use the information?** I will guess the length and width of the deck. Then I will check my guess and revise it if it is not correct.

Solve the Problem

I can try different values for the length of the deck, each that is $1\frac{1}{3}$ times as long as the width. Then I can multiply the length and width and compare to the correct area.

Guess		**Check**	**Revise**
Width (in feet)	**Length (in feet) ($1\frac{1}{3}$ times the width)**	**Area of Deck (in square feet)**	
12	$1\frac{1}{3} \times 12 =$ 16	$12 \times 16 =$ 192 too low	Try a longer width.
18	$1\frac{1}{3} \times 18 =$ 24	$18 \times 24 =$ 432 too high	Try a shorter width.
15	$1\frac{1}{3} \times 15 =$ 20	$15 \times 20 =$ 300 correct	

So, the dimensions of the deck are 20 feet by 15 feet.

1. Abigail made a quilt that has an area of 4,800 square inches. The length of the quilt is $1\frac{1}{3}$ times the width of the quilt. What are the dimensions of the quilt?

____

2. The width of the mirror in Shannon's bathroom is $\frac{4}{9}$ its length. The area of the mirror is 576 square inches. What are the dimensions of the mirror?

____

Name ______________________

Problem Solving • Find Unknown Lengths

1. Kamal's bedroom has an area of 120 square feet. The width of the room is $\frac{5}{6}$ the length of the room. What are the dimensions of Kamal's bedroom?

Guess: $6 \times 20 = 120$
Check: $\frac{5}{6} \times 20 = 16\frac{2}{3}$; try a longer width.
Guess: $10 \times 12 = 120$
Check: $\frac{5}{6} \times 12 = 10$. Correct!

10 feet by 12 feet

2. Marisol is painting on a piece of canvas that has an area of 180 square inches. The length of the painting is $1\frac{1}{4}$ times the width. What are the dimensions of the painting?

____

3. A small plane is flying a banner in the shape of a rectangle. The area of the banner is 144 square feet. The width of the banner is $\frac{1}{4}$ the length of the banner. What are the dimensions of the banner?

____

4. An artificial lake is in the shape of a rectangle and has an area of $\frac{9}{20}$ square mile. The width of the lake is $\frac{1}{5}$ the length of the lake. What are the dimensions of the lake?

____

Name ____________________

Lesson 73

COMMON CORE STANDARD CC.5.NF.6

Lesson Objective: Multiply mixed numbers.

Multiply Mixed Numbers

You can use a multiplication square to multiply mixed numbers.

Multiply. $1\frac{2}{7} \times 1\frac{3}{4}$ **Write the product in simplest form.**

Step 1 Write the mixed numbers outside the square.

$\times$	1	$\frac{2}{7}$
1		
$\frac{3}{4}$		

Step 2 Multiply the number in each column by the number in each row.

$\times$	1	$\frac{2}{7}$
1	1×1	$\frac{2}{7} \times 1$
$\frac{3}{4}$	$1 \times \frac{3}{4}$	$\frac{2}{7} \times \frac{3}{4}$

Step 3 Write each product inside the square.

$\times$	1	$\frac{2}{7}$
1	1	$\frac{2}{7}$
$\frac{3}{4}$	$\frac{3}{4}$	$\frac{3}{14}$

Step 4 Add the products inside the multiplication square. $1 + \frac{2}{7} + \frac{3}{4} + \frac{3}{14}$

Find the least common denominator. $\frac{28}{28} + \frac{8}{28} + \frac{21}{28} + \frac{6}{28} = \frac{63}{28}$

Simplify. $\frac{63}{28} = 2\frac{7}{28}$, or $2\frac{1}{4}$

So, $1\frac{2}{7} \times 1\frac{3}{4}$ is $2\frac{1}{4}$.

Find the product. Write the product in simplest form.

1. $2\frac{5}{8} \times 1\frac{1}{7}$ ____________

2. $3\frac{1}{2} \times 12$ ____________

3. $10\frac{5}{6} \times \frac{3}{5}$ ____________

4. $7\frac{7}{10} \times \frac{10}{11}$ ____________

Use the Distributive Property to find the product.

5. $12 \times 2\frac{1}{2}$ ____________

6. $15 \times 5\frac{1}{3}$ ____________

Name ____________________

Lesson 73
CC.5.NF.6

Multiply Mixed Numbers

Find the product. Write the product in simplest form.

1. $1\frac{2}{3} \times 4\frac{2}{5}$

$1\frac{2}{3} \times 4\frac{2}{5} = \frac{5}{3} \times \frac{22}{5}$

$= \frac{110}{15} = \frac{22}{3}$

$= 7\frac{1}{3}$

2. $1\frac{1}{7} \times 1\frac{3}{4}$ ________

3. $8\frac{1}{3} \times \frac{3}{5}$ ________

4. $2\frac{5}{8} \times 1\frac{2}{3}$ ________

5. $5\frac{1}{2} \times 3\frac{1}{3}$ ________

6. $7\frac{1}{5} \times 2\frac{1}{6}$ ________

7. $\frac{2}{3} \times 4\frac{1}{5}$ ________

8. $2\frac{2}{5} \times 1\frac{1}{4}$ ________

Use the Distributive Property to find the product.

9. $4\frac{2}{5} \times 10$ ________

10. $26 \times 2\frac{1}{2}$ ________

11. $6 \times 3\frac{2}{3}$ ________

Problem Solving REAL WORLD

12. Jake can carry $6\frac{1}{4}$ pounds of wood in from the barn. His father can carry $1\frac{5}{7}$ times as much as Jake. How many pounds can Jake's father carry?

____

13. A glass can hold $3\frac{1}{3}$ cups of water. A bowl can hold $2\frac{3}{5}$ times the amount in the glass. How many cups can a bowl hold?

____

Name ________________________________

Lesson 74

COMMON CORE STANDARDS
CC.5.NF.7a, CC.5.NF.7b

Lesson Objective: Divide a whole number by a fraction and divide a fraction by a whole number.

Divide Fractions and Whole Numbers

You can use a number line to help you divide a whole number by a fraction.

Divide. $6 \div \frac{1}{2}$

Step 1 Draw a number line from 0 to 6. Divide the number line into halves. Label each half on your number line, starting with $\frac{1}{2}$.

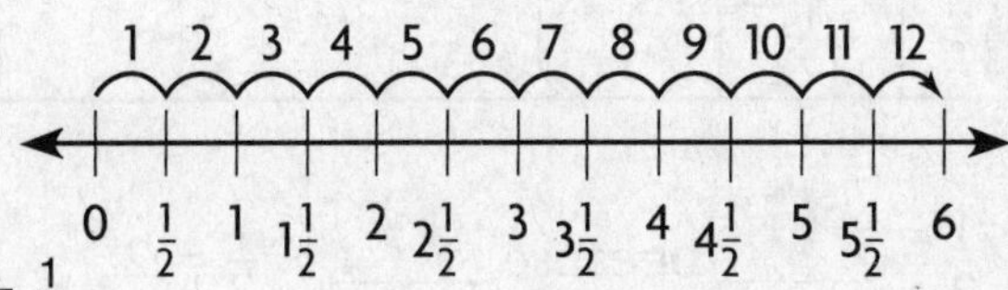

Step 2 Skip count by halves from 0 to 6 to find $6 \div \frac{1}{2}$.

Step 3 Count the number of skips. It takes 12 skips to go from 0 to 6. So the quotient is 12.

$6 \div \frac{1}{2} =$ <u>12</u> because <u>12</u> $\times \frac{1}{2} = 6$.

You can use fraction strips to divide a fraction by a whole number.

Divide. $\frac{1}{2} \div 5$

Step 1 Place a $\frac{1}{2}$ strip under a 1-whole strip.

Step 2 Find 5 fraction strips, all with the same denominator, that fit exactly under the $\frac{1}{2}$ strip.

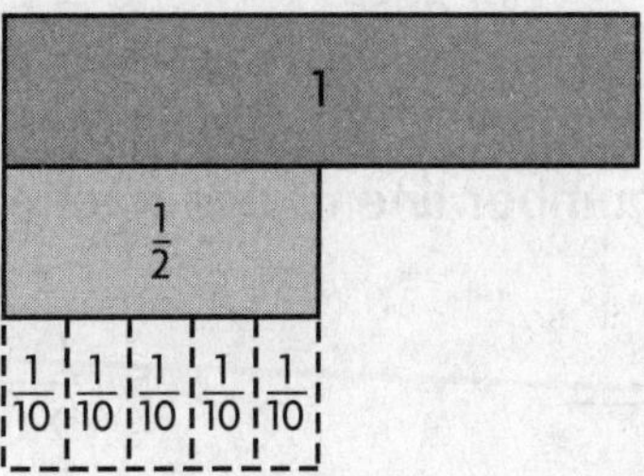

Each part is $\frac{1}{10}$ of the whole.

Step 3 Record and check the quotient.

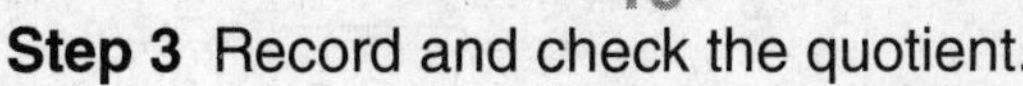

$\frac{1}{2} \div 5 =$ <u>$\frac{1}{10}$</u> because <u>$\frac{1}{10}$</u> $\times 5 = \frac{1}{2}$.

So, $\frac{1}{2} \div 5 =$ <u>$\frac{1}{10}$</u>.

Divide. Draw a number line or use fraction strips.

1. $1 \div \frac{1}{2} =$ ________

2. $2 \div \frac{1}{3} =$ ________

3. $4 \div \frac{1}{4} =$ ________

4. $\frac{1}{5} \div 3 =$ ________

5. $\frac{1}{3} \div 2 =$ ________

6. $4 \div \frac{1}{5} =$ ________

Name ______________________________

Lesson 74

CC.5.NF.7a, CC.5.NF.7b

Divide Fractions and Whole Numbers

Divide and check the quotient.

1.

1			1		
$\frac{1}{3}$	$\frac{1}{3}$	$\frac{1}{3}$	$\frac{1}{3}$	$\frac{1}{3}$	$\frac{1}{3}$

$2 \div \frac{1}{3} =$ 6 because 6 $\times \frac{1}{3} = 2.$

2.

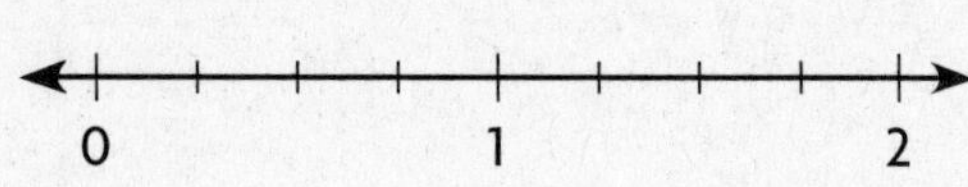

$2 \div \frac{1}{4} =$ ______ because ______ $\times \frac{1}{4} = 2.$

3.

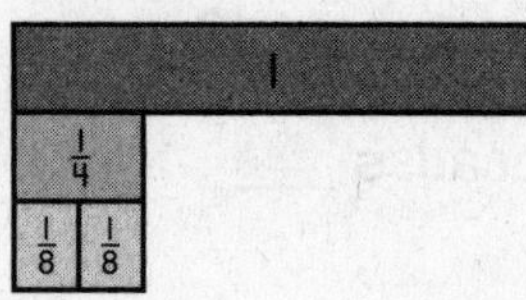

$\frac{1}{4} \div 2 =$ ______ because ______ $\times 2 = \frac{1}{4}.$

Divide. Draw a number line or use fraction strips.

4. $1 \div \frac{1}{5} =$ ______

5. $\frac{1}{6} \div 3 =$ ______

6. $4 \div \frac{1}{6} =$ ______

7. $3 \div \frac{1}{3} =$ ______

8. $\frac{1}{4} \div 6 =$ ______

9. $5 \div \frac{1}{4} =$ ______

Problem Solving REAL WORLD

10. Amy can run $\frac{1}{10}$ mile per minute. How many minutes will it take Amy to run 3 miles?

____

11. Jeremy has 3 yards of ribbon to use for wrapping gifts. He cuts the ribbon into pieces that are $\frac{1}{4}$ yard long. How many pieces of ribbon does Jeremy have?

____

Name ______________________

Lesson 75

COMMON CORE STANDARD CC.5.NF.7b

Lesson Objective: Solve problems using the strategy *draw a diagram.*

Problem Solving • Use Multiplication

Nathan makes 4 batches of soup and divides each batch into halves. How many $\frac{1}{2}$-batches of soup does he have?

Read the Problem	Solve the Problem
What do I need to find? I need to find the number of $\frac{1}{2}$-batches of soup Nathan has.	Since Nathan makes 4 batches of soup, my diagram needs to show 4 circles to represent the 4 batches. I can divide each of the 4 circles in half. 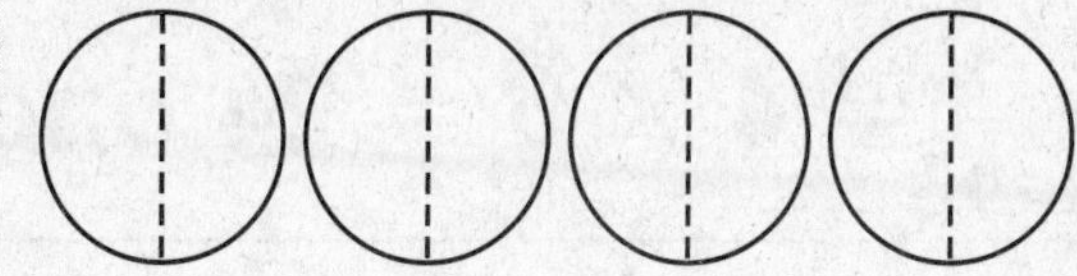
What information do I need to use? I need to use the size of each batch of soup and the total number of batches of soup Nathan makes.	
How will I use the information? I can make a diagram to organize the information from the problem. Then I can use the diagram to find the number of $\frac{1}{2}$-batches of soup Nathan has after he divides the 4 batches of soup.	To find the total number of halves in the 4 batches, I can multiply 4 by the number of halves in each circle. $4 \div \frac{1}{2} = 4 \times \underline{2} = \underline{8}$ So, Nathan has 8 one-half-batches of soup.

Draw a diagram to help you solve the problem.

1. A nearby park has 8 acres of land to use for gardens. The park divides each acre into fourths. How many $\frac{1}{4}$-acre gardens does the park have?

   ____

2. Clarissa has 3 pints of ice tea that she divides into $\frac{1}{2}$-pint servings. How many $\frac{1}{2}$-pint servings does she have?

   ____

Name ______________________________

Lesson 75
CC.5.NF.7b

Problem Solving • Use Multiplication

1. Sebastian bakes 4 pies and cuts each pie into sixths. How many $\frac{1}{6}$ pie slices does he have?

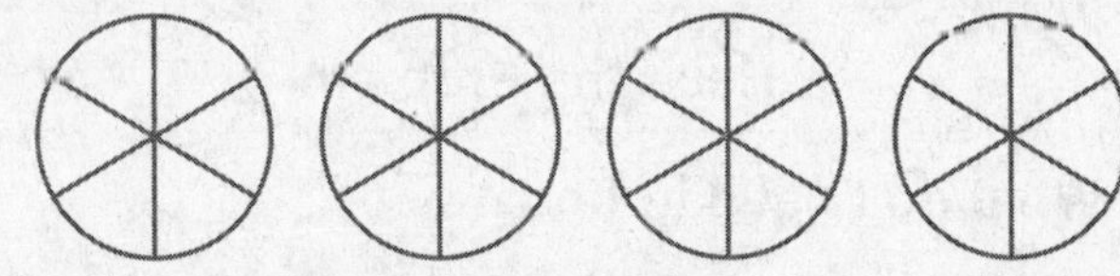

To find the total number of sixths in the 4 pies, multiply 4 by the number of sixths in each pie.

$4 \div \frac{1}{6} = 4 \times 6 = 24$ one-sixth-pie slices

2. Ali has 2 vegetable pizzas that she cuts into eighths. How many $\frac{1}{8}$-size pieces does she have?

____

3. A baker has 6 loaves of bread. Each loaf weighs 1 pound. He cuts each loaf into thirds. How many $\frac{1}{3}$-pound loaves of bread does the chef now have?

____

4. Suppose the baker has 4 loaves of bread and cuts the loaves into halves. How many $\frac{1}{2}$-pound loaves of bread would the baker have?

____

5. Madalyn has 3 watermelons that she cuts into halves to give to her neighbors. How many neighbors will get a $\frac{1}{2}$-size piece of watermelon?

____

6. A landscaper had 5 tons of rock to build decorative walls. He used $\frac{1}{4}$ ton of rock for each wall. How many decorative walls did he build?

____

Name ______________________________

Lesson 76

COMMON CORE STANDARD CC.5.NF.7c

Lesson Objective: Divide a whole number by a fraction and divide a fraction by a whole number.

Fraction and Whole-Number Division

You can divide fractions by solving a related multiplication sentence.

Divide. $4 \div \frac{1}{3}$

Step 1 Draw 4 circles to represent the dividend, 4.

Step 2 Since the divisor is $\frac{1}{3}$, divide each circle into thirds.

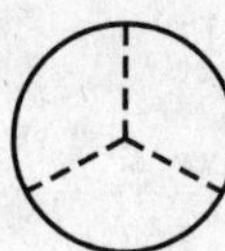 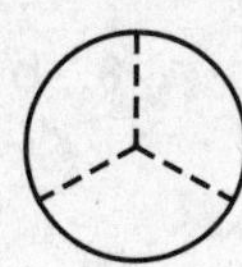 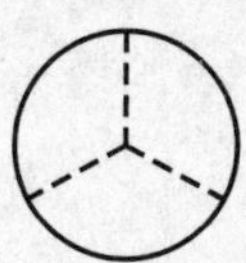 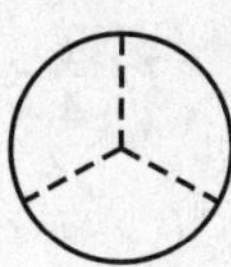

Step 3 Count the total number of thirds.

When you divide the __4__ circles into thirds, you are finding the number of thirds in 4 circles, or finding 4 groups of __3__.

There are __12__ thirds.

Step 4 Complete the number sentence.

$4 \div \frac{1}{3} = 4 \times$ __3__ $=$ __12__

Use the model to complete the number sentence.

1. 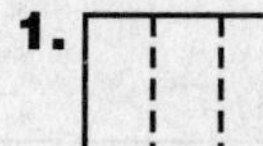 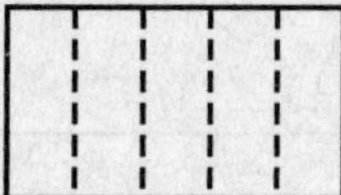 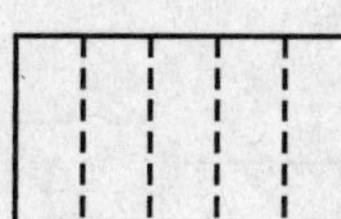 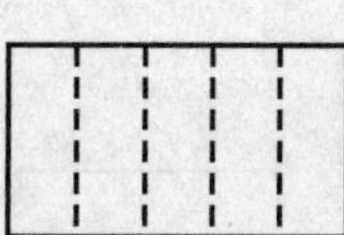

$3 \div \frac{1}{5} = 3 \times$ ______ $=$ ______

2.  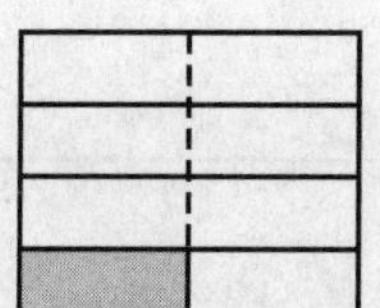

$\frac{1}{4} \div 2 = \frac{1}{4} \times$ ______ $=$ ______

Write a related multiplication sentence to solve.

3. $2 \div \frac{1}{5}$

4. $\frac{1}{3} \div 3$

5. $\frac{1}{6} \div 2$

6. $5 \div \frac{1}{4}$

______ ______ ______ ______

Name ______________________________

Lesson 76
CC.5.NF.7c

Fraction and Whole-Number Division

Write a related multiplication sentence to solve.

1. $3 \div \frac{1}{2}$

$3 \times 2 = 6$

2. $\frac{1}{5} \div 3$

3. $2 \div \frac{1}{8}$

4. $\frac{1}{3} \div 4$

5. $5 \div \frac{1}{4}$

6. $\frac{1}{2} \div 2$

7. $\frac{1}{4} \div 6$

8. $6 \div \frac{1}{5}$

9. $\frac{1}{5} \div 5$

10. $4 \div \frac{1}{8}$

11. $\frac{1}{3} \div 7$

12. $9 \div \frac{1}{2}$

Problem Solving REAL WORLD

13. Isaac has a piece of rope that is 5 yards long. Into how many $\frac{1}{2}$-yard pieces of rope can Isaac cut the rope?

14. Two friends share $\frac{1}{2}$ of a pineapple equally. What fraction of a whole pineapple does each friend get?

Name ______________________

Lesson 77

COMMON CORE STANDARD CC.5.NF.7c

Lesson Objective: Represent division by drawing diagrams and writing story problems and equations.

Interpret Division with Fractions

You can draw a diagram or write an equation to represent division with fractions.

Beatriz has 3 cups of applesauce. She divides the applesauce into $\frac{1}{4}$-cup servings. How many servings of applesauce does she have?

One Way Draw a diagram to solve the problem.

Draw 3 circles to represent the 3 cups of applesauce. Since Beatriz divides the applesauce into $\frac{1}{4}$-cup servings, draw lines to divide each "cup" into fourths.

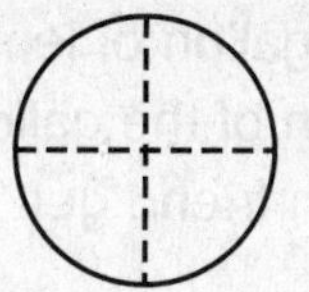 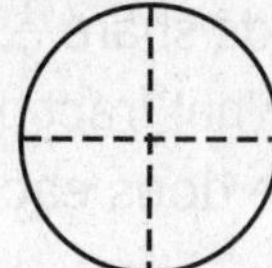 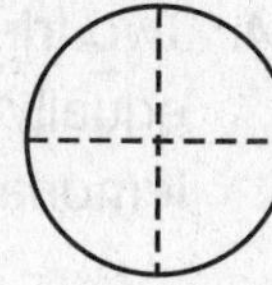

To find $3 \div \frac{1}{4}$, count the total number of fourths in the 3 circles.

So, Beatriz has 12 one-fourth-cup servings of applesauce.

Another Way Write an equation to solve.

Write an equation. $3 \div \frac{1}{4} = n$

Write a related multiplication equation. $3 \times 4 = n$

Then solve. $12 = n$

So, Beatriz has 12 one-fourth-cup servings of applesauce.

1. Draw a diagram to represent the problem. Then solve.

Drew has 5 granola bars. He cuts the bars into halves. How many $\frac{1}{2}$-bar pieces does he have?

____

2. Write an equation to represent the problem. Then solve.

Three friends share $\frac{1}{4}$ pan of brownies. What fraction of the whole pan of brownies does each friend get?

____

____

Name ______________________

Lesson 77
CC.5.NF.7c

Interpret Division with Fractions

Write an equation to represent the problem. Then solve.

1. Daniel has a piece of wire that is $\frac{1}{2}$ yard long. He cuts the wire into 3 equal pieces. What fraction of a yard is each piece?

   $\frac{1}{2} \div 3 = n$; $\frac{1}{2} \times \frac{1}{3} = n$;

   $n = \frac{1}{6}$; $\frac{1}{6}$ yard

2. Vita has a piece of ribbon that is 5 meters long. She cuts the ribbon into pieces that are each $\frac{1}{3}$ meter long. How many pieces does she cut?

   ____

Draw a diagram to represent the problem. Then solve.

3. Leah has 3 muffins. She cuts each muffin into fourths. How many $\frac{1}{4}$-muffin pieces does she have?

   ____

4. Two friends share $\frac{1}{4}$ gallon of lemonade equally. What fraction of the gallon of lemonade does each friend get?

   ____

5. Write a story problem to represent $3 \div \frac{1}{2}$.

   ____

   ____

6. Write a story problem to represent $\frac{1}{4} \div 2$.

   ____

   ____

Problem Solving REAL WORLD

7. Spencer has $\frac{1}{3}$ pound of nuts. He divides the nuts equally into 4 bags. What fraction of a pound of nuts is in each bag?

   ____

8. Humma has 3 apples. She slices each apple into eighths. How many $\frac{1}{8}$-apple slices does she have?

   ____

Name ___________________________

Lesson 78

COMMON CORE STANDARD CC.5.MD.1

Lesson Objective: Compare, contrast, and convert customary units of length.

Customary Length

You can convert one customary unit of length to another customary unit of length by multiplying or dividing.

Multiply to change from larger to smaller units of length.

Divide to change from smaller to larger units of length.

Customary Units of Length

1 foot (ft) = 12 inches (in.)
1 yard (yd) = 3 feet
1 mile (mi) = 5,280 feet
1 mile = 1,760 yards

Convert 3 feet to inches.

Step 1	**Step 2**	**Step 3**
Decide: (Multiply) or Divide feet → inches larger → smaller	Think: 1 ft = 12 in., so 3 ft = (3 × <u>12</u>) in.	Multiply. 3 × 12 = 36

So, 3 feet = <u>36</u> inches.

Convert 363 feet to yards.

Step 1	**Step 2**	**Step 3**
Decide: Multiply or (Divide) feet → yards smaller → larger	Think: 3 ft = 1 yd, so 363 ft = (363 ÷ <u>3</u>) yd.	Divide. 363 ÷ <u>3</u> = <u>121</u>

So, 363 feet = <u>121</u> yards.

Convert.

1. 33 yd = ________ ft
2. 300 mi = ________ yd
3. 46 in. = ____ ft ____ in.
4. 96 yd = ________ ft
5. 48 ft = ________ yd
6. 2 mi 20 yd = ________ yd

Compare. Write <, >, or =.

7. 2 yd ◯ 7 ft
8. 67 mi ◯ 117,920 yd
9. 250 yd ◯ 800 ft
10. 14 yd 2 ft ◯ 16 ft
11. 34 ft 10 in. ◯ 518 in.
12. 5 mi 8 ft ◯ 8,800 yd

Name ______________________

Customary Length

Lesson 78
CC.5.MD.1

Convert.

1. 12 yd = **36** ft

total yards | feet in 1 yard | total feet

12 × 3 = 36

12 yards = 36 feet

2. 5 ft = ________ in.

3. 5 mi = ________ ft

4. 240 in. = ________ ft

5. 100 yd = ________ ft

6. 10 ft = ________ in.

7. 150 in. = _____ ft _____ in.

8. 7 yd 2 ft = ________ ft

9. 10 mi = ________ ft

Compare. Write <, >, or =.

10. 23 in. ◯ 2 ft

11. 25 yd ◯ 75 ft

12. 6,200 ft ◯ 1 mi 900 ft

13. 100 in. ◯ 3 yd 1 ft

14. 1,000 ft ◯ 300 yd

15. 500 in. ◯ 40 ft

Problem Solving REAL WORLD

16. Marita orders 12 yards of material to make banners. If she needs 1 foot of fabric for each banner, how many banners can she make?

____

17. Christy bought an 8-foot piece of lumber to trim a bookshelf. Altogether, she needs 100 inches of lumber for the trim. Did Christy buy enough lumber? Explain.

____

____

Name ______________________________

Lesson 79

COMMON CORE STANDARD CC.5.MD.1

Lesson Objective: Compare, contrast, and convert customary units of capacity.

Customary Capacity

You can convert one unit of customary capacity to another by multiplying or dividing.

Multiply to change from larger to smaller units.

Divide to change from smaller to larger units.

Customary Units of Capacity
1 cup (c) = 8 fluid ounces (fl oz)
1 pint (pt) = 2 cups
1 quart (qt) = 2 pints
1 quart = 4 cups
1 gallon (gal) = 4 quarts

Convert 8 cups to quarts.

Step 1	**Step 2**	**Step 3**
Decide: Multiply or (Divide) cups → quarts smaller → larger	Think: 4 c = 1 qt, so 8 c = (8 ÷ 4) qt.	Divide. 8 ÷ 4 = 2

So, 8 cups = 2 quarts.

Convert 19 gallons to quarts.

Step 1	**Step 2**	**Step 3**
Decide: (Multiply) or Divide gallons → quarts larger → smaller	Think: 1 gal = 4 qt, so 19 gal = (19 × 4) qt.	Multiply. 19 × 4 = 76

So, 19 gallons = 76 quarts.

Convert.

1. 14 pt = __________ qt
2. 32 qt = __________ c
3. 7 c = __________ fl oz
4. 28 c = __________ pt
5. 9 gal = __________ qt
6. 16 c = __________ qt

Compare. Write <, >, or =.

7. 16 qt ◯ 60 c
8. 88 fl oz ◯ 11 c
9. 3 gal ◯ 10 qt
10. 36 qt ◯ 54 c
11. 66 fl oz ◯ 9 c
12. 16 gal ◯ 64 qt

Name ____________________

Lesson 79
CC.5.MD.1

Customary Capacity

Convert.

1. 5 gal = 40 pt

   Think: 1 gallon = 4 quarts
   1 quart = 2 pints

2. 192 fl oz = ______ pt

3. 15 pt = ______ c

4. 240 fl oz = ______ c

5. 32 qt = ______ gal

6. 10 qt = ______ c

7. 48 c = ______ qt

8. 72 pt = ______ gal

9. 128 fl oz = ______ pt

Compare. Write <, >, or =.

10. 17 qt ◯ 4 gal

11. 96 fl oz ◯ 8 pt

12. 400 pt ◯ 100 gal

13. 100 fl oz ◯ 16 pt

14. 74 fl oz ◯ 8 c

15. 12 c ◯ 3 qt

Problem Solving REAL WORLD

16. Vickie made a recipe for 144 fluid ounces of scented candle wax. How many 1-cup candle molds can she fill with the recipe?

    ____

17. A recipe calls for 32 fluid ounces of heavy cream. How many 1-pint containers of heavy cream are needed to make the recipe?

    ____

Name ______________________________

Lesson 80

COMMON CORE STANDARD CC.5.MD.1

Lesson Objective: Compare, contrast, and convert customary units of weight.

Weight

You can convert one customary unit of weight to another by multiplying or dividing.

Multiply to change from larger to smaller units.

Divide to change from smaller to larger units.

Customary Units of Weight

1 pound (lb) = 16 ounces (oz)
1 ton (T) = 2,000 pounds

Convert 96 ounces to pounds.

Step 1 Decide: Multiply or (Divide)	**Step 2** Think:	**Step 3** Divide.
ounces ⟶ pounds smaller ⟶ larger	16 oz = 1 lb so 96 oz = (96 ÷ **16**) lb.	96 ÷ **16** = **6**

So, 96 ounces = **6** pounds.

Convert 4 pounds to ounces.

Step 1 Decide: (Multiply) or Divide	**Step 2** Think:	**Step 3** Multiply.
pounds ⟶ ounces larger ⟶ smaller	1 lb = 16 oz, so 4 lb = (4 × **16**) oz.	4 × **16** = **64**

So, 4 pounds = **64** ounces.

Convert.

1. 14 lb = ________ oz

2. 12,000 lb = ________ T

3. 2 T = ________ lb

4. 7 lb = ________ oz

5. 22 lb = ________ oz

6. 16 oz = ________ lb

Compare. Write <, >, or =.

7. 1 T ◯ 3,000 lb

8. 3 lb ◯ 43 oz

9. 5 T ◯ 10,000 lb

10. 3 T ◯ 6,000 lb

11. 6 lb ◯ 96 oz

12. 16 T ◯ 6,400 lb

Name ______________________________

Weight

Lesson 80
CC.5.MD.1

Convert.

1. 96 oz = <u>6</u> lb

   total oz → 96 ÷ oz in 1 lb → 16 = total lb → 6

2. 6 T = __________ lb

3. 18 lb = __________ oz

4. 3,200 oz = __________ lb

5. 12 T = __________ lb

6. 9 lb = __________ oz

7. 7 lb = __________ oz

8. 100 lb = __________ oz

9. 60,000 lb = __________ T

Compare. Write <, >, or =.

10. 40 oz ◯ 4 lb

11. 80 oz ◯ 5 lb

12. 5,000 lb ◯ 5 T

13. 18,000 lb ◯ 9 T

14. 25 lb ◯ 350 oz

15. 27 oz ◯ 2 lb

Problem Solving

16. Mr. Fields ordered 3 tons of gravel for a driveway at a factory. How many pounds of gravel did he order?

    ____

17. Sara can take no more than 22 pounds of luggage on a trip. Her suitcase weighs 112 ounces. How many more pounds can she pack without going over the limit?

    ____

Name ____________________

Lesson 81

COMMON CORE STANDARD CC.5.MD.1

Lesson Objective: Convert measurement units to solve multistep problems.

Multistep Measurement Problems

An ice cream parlor donated 6 containers of ice cream to a local elementary school. Each container holds 3 gallons of ice cream. If each student is served 1 cup of ice cream, how many students can be served?

Step 1 Record the information you are given.

There are __6__ containers of ice cream.

Each container holds __3__ gallons of ice cream.

Step 2 Find the total amount of ice cream in the 6 containers.

6×3 gallons = __18__ gallons of ice cream

Step 3 Convert from gallons to cups.

There are __4__ quarts in 1 gallon, so 18 gallons = __72__ quarts.

There are __2__ pints in 1 quart, so 72 quarts = __144__ pints.

There are __2__ cups in 1 pint, so 144 pints = __288__ cups.

So, __288__ students can be served 1 cup of ice cream.

Solve.

1. A cargo truck weighs 8,750 pounds. The weight limit for a certain bridge is 5 tons. How many pounds of cargo can be added to the truck before it exceeds the weight limit for the bridge?

____

2. A plumber uses 16 inches of tubing to connect each washing machine in a laundry to the water source. He wants to install 18 washing machines. How many yards of tubing will he need?

____

3. Larry has 9 gallons of paint. He uses 10 quarts to paint his kitchen and 3 gallons to paint his living room. How many pints of paint will be left?

____

4. Ketisha is practicing for a marathon by running around a track that is 440 yards long. Yesterday she ran around the track 20 times. How many miles did she run?

____

Name ________________

Multistep Measurement Problems

Solve.

1. A cable company has 5 miles of cable to install. How many 100-yard lengths of cable can be cut?

   Think: 1,760 yards = 1 mile.
   So the cable company has 5 × 1,760, or 8,800 yards of cable.

   Divide. 8,800 ÷ 100 = 88

   88 lengths

2. Afton made a chicken dish for dinner. She added a 10-ounce package of vegetables and a 14-ounce package of rice to 40 ounces of chicken. What was the total weight of the chicken dish in pounds?

   ____

3. A jar contains 26 fluid ounces of spaghetti sauce. How many cups of spaghetti sauce do 4 jars contain?

   ____

4. Coach Kent brings 3 quarts of sports drink to soccer practice. He gives the same amount of the drink to each of his 16 players. How many ounces of the drink does each player get?

   ____

5. Leslie needs 324 inches of fringe to put around the edge of a tablecloth. The fringe comes in lengths of 10 yards. If Leslie buys 1 package of fringe, how many feet of fringe will she have left over?

   ____

6. Darnell rented a moving truck. The weight of the empty truck was 7,860 pounds. When Darnell filled the truck with his items, it weighed 6 tons. What was the weight in pounds of the items that Darnell placed in the truck?

   ____

Problem Solving REAL WORLD

7. A pitcher contains 40 fluid ounces of iced tea. Shelby pours 3 cups of iced tea. How many pints of iced tea are left in the pitcher?

   ____

8. Olivia ties 2.5 feet of ribbon onto one balloon. How many yards of ribbon does Olivia need for 18 balloons?

   ____

Name ______________________________

Lesson 82

COMMON CORE STANDARD CC.5.MD.1

Lesson Objective: Compare, contrast, and convert metric units.

Metric Measures

The metric system is based on place value. To convert between units, you multiply or divide by a power of 10. You **multiply** to change larger units to smaller units, such as liters to centiliters. You **divide** to change smaller units to larger units, such as meters to kilometers.

Metric Units of Length
1 centimeter (cm) = 10 millimeters (mm)
1 decimeter (dm) = 10 centimeters (cm)
1 meter (m) = 1,000 millimeters (mm)
1 kilometer (km) = 1,000 meters (m)

Convert 566 millimeters to decimeters.

- Think about how the two units are related.

  1 decimeter = 100 millimeters

- **Think:** Should I multiply or divide?

  Millimeters are smaller than decimeters.

  So divide, or move the decimal point left for each power of 10.

				5	• 6	6
kilo- (k)	hecto- (h)	deka- (da)	meter liter gram	deci- (d)	centi- (c)	milli- (m)

566 *millimeters* ÷ 100 *mm in 1 dm* = **5.66** *total decimeters*

So, 566 mm = **5.66** dm.

Complete the equation to show the conversion.

1. 115 km ◯ 10 = __________ hm

115 km ◯ 100 = __________ dam

115 km ◯ 1,000 = __________ m

2. 418 cL ◯ 10 = __________ dL

418 cL ◯ 100 = __________ L

418 cL ◯ 1,000 = __________ daL

Convert.

3. 40 cm = ______ mm **4.** 500 mL = ______ dL **5.** 6 kg = ______ g

6. 5,000 cL = ______ L **7.** 4 kg = ______ hg **8.** 200 mm = ______ cm

Name ______________________________

Lesson 82
CC.5.MD.1

Metric Measures

Convert.

1. 16 m = 16,000 mm

number of meters		millimeters in 1 meter		number of millimeters
16	×	1,000	=	16,000

   16 m = 16,000 mm

2. 6,500 cL = __________ L

3. 15 cm = __________ mm

4. 3,200 g = __________ kg

5. 12 L = __________ mL

6. 200 cm = __________ m

7. 70,000 g = __________ kg

8. 100 dL = __________ L

9. 60 m = __________ mm

Compare. Write <, >, or =.

10. 900 cm ◯ 9,000 mm

11. 600 km ◯ 5 m

12. 5,000 cm ◯ 5 m

13. 18,000 g ◯ 10 kg

14. 8,456 mL ◯ 9 L

15. 2 m ◯ 275 cm

Problem Solving REAL WORLD

16. Bria ordered 145 centimeters of fabric. Jayleen ordered 1.5 meters of fabric. Who ordered more fabric?

    ____

17. Ed fills his sports bottle with 1.2 liters of water. After his bike ride, he drinks 200 milliliters of the water. How much water is left in Ed's sports bottle?

    ____

Name ___________________________

Lesson 83

COMMON CORE STANDARD CC.5.MD.1

Lesson Objective: Solve problems about customary and metric conversions using the strategy *make a table*.

Problem Solving • Customary and Metric Conversions

You can use the strategy *make a table* to help you solve problems about customary and metric conversions.

Jon's faucet is dripping at the rate of 24 centiliters in a day. How many milliliters of water will have dripped from Jon's faucet in 24 hours?

Read the Problem

What do I need to find?

I need to find how many milliliters of water will have dripped from Jon's faucet in 24 hours.

What information do I need to use?

I need to use the number of cL that have dripped in 24 hr and the number of mL in a cL.

How will I use the information?

I will make a table to show the relationship between the number of centiliters and the number of milliliters.

Conversion Table

	L	dL	cL	mL
1 L	1	10	100	1,000
1 dL	$\frac{1}{10}$	1	10	100
1 cL	$\frac{1}{100}$	$\frac{1}{10}$	1	10
1 mL	$\frac{1}{1,000}$	$\frac{1}{100}$	$\frac{1}{10}$	1

I can use the Conversion Table to find the number of milliliters in 1 centiliter.

There are 10 milliliters in 1 centiliter.

cL	1	2	4	24
mL	10	20	40	240

So, 240 milliliters of water will have dripped from Jon's faucet in 24 hours.

Make a table to help you solve the problems.

1. Fernando has a bucket that holds 3 gallons of water. He is filling the bucket using a 1-pint container. How many times will he have to fill the pint container in order to fill the bucket?

____

2. Lexi has a roll of shelf paper that is 800 cm long. She wants to cut the paper into 1-m strips to line the shelves in her pantry. How many 1-meter strips can she cut?

____

Name ____________________

Problem Solving • Customary and Metric Conversions

Solve each problem by making a table.

1. Thomas is making soup. His soup pot holds 8 quarts of soup. How many 1-cup servings of soup will Thomas make?

Number of Quarts	1	2	3	4	8
Number of Cups	4	8	12	16	32

32 1-cup servings

2. Paulina works out with a 2.5-kilogram mass. What is the mass of the 2.5-kilogram mass in grams?

____

3. Alex lives 500 yards from the park. How many inches does Alex live from the park?

____

4. Emma uses a 250-meter roll of crepe paper to make streamers. How many dekameters of crepe paper does Emma use?

____

5. A flatbed truck is loaded with 7,000 pounds of bricks. How many tons of brick are on the truck?

____

Name ______________________________

Lesson 84

COMMON CORE STANDARD CC.5.MD.1

Lesson Objective: Convert units of time to solve elapsed time problems.

Elapsed Time

You can solve elapsed time problems by converting units of time.

Units of Time
60 seconds (s) = 1 minute (min)
60 minutes = 1 hour (hr)
24 hours = 1 day (d)
7 days = 1 week (wk)
52 weeks = 1 year (yr)
12 months (mo) = 1 year
365 days = 1 year

Starting at 4:20 P.M., Connie practiced piano for 90 minutes. At what time did Connie stop practicing piano?

Convert 90 minutes to hours and minutes. Then find the end time.

Step 1 To convert minutes to hours, divide.

90 ÷ 60 is 1 with a remainder of 30

90 min = __1__ hr __30__ min

Step 2 Count forward by hours until you reach 1 hour.

4:20 → 5:20 = 1 hour

Step 3 Count forward by minutes until you reach 30 minutes.

5:20 → 5:30 = 1 hour 10 minutes
5:30 → 5:40 = 1 hour 20 minutes
5:40 → 5:50 = 1 hour 30 minutes

Connie stops practicing piano at __5:50 P.M.__.

Convert.

1. 480 min = ________ hr

2. 4 d = ________ hr

3. 125 hr = _____ d _____ hr

Find the start, elapsed, or end time.

4. Start time: 7:15 A.M.

Elapsed time: 2 hr 20 min

End time: ____________

5. Start time: 6:28 A.M.

Elapsed time: ____________

End time: 10:08 A.M.

6. Start time: ____________

Elapsed time: 5 hr 50 min

End time: 7:55 P.M.

7. Start time: 5:24 P.M.

Elapsed time: 6 hr

End time: ____________

Name ______________________

Elapsed Time

Convert.

1. 5 days = **120** hr
2. 8 hr = __________ min
3. 30 min = __________ s

Think: 1 day = 24 hours
$5 \times 24 = 120$

4. 15 hr = __________ min
5. 5 yr = __________ d
6. 7 d = __________ hr

7. 24 hr = __________ min
8. 600 s = __________ min
9. 60,000 min = __________ hr

Find the start, elapsed, or end time.

10. Start time: 11:00 A.M.

Elapsed time: 4 hours 5 minutes

End time: __________

11. Start time: 6:30 P.M.

Elapsed time: 2 hours 18 minutes

End time: __________

12. Start time: __________

Elapsed time: $9\frac{3}{4}$ hours

End time: 6:00 P.M.

13. Start time: 2:00 P.M.

Elapsed time: __________

End time: 8:30 P.M.

Problem Solving REAL WORLD

14. Kiera's dance class starts at 4:30 P.M. and ends at 6:15 P.M. How long is her dance class?

____

15. Julio watched a movie that started at 11:30 A.M. and ended at 2:12 P.M. How long was the movie?

____

Name ____________________

Lesson 85

COMMON CORE STANDARD CC.5.MD.2

Lesson Objective: Make and use line plots with fractions to solve problems.

Line Plots

A **line plot** is a graph that shows the shape of a data set by placing *X*s above each data value on a number line. You can make a line plot to represent a data set and then use the line plot to answer questions about the data set.

Students measure the lengths of several seeds. The length of each seed is listed below.

$\frac{1}{2}$ inch, $\frac{3}{4}$ inch, $\frac{1}{2}$ inch, $\frac{1}{4}$ inch, $\frac{3}{4}$ inch, $\frac{3}{4}$ inch, $\frac{3}{4}$ inch, $\frac{1}{4}$ inch, $\frac{1}{2}$ inch

What is the combined length of the seeds that are $\frac{1}{4}$ inch long?

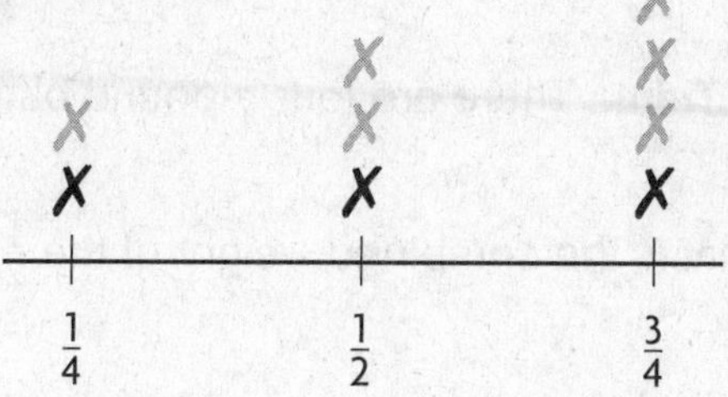

Step 1 To represent the different lengths of the seeds, draw and label a line plot with the data values $\frac{1}{4}$, $\frac{1}{2}$, and $\frac{3}{4}$. Then use an *X* to represent each seed. The line plot has been started for you.

Step 2 There are __2__ *X*s above $\frac{1}{4}$ on the line plot.

Multiply to find the combined length of the seeds:

__2__ × __$\frac{1}{4}$__ = __$\frac{2}{4}$, or $\frac{1}{2}$__ inch

The combined length of the seeds that are $\frac{1}{4}$ inch long is $\frac{1}{2}$ inch.

You can use the same process to find the combined lengths of the seeds that are $\frac{1}{2}$ inch long and $\frac{3}{4}$ inch long.

Use the data and the line plot above to answer the questions.

1. What is the total length of all the seeds that the students measured?

____

2. What is the average length of one of the seeds that the students measured?

____

Name ________________________

Line Plots

Use the data to complete the line plot. Then answer the questions.

A clerk in a health food store makes bags of trail mix. The amount of trail mix in each bag is listed below.

$\frac{1}{4}$ lb, $\frac{1}{4}$ lb, $\frac{3}{4}$ lb, $\frac{1}{2}$ lb, $\frac{1}{4}$ lb, $\frac{3}{4}$ lb,
$\frac{3}{4}$ lb, $\frac{3}{4}$ lb, $\frac{1}{2}$ lb, $\frac{1}{4}$ lb, $\frac{1}{2}$ lb, $\frac{1}{2}$ lb

1. What is the combined weight of the $\frac{1}{4}$-lb bags? 1 lb

   Think: There are four $\frac{1}{4}$-pound bags.

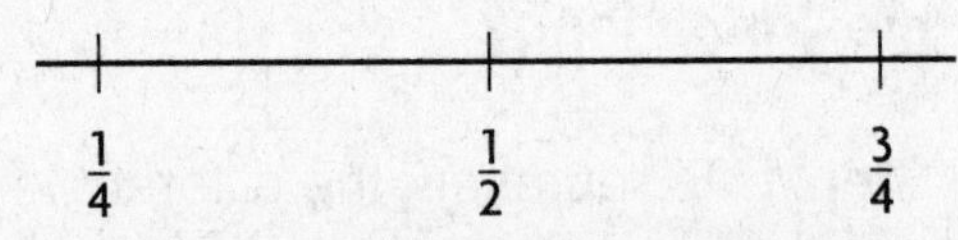

Weight of Trail Mix (in pounds)

2. What is the combined weight of the $\frac{1}{2}$-lb bags? ________

3. What is the combined weight of the $\frac{3}{4}$-lb bags? ________

4. What is the total weight of the trail mix used in all the bags? ________

5. What is the average amount of trail mix in each bag? ________

Julie uses crystals to make a bracelet. The lengths of the crystals are shown below.

$\frac{1}{2}$ in., $\frac{5}{8}$ in., $\frac{3}{4}$ in., $\frac{1}{2}$ in., $\frac{3}{8}$ in., $\frac{1}{2}$ in., $\frac{3}{4}$ in.,
$\frac{3}{8}$ in., $\frac{3}{4}$ in., $\frac{5}{8}$ in., $\frac{1}{2}$ in., $\frac{3}{8}$ in., $\frac{5}{8}$ in., $\frac{3}{4}$ in.

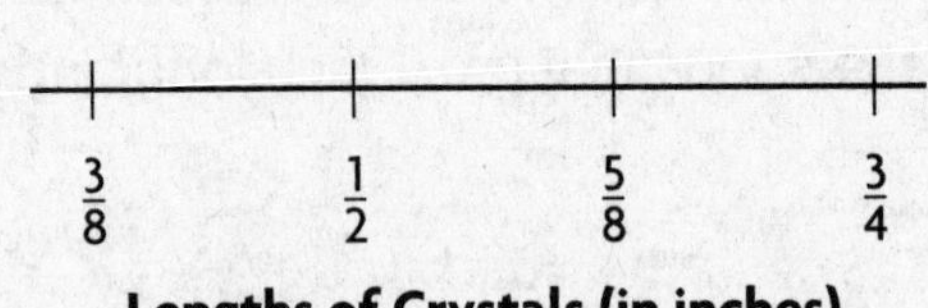

Lengths of Crystals (in inches)

6. What is the combined length of the $\frac{1}{2}$-in. crystals? ________

7. What is the combined length of the $\frac{5}{8}$-in. crystals? ________

8. What is the total length of all the crystals in the bracelet? ________

9. What is the average length of each crystal in the bracelet? ________

Name ______________________________

Three-Dimensional Figures

Lesson 86

COMMON CORE STANDARD CC.5.MD.3

Lesson Objective: Identify, describe, and classify three-dimensional figures.

A **polyhedron** is a solid figure with faces that are polygons. You can identify a polyhedron by the shape of its faces.

A **pyramid** is a polyhedron with one polygon base. The lateral faces of a pyramid are triangles that meet at a common vertex.

triangular pyramid — The base and faces are triangles.

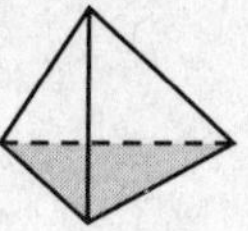

rectangular pyramid — The base is a rectangle.

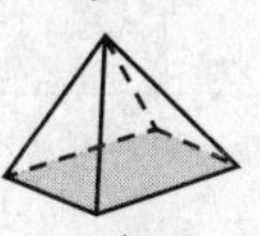

square pyramid — The base is a square.

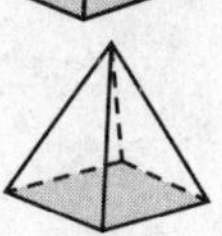

pentagonal pyramid — The base is a pentagon.

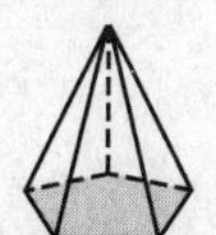

hexagonal pyramid — The base is a hexagon.

A **prism** is a polyhedron with two congruent polygons as bases. The lateral faces of a prism are rectangles.

triangular prism — The two bases are triangles.

rectangular prism — All faces are rectangles.

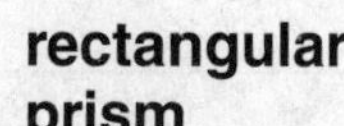

square prism or cube — All faces are squares.

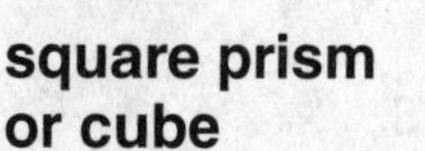

pentagonal prism — The two bases are pentagons.

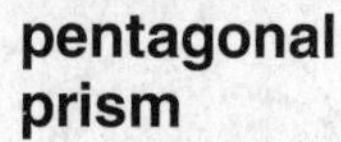

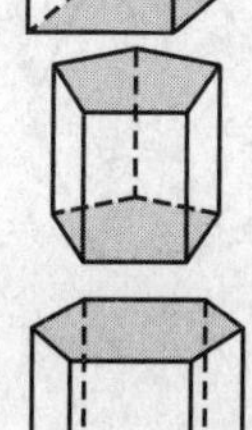

hexagonal prism — The two bases are hexagons.

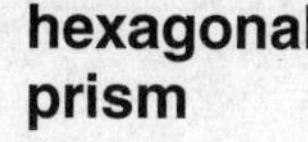

A solid figure with curved surfaces is **not a polyhedron**.

cone — The one base is a circle.

cylinder — The two bases are circles.

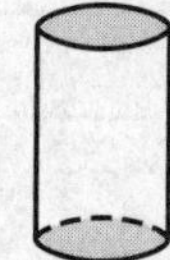

sphere — There is no base.

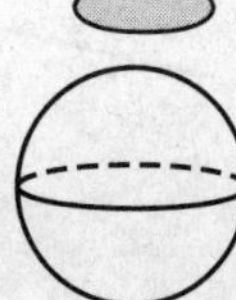

Classify the solid figure. Write *prism, pyramid, cone, cylinder,* or *sphere.*

The solid figure has one base.

The rest of its faces are triangles.

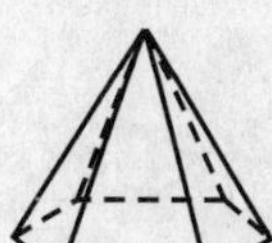

So, the solid figure is a pyramid.

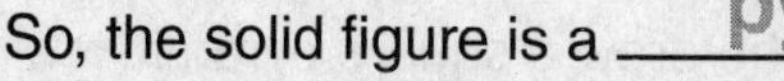

Classify each solid figure. Write *prism, pyramid, cone, cylinder,* or *sphere.*

1. 

2. 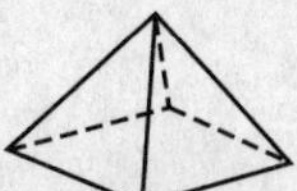

3. 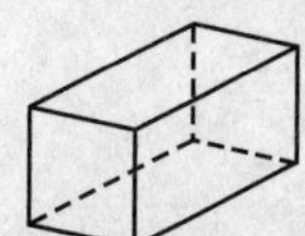

4. 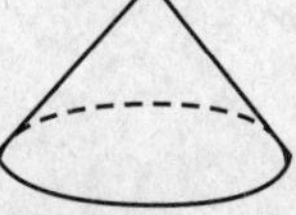

Name ______________________

Lesson 86
CC.5.MD.3

Three-Dimensional Figures

Classify the solid figure. Write *prism, pyramid, cone, cylinder,* or *sphere.*

1.

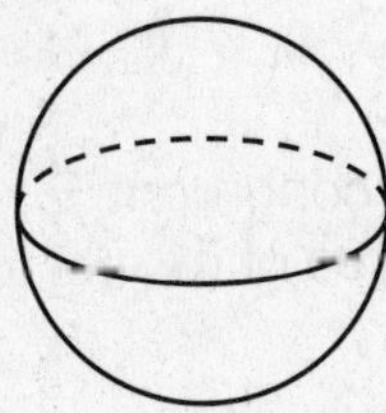

There are no bases. There is 1 curved surface. It is a

sphere.

2.

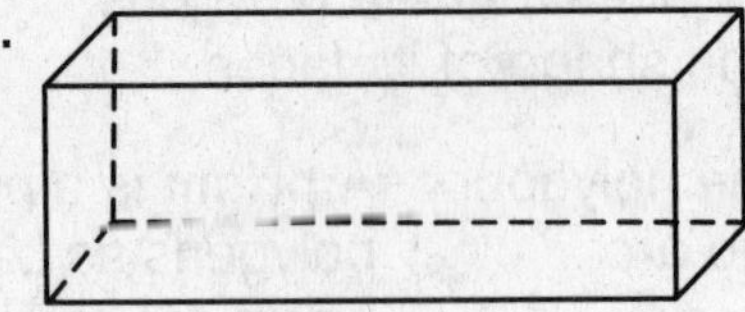

____

3.

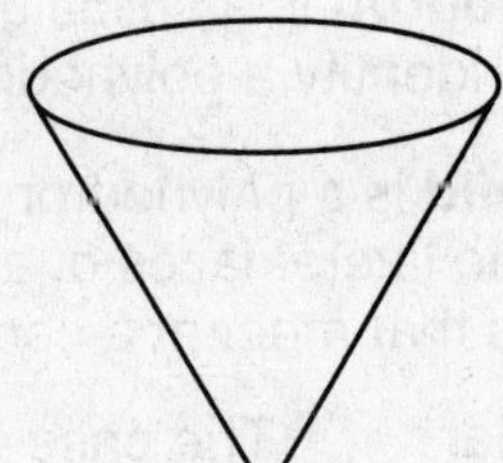

____

Name the solid figure.

4.

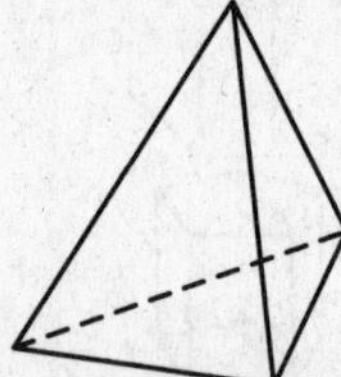

____

5.

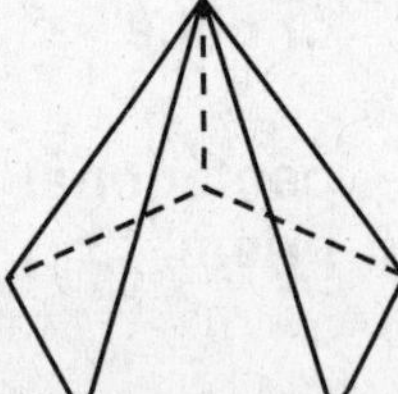

____

6.

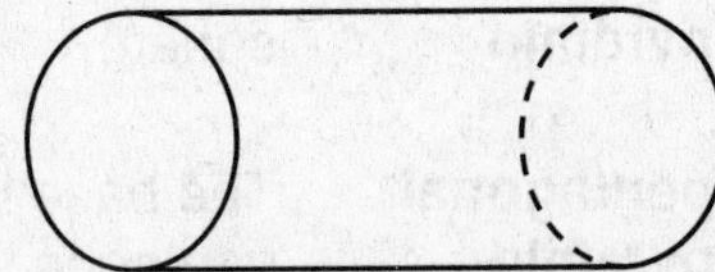

____

7.

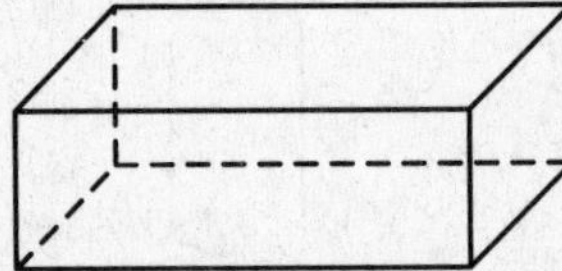

____

8.

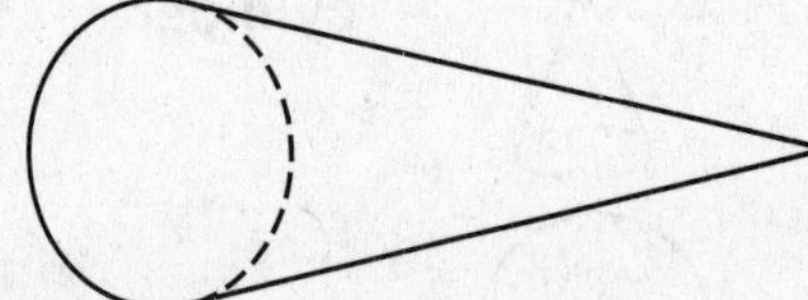

____

9.

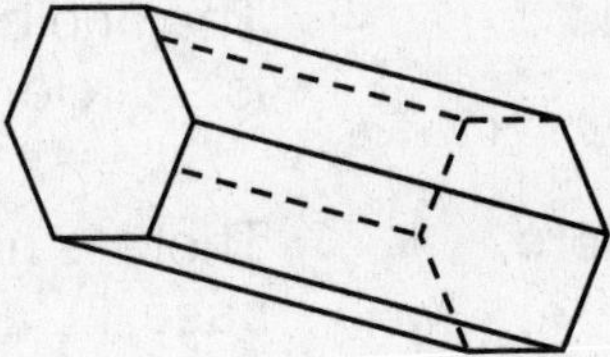

____

Problem Solving REAL WORLD

10. Darrien is making a solid figure out of folded paper. His solid figure has six congruent faces that are all squares. What solid figure did Darrien make?

____

11. Nanako said she drew a square pyramid and that all of the faces are triangles. Is this possible? **Explain.**

____

Name ______________________________

Lesson 87

COMMON CORE STANDARD CC.5.MD.3a

Lesson Objective: Understand unit cubes and how they can be used to build a solid figure.

Unit Cubes and Solid Figures

A **unit cube** is a cube that has a length, width, and height of 1 unit. You can use unit cubes to build a rectangular prism.

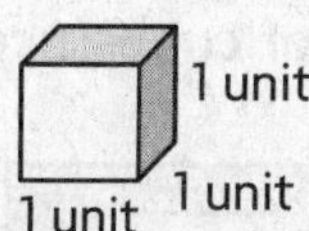

Count the number of cubes used to build the rectangular prism.

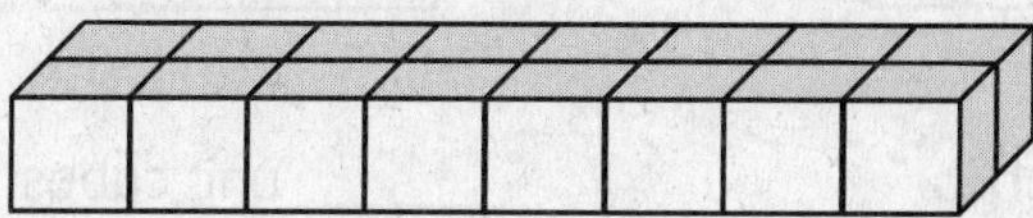

The length of the prism is made up of __8__ unit cubes.

The width of the prism is made up of __2__ unit cubes.

The height of the prism is made up of __1__ unit cube.

The number of unit cubes used to build the rectangular prism is __16__.

Count the number of unit cubes used to build each solid figure.

1.

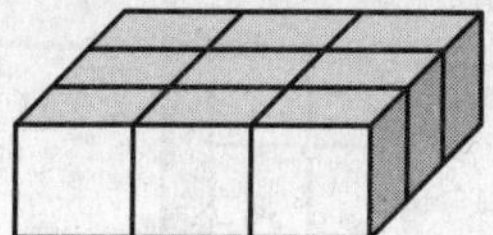

____________ unit cubes

2.

____________ unit cubes

3.

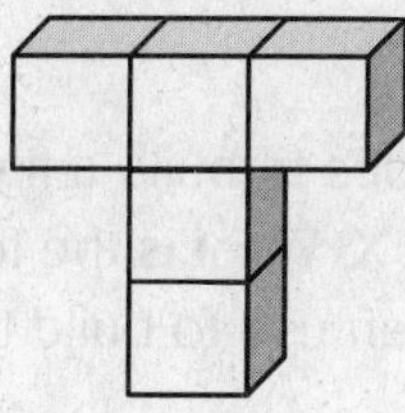

____________ unit cubes

4.

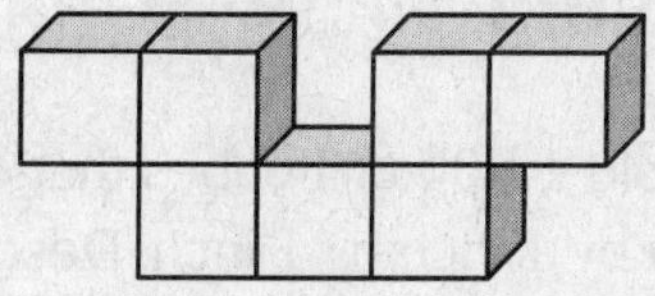

____________ unit cubes

Name ______________________________

Lesson 87

CC.5.MD.3a

Unit Cubes and Solid Figures

Count the number of cubes used to build each solid figure.

1.

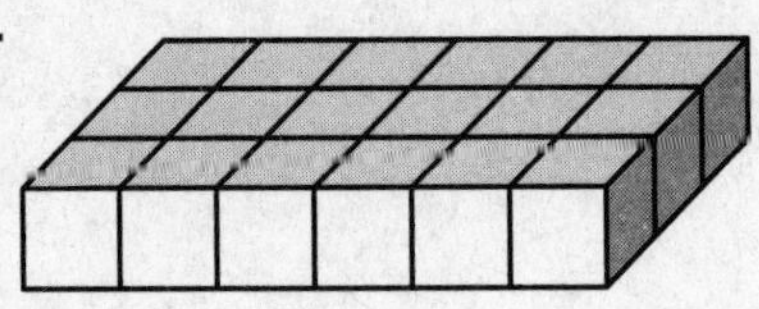

18 unit cubes

2.

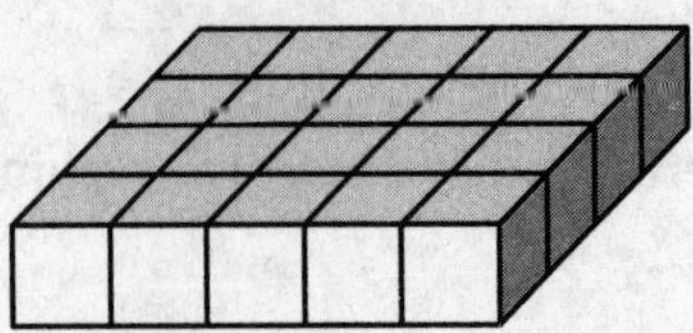

_____ unit cubes

3.

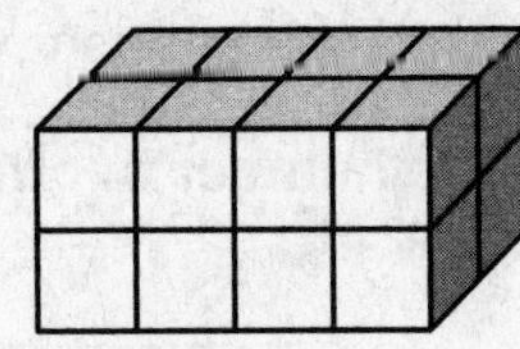

_____ unit cubes

4.

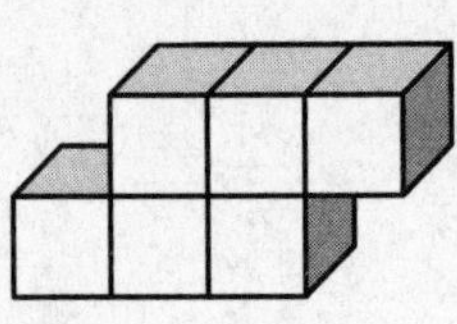

_____ unit cubes

5.

_____ unit cubes

6.

_____ unit cubes

Compare the number of unit cubes in each solid figure. Use <, >, or =.

7.

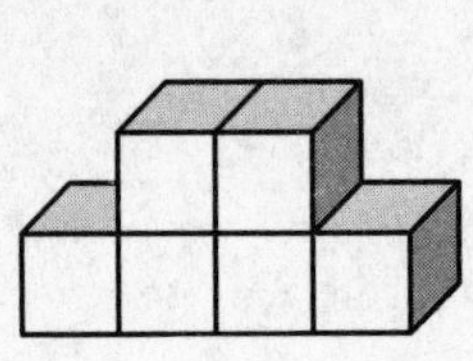

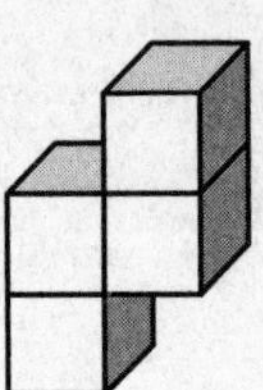

_____ unit cubes ◯ _____ unit cubes

8.

_____ unit cubes ◯ _____ unit cubes

Problem Solving REAL WORLD

9. A carton can hold 1,000 unit cubes that measure 1 inch by 1 inch by 1 inch. Describe the dimensions of the carton using unit cubes.

____

____

____

____

10. Peter uses unit cubes to build a figure in the shape of the letter X. What is the fewest unit cubes that Peter can use to build the figure?

____

Name ______________________________

Lesson 88

COMMON CORE STANDARD CC.5.MD.3b

Lesson Objective: Count unit cubes that fill a solid figure to find volume.

Understand Volume

The **volume** of a rectangular prism is equal to the number of unit cubes that make up the prism. Each unit cube has a volume of 1 cubic unit.

Find the volume of the prism. 1 unit cube = 1 cubic inch

Step 1 Count the number of unit cubes in the bottom layer of the prism.

There are __4__ unit cubes that make up the length of the first layer.

There are __2__ unit cubes that make up the width of the first layer.

There is __1__ unit cube that makes up the height of the first layer.

So, altogether, there are __8__ unit cubes that make up the bottom layer of the prism.

Step 2 Count the number of layers of cubes that make up the prism.

The prism is made up of __3__ layers of unit cubes.

Step 3 Find the total number of cubes that fill the prism.

Multiply the number of layers by the number of cubes in each layer.

$3 \times 8 =$ __24__ unit cubes

Each unit cube has a volume of 1 cubic inch. So, the volume of the prism is 24×1, or __24__ cubic inches.

Use the unit given. Find the volume.

1.

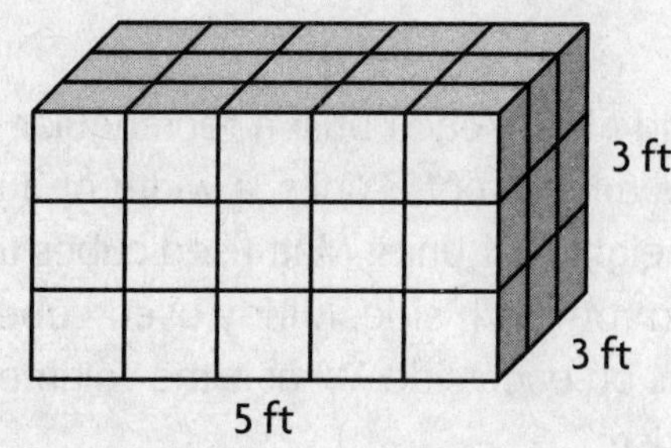

Each cube = 1 cu ft

Volume = ________ cu ________

2.

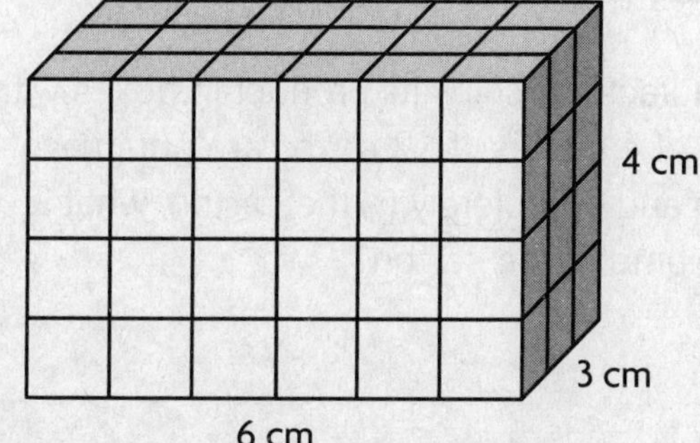

Each cube = 1 cu cm

Volume = ________ cu ________

Name ______________________

Lesson 88

CC.5.MD.3b

Understand Volume

Use the unit given. Find the volume.

1.

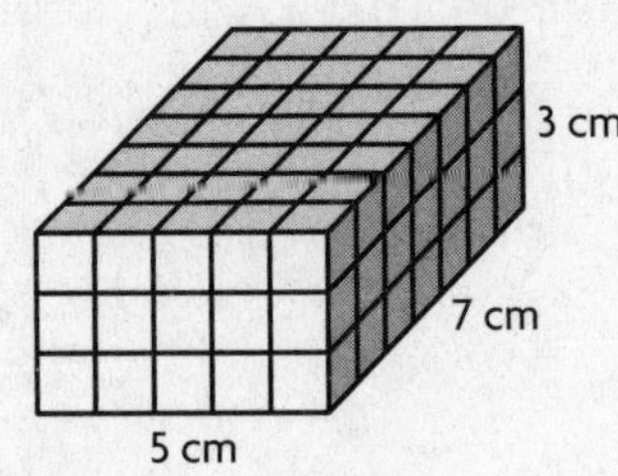

Each cube = 1 cu cm

Volume = 105 cu cm

2.

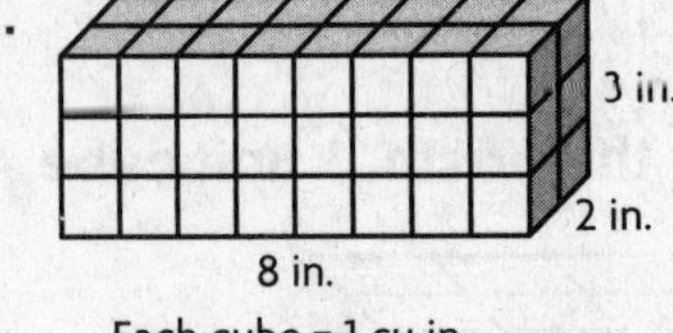

Each cube = 1 cu in.

Volume = ______ cu ______

3.

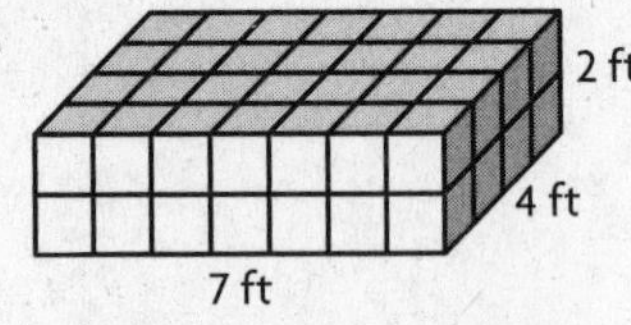

Each cube = 1 cu ft

Volume = ______ cu ______

4.

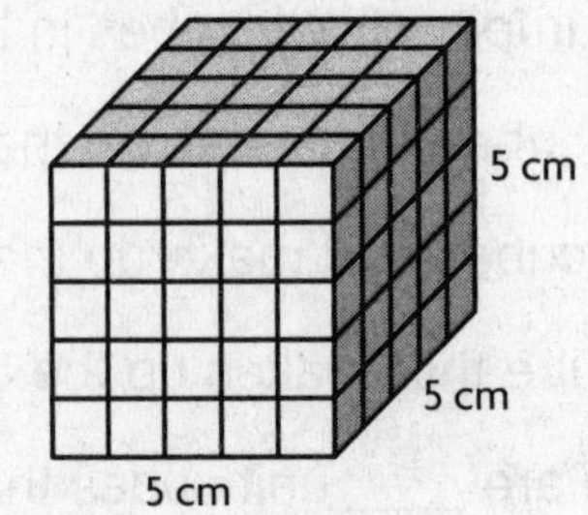

Each cube = 1 cu cm

Volume = ______ cu ______

5. Compare the volumes. Write <, >, or =.

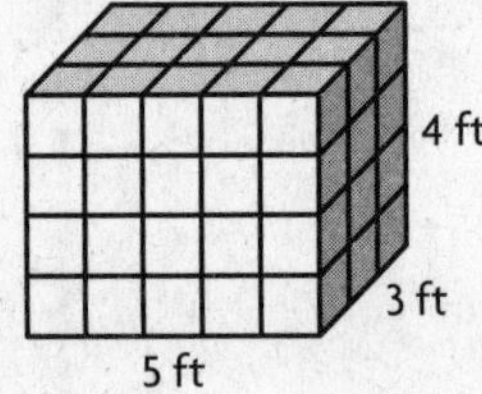

Each cube = 1 cu ft

______ cu ft ◯ ______ cu ft

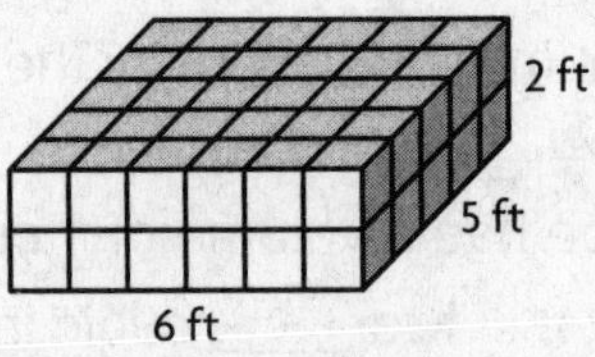

Each cube = 1 cu ft

Problem Solving REAL WORLD

6. A manufacturer ships its product in boxes with edges of 4 inches. If 12 boxes are put in a carton and completely fill the carton, what is the volume of the carton?

____

7. Matt and Mindy each built a rectangular prism that has a length of 5 units, a width of 2 units, and a height of 4 units. Matt used cubes that are 1 cm on each side. Mindy used cubes that are 1 in. on each side. What is the volume of each prism?

____

____

Name ________________________________

COMMON CORE STANDARD CC.5.MD.4

Lesson Objective: Estimate the volume of a rectangular prism.

Estimate Volume

You can estimate the volume of a larger box by filling it with smaller boxes.

Mario packs boxes of markers into a large box. The volume of each box of markers is 15 cubic inches. Estimate the volume of the large box.

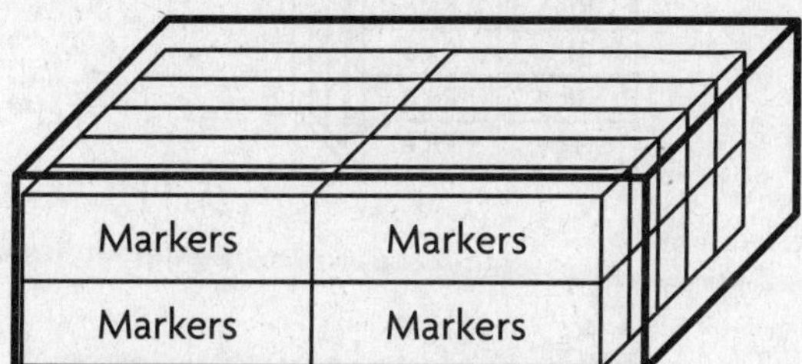

The volume of one box of markers is __15__ cubic inches.

Use the box of markers to estimate the volume of the large box.

- The large box holds __2__ layers of boxes of markers, a top layer and a bottom layer. Each layer contains __10__ boxes of markers. So, the large box holds about 2 × 10, or __20__ boxes of markers.
- Multiply the volume of 1 box of markers by the estimated number of boxes of markers that fit in the large box.
  __20__ × __15__ = __300__

So, the volume of the large box is about __300__ cubic inches.

Estimate the volume.

1. Each box of toothpaste has a volume of 25 cubic inches.

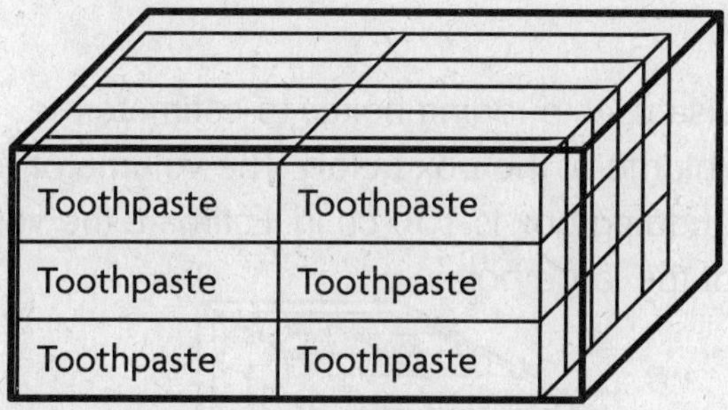

There are ______ boxes of toothpaste in the large box.

The estimated volume of the large box

is ______ × 25 = ______ cubic inches.

2. Volume of CD case: 80 cu cm

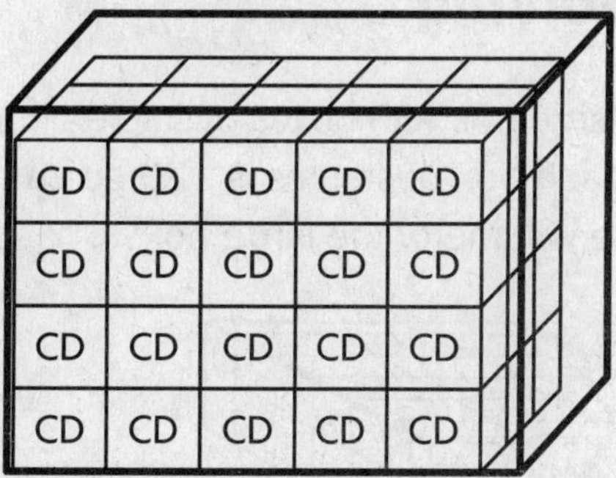

Volume of large box: ______________

Name ___________________________

Lesson 89

CC.5.MD.4

Estimate Volume

Estimate the volume.

1. Volume of package of paper: 200 cu in.

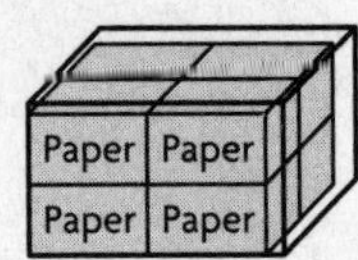

Think: Each package of paper has a volume of 200 cu in. There are __8__ packages of paper in the larger box. So, the volume of the large box is about __8__ × 200, or __1,600__ cubic inches.

Volume of large box: __1,600 cu in.__

2. Volume of rice box: 500 cu cm

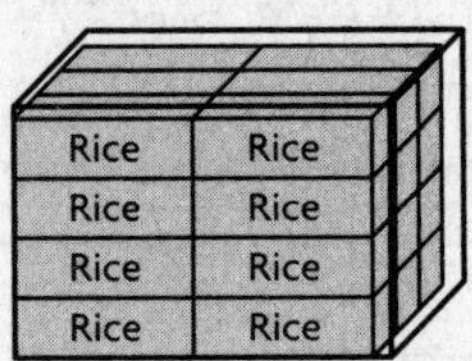

Volume of large box: ___________________

3. Volume of tea box: 40 cu in.

Volume of large box: ___________________

4. Volume of DVD case: 20 cu in.

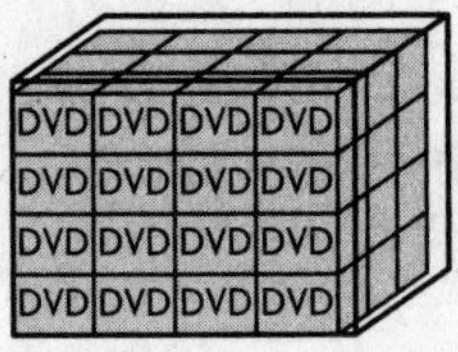

Volume of large box: ___________________

Problem Solving

5. Theo fills a large box with boxes of staples. The volume of each box of staples is 120 cu cm. Estimate the volume of the large box.

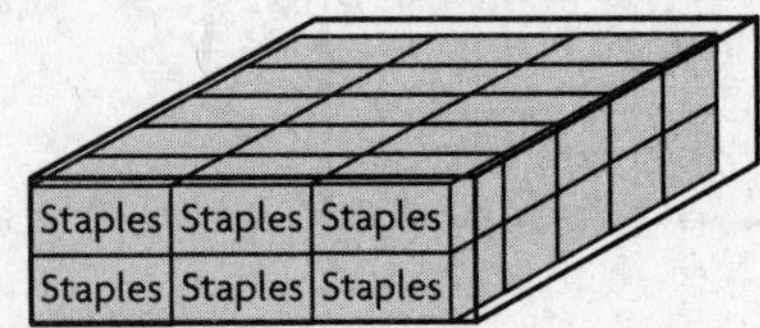

____

6. Lisa uses pudding boxes to estimate the volume of the box below. The volume of each pudding box is 150 cu in. Estimate the volume of the large box.

____

Name ______________________________

Lesson 40

COMMON CORE STANDARD CC.5.MD.5a

Lesson Objective: Find the volume of rectangular prisms.

Volume of Rectangular Prisms

Jorge wants to find the volume of this rectangular prism. He can use cubes that measure 1 centimeter on each side to find the volume.

Step 1 The base has a length of 2 centimeters and a width of 3 centimeters. Multiply to find the area of the base.

Base = __2__ × __3__

Base = __6__ cm²

Step 2 The height of the prism is 4 centimeters. Add the number of cubes in each layer to find the volume.

Remember: Each layer has 6 cubes.

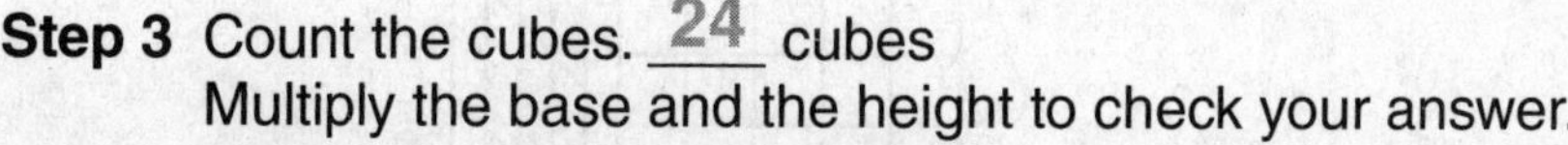

Step 3 Count the cubes. __24__ cubes

Multiply the base and the height to check your answer.

Volume = __6__ × __4__

Volume = __24__ cubic centimeters

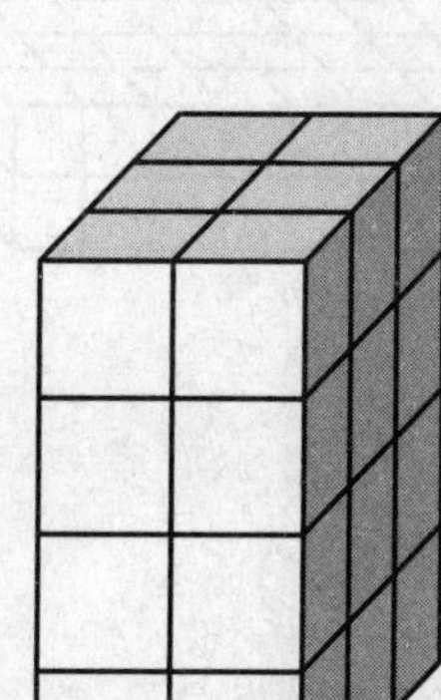

So, the volume of Jorge's rectangular prism is __24__ cubic centimeters.

Find the volume.

1.

Volume: ________

2.

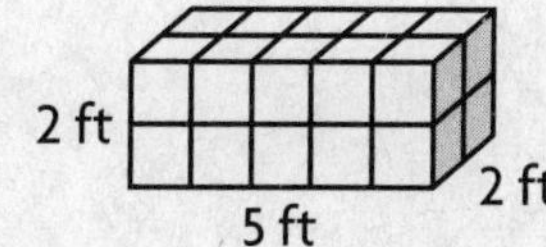

Volume: ________

3.

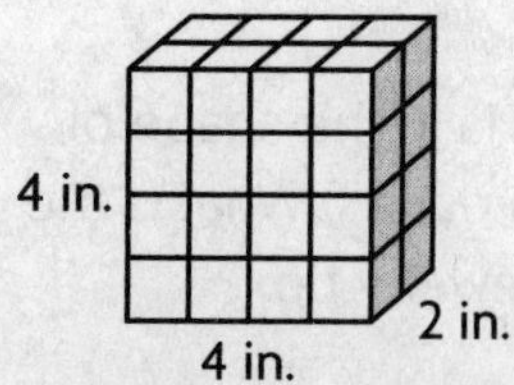

Volume: ________

4.

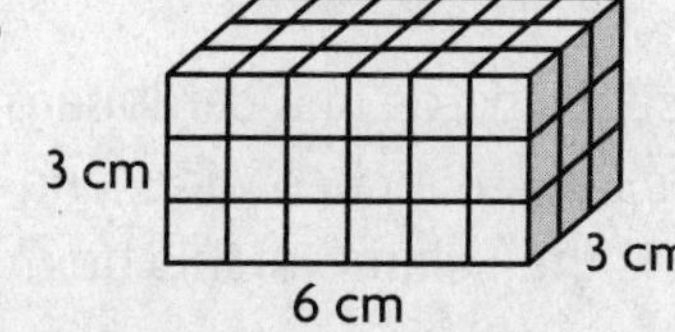

Volume: ________

Name ___________________________

Volume of Rectangular Prisms

Find the volume.

1.

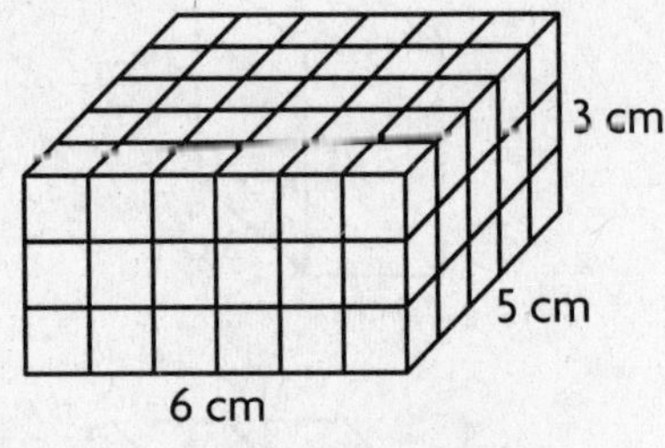

Volume: 90 cm^3

2.

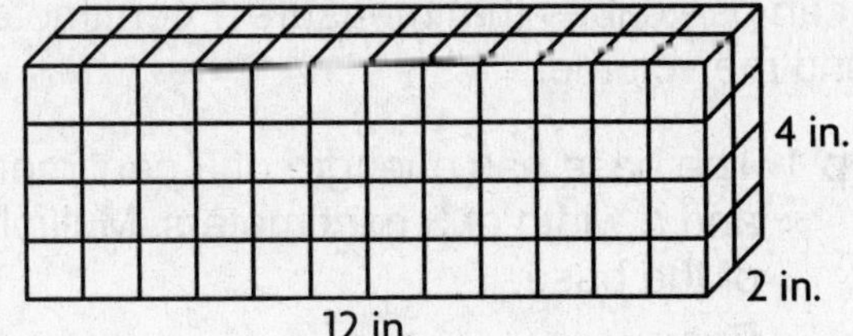

Volume: ___________

3.

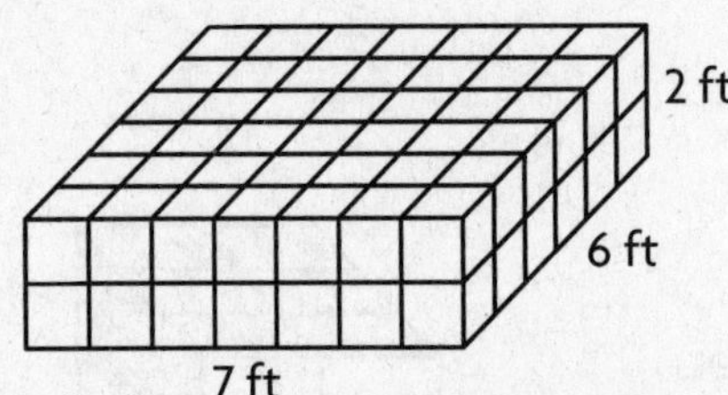

Volume: ___________

4.

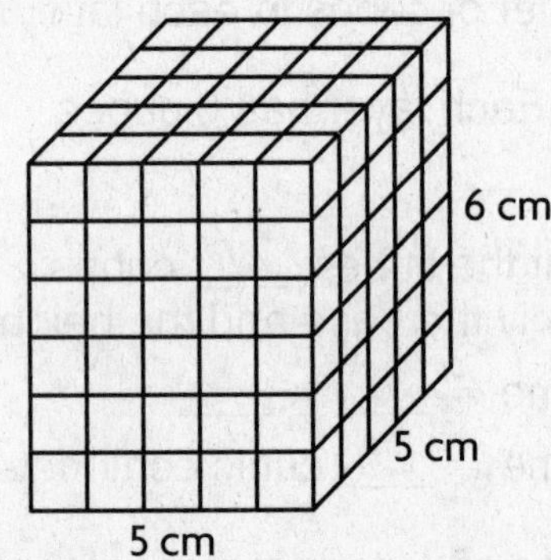

Volume: ___________

5.

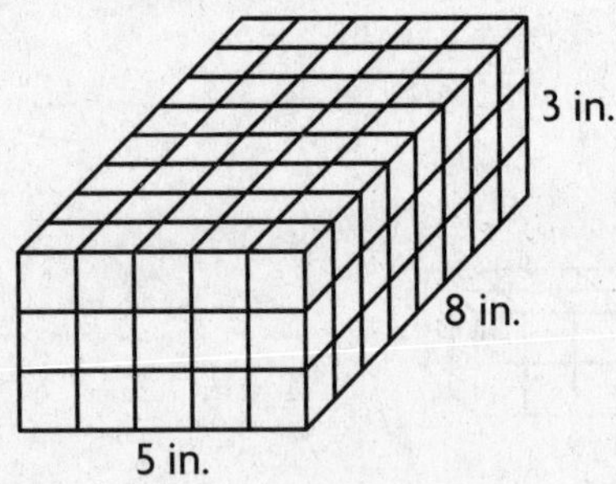

Volume: ___________

6.

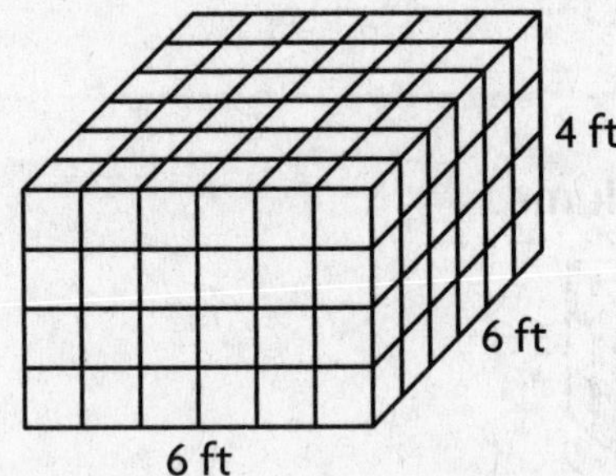

Volume: ___________

Problem Solving REAL WORLD

7. Aaron keeps his baseball cards in a cardboard box that is 12 inches long, 8 inches wide, and 3 inches high. What is the volume of this box?

____

8. Amanda's jewelry box is in the shape of a cube that has 6-inch edges. What is the volume of Amanda's jewelry box?

____

Name ________________________________

Lesson 91

COMMON CORE STANDARD CC.5.MD.5b

Lesson Objective: Use a formula to find the volume of a rectangular prism.

Algebra • Apply Volume Formulas

You can use a formula to find the volume of a rectangular prism.

Volume = *length* × *width* × *height*

$V = (l \times w) \times h$

Find the volume of the rectangular prism.

4 in.
3 in.
9 in.

Step 1 Identify the length, width, and height of the rectangular prism.

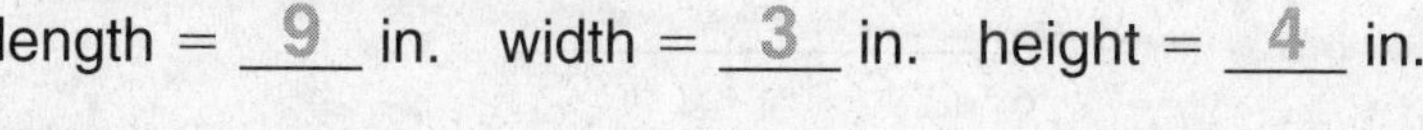

length = <u>9</u> in. width = <u>3</u> in. height = <u>4</u> in.

Step 2 Substitute the values of the length, width, and height into the formula.

$V = (l \times w) \times h$

$V = (\underline{\ 9\ } \times \underline{\ 3\ }) \times \underline{\ 4\ }$

Step 3 Multiply the length by the width.

$V = (9 \times 3) \times 4$

$V = \underline{\ 27\ } \times 4$

Step 4 Multiply the product of the length and width by the height.

$V = 27 \times \underline{\ 4\ }$

$= \underline{\ 108\ }$

So, the volume of the rectangular prism is <u>108</u> cubic inches.

Find the volume.

1.

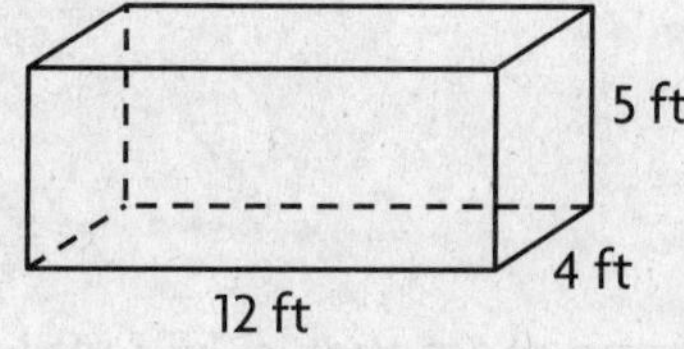

$V =$ ____________

2.

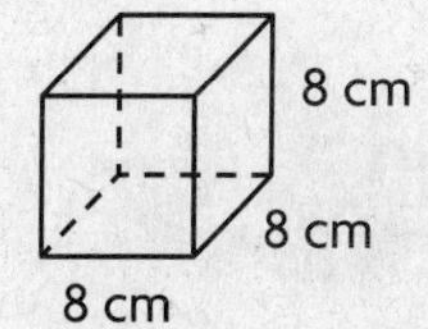

$V =$ ____________

Name ____________________

Apply Volume Formulas

Find the volume.

1.

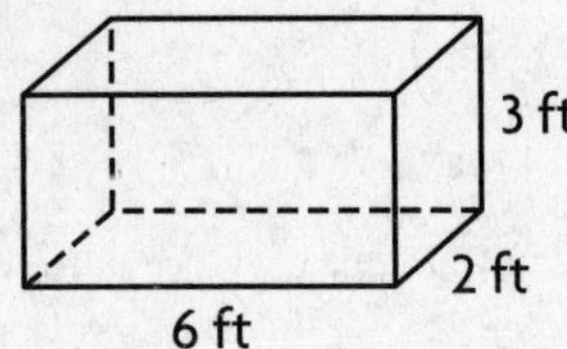

$V =$ l × w × h

$V =$ 6 × 2 × 3

$V =$ 36 ft³

2.

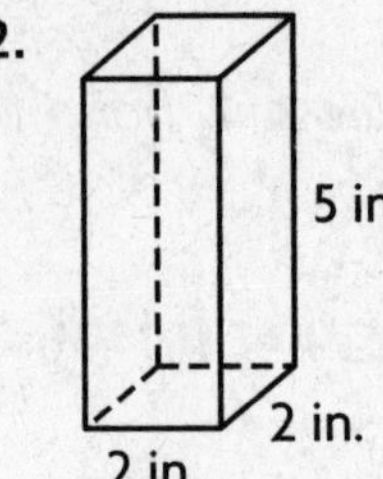

$V =$ ____________

3.

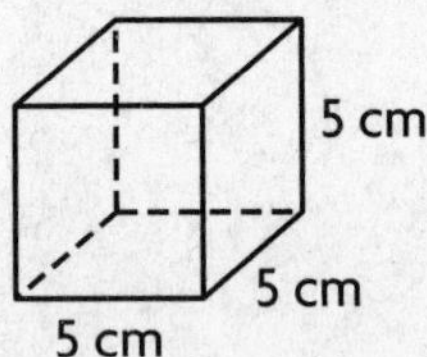

$V =$ ____________

4.

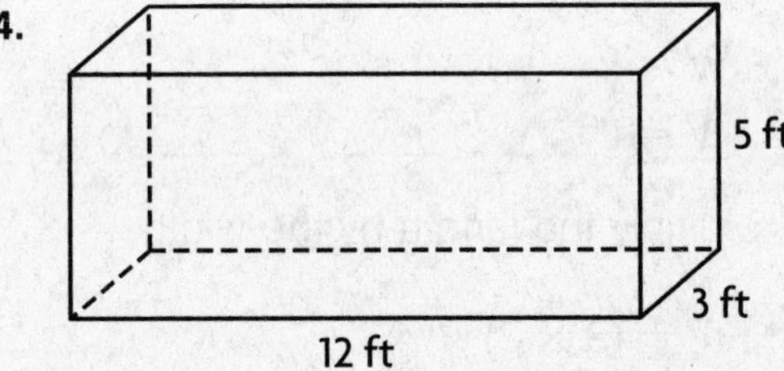

$V =$ ____________

5.

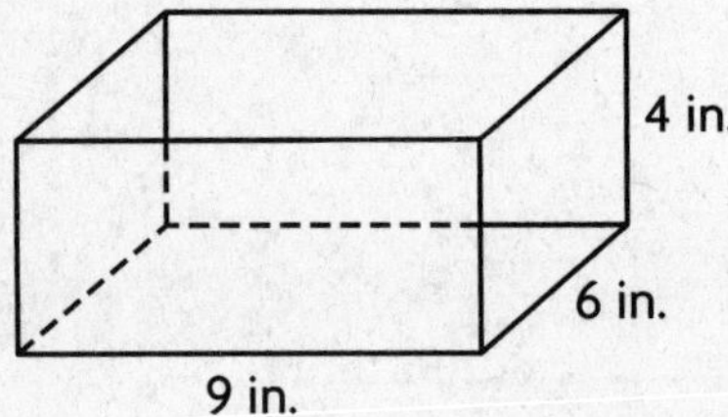

$V =$ ____________

6.

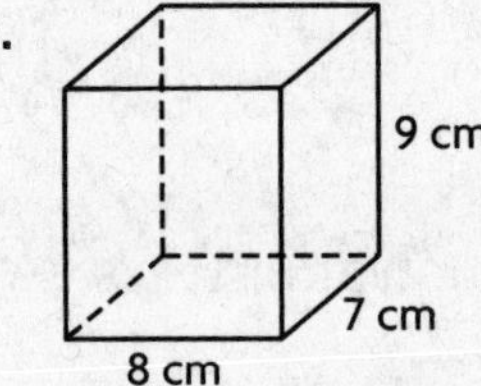

$V =$ ____________

Problem Solving REAL WORLD

7. A construction company is digging a hole for a swimming pool. The hole will be 12 yards long, 7 yards wide, and 3 yards deep. How many cubic yards of dirt will the company need to remove?

____

8. Amy rents a storage room that is 15 feet long, 5 feet wide, and 8 feet. What is the volume of the storage room?

____

Name ____________________

Lesson 92

COMMON CORE STANDARD CC.5.MD.5b

Lesson Objective: Use the strategy *make a table* to compare volumes.

Problem Solving • Compare Volumes

A company makes aquariums that come in three sizes of rectangular prisms. The length of each aquarium is three times its width and depth. The depths of the aquariums are 1 foot, 2 feet, and 3 feet. What is the volume of each aquarium?

<table>
<tr><th>Read the Problem</th><th>Solve the Problem</th></tr>
<tr><td>

What do I need to find?

I need to find the volume of each aquarium.

What information do I need to use?

I can use the formula for volume, $V = l \times w \times h$, or $V = B \times h$. I can use 1 ft, 2 ft, and 3 ft as the depths.

I can use the clues the length is three times the width and depth.

How will I use the information?

I will use the volume formula and a table to list all of the possible combinations of lengths, widths, and depths.

</td><td>

Think: The depth of an aquarium is the same as the height of the prism formed by the aquarium

Length (ft)	Width (ft)	Depth, or Height (ft)	Volume (cu ft)
3	1	1	3
6	2	2	24
9	3	3	81

So, the volumes of the aquariums are 3 cubic feet, 24 cubic feet, and 81 cubic feet.

</td></tr>
</table>

1. Jamie needs a bin for her school supplies. A blue bin has a length of 12 inches, a width of 5 inches, and a height of 4 inches. A green bin has a length of 10 inches, a width of 6 inches, and a height of 5 inches. What is the volume of the bin with the greatest volume?

   ____

2. Suppose the blue bin that Jamie found had a length of 5 inches, a width of 5 inches, and a height of 12 inches. Would one bin have a greater volume than the other? **Explain.**

   ____

   ____

Name ______________________

Problem Solving • Compare Volumes

Make a table to help you solve each problem.

1. Amita wants to make a mold for a candle. She wants the shape of the candle to be a rectangular prism with a volume of exactly 28 cubic centimeters. She wants the sides to be in whole centimeters. How many different molds can she make?

   10 molds

2. Amita decides that she wants the molds to have a square base. How many of the possible molds can she use?

   ____

3. Raymond wants to make a box that has a volume of 360 cubic inches. He wants the height to be 10 inches and the other two dimensions to be whole numbers of inches. How many different-sized boxes can he make?

   ____

4. Jeff put a small box that is 12 inches long, 8 inches wide, and 4 inches tall inside a box that is 20 inches long, 15 inches wide, and 9 inches high. How much space is left in the larger box?

   ____

5. Mrs. Nelson has a rectangular flower box that is 5 feet long and 2 feet tall. She wants the width of the box to be no more than 5 feet. If the width is a whole number, what are the possible volumes for the flower box?

   ____

6. Sophina bought 3 yards of trim to put around a rectangular scarf. She wants the width of the scarf to be a whole number that is at least 6 inches and at most 12 inches. If she uses all the trim, what are the possible dimensions of her scarf? Write your answers in inches.

   ____

Name ______________________

Lesson 93

COMMON CORE STANDARD CC.5.MD.5c

Lesson Objective: Find the volume of combined rectangular prisms.

Find Volume of Composed Figures

A composite figure is a solid made up of two or more solids. To find the volume of a composite figure, first find the volume of each solid that makes up the figure. Then find the sum of the volumes of the figures.

Find the volume of the composite figure at right.

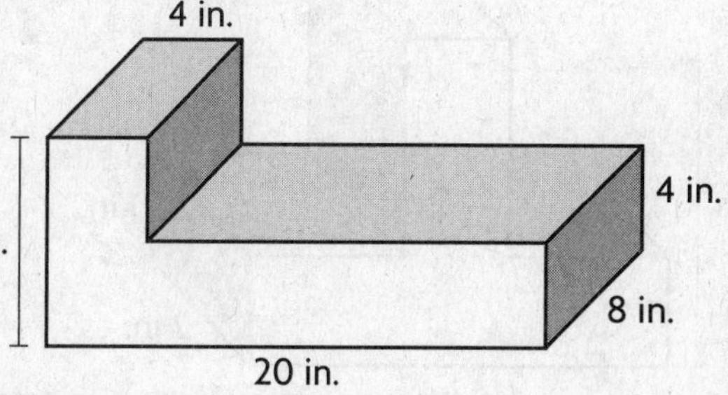

Step 1 Break apart the composite figure into two rectangular prisms. Label the dimensions of each prism.

Prism 1 **Prism 2**

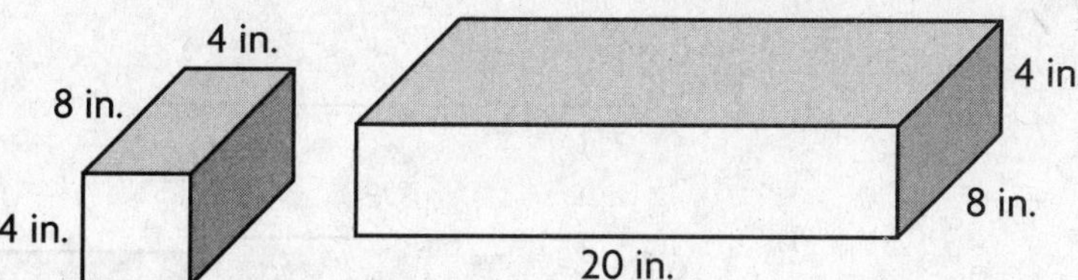

Step 2 Find the volume of each prism.

Prism 1

$V = (l \times w) \times h$

$V = \underline{4} \times \underline{8} \times \underline{4}$

$V = 128 \text{ in.}^3$

Prism 2

$V = (l \times w) \times h$

$V = \underline{20} \times \underline{8} \times \underline{4}$

$V = 640 \text{ in.}^3$

Step 3 Find the sum of the volumes of the two prisms.

Volume of Prism 1 + Volume of Prism 2 = Volume of Composite Figure

128 + 640 = Volume of Composite Figure

768 = Volume of Composite Figure

So, the volume of the composite figure is 768 in.^{3}

Find the volume of the composite figure.

1.

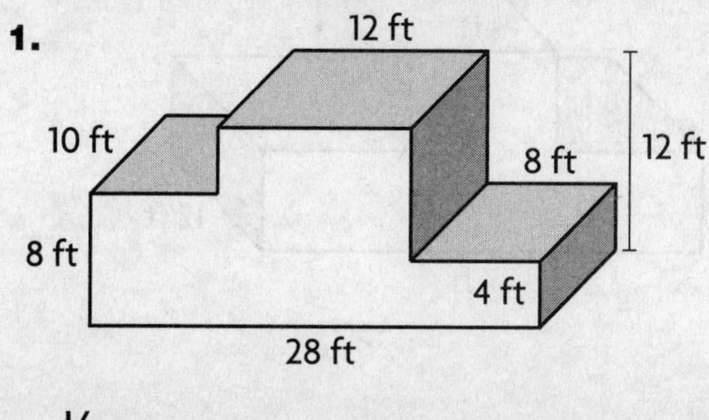

$V =$ ______________

2.

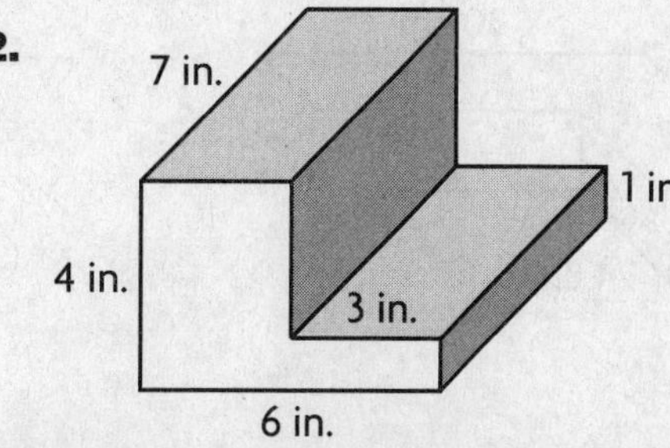

$V =$ ______________

Name ____________________

Lesson 93
CC.5.MD.5c

Find Volume of Composed Figures

Find the volume of the composite figure.

1.

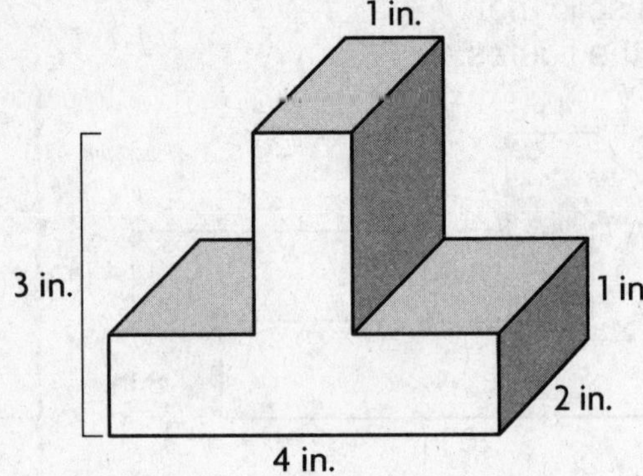

$V =$ ____________

2.

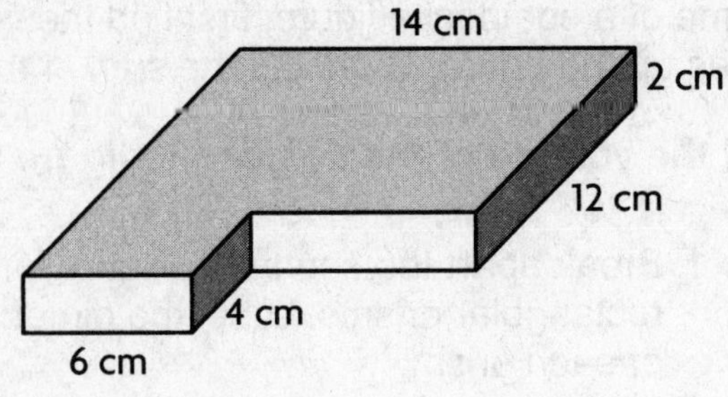

$V =$ ____________

3.

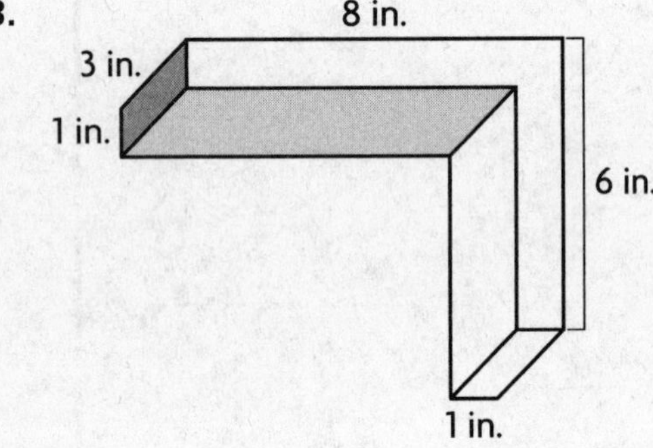

$V =$ ____________

4.

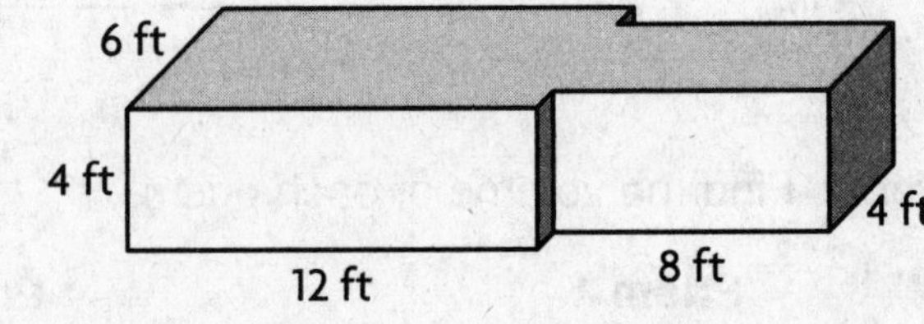

$V =$ ____________

Problem Solving REAL WORLD

5. As part of her shop class, Jules made the figure below out of pieces of wood. How much space does the figure she made take up?

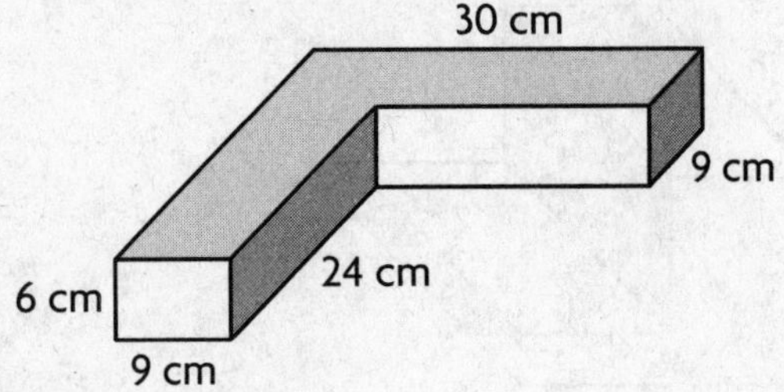

____

6. What is the volume of the composite figure below?

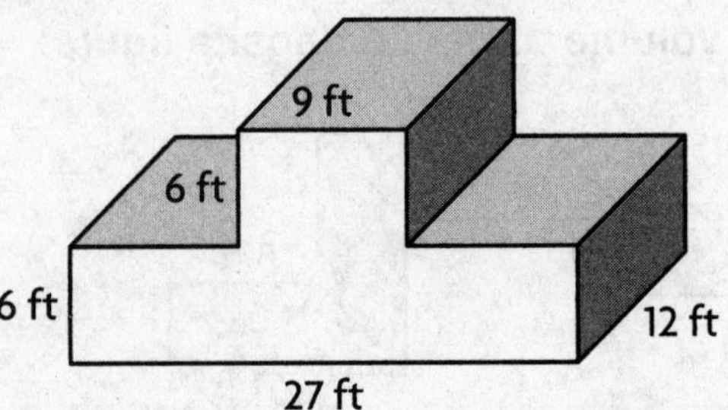

____

Name ______________________________

Lesson 94

COMMON CORE STANDARD CC.5.G.1

Lesson Objective: Graph and name points on a coordinate grid using ordered pairs.

Ordered Pairs

A coordinate grid is like a sheet of graph paper bordered at the left and at the bottom by two perpendicular number lines. The **x-axis** is the horizontal number line at the bottom of the grid. The **y-axis** is the vertical number line on the left side of the grid.

An ordered pair is a pair of numbers that describes the location of a point on the grid. An ordered pair contains two coordinates, *x* and *y*. The **x-coordinate** is the first number in the ordered pair, and the **y-coordinate** is the second number.

$(x, y) \longrightarrow (10, 4)$

Plot and label (10, 4) on the coordinate grid.

To graph an ordered pair:

- Start at the origin, (0, 0).
- Think: The letter *x* comes before *y* in the alphabet. Move across the *x*-axis first.
- The *x*-coordinate is 10, so move 10 units right.
- The *y*-coordinate is 4, so move 4 units up.
- Plot and label the ordered pair (10, 4).

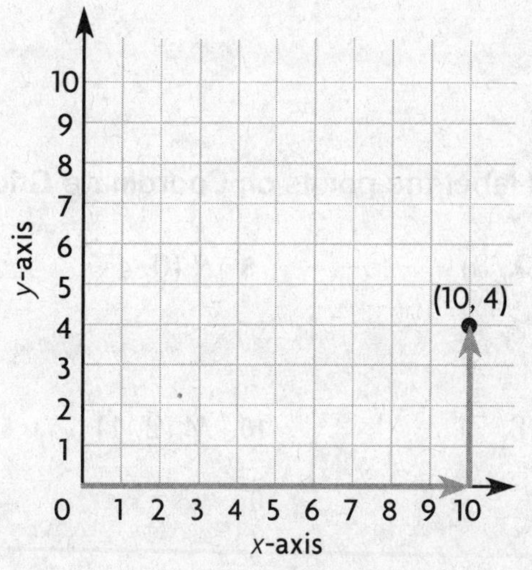

Use the coordinate grid to write an ordered pair for the given point.

1. *G* __________ **2.** *H* __________

3. *J* __________ **4.** *K* __________

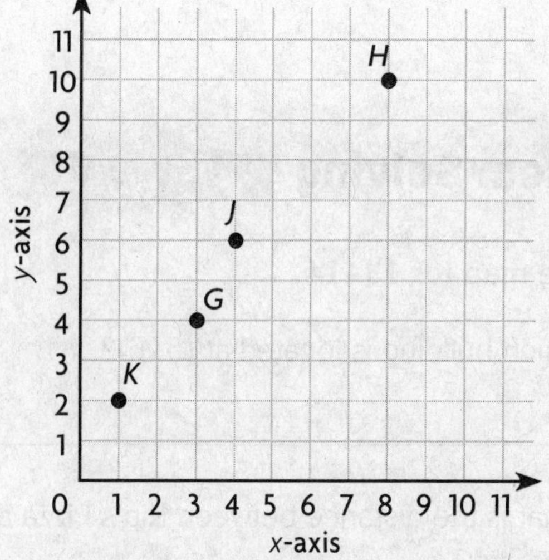

Plot and label the points on the coordinate grid.

5. *A* (1, 6) **6.** *B* (1, 9)

7. *C* (3, 7) **8.** *D* (5, 5)

9. *E* (9, 3) **10.** *F* (6, 2)

Name ______________________________

Ordered Pairs

Use Coordinate Grid A to write an ordered pair for the given point.

1. *A* (2, 3)
2. *B*
3. *C*
4. *D*
5. *E*
6. *F*

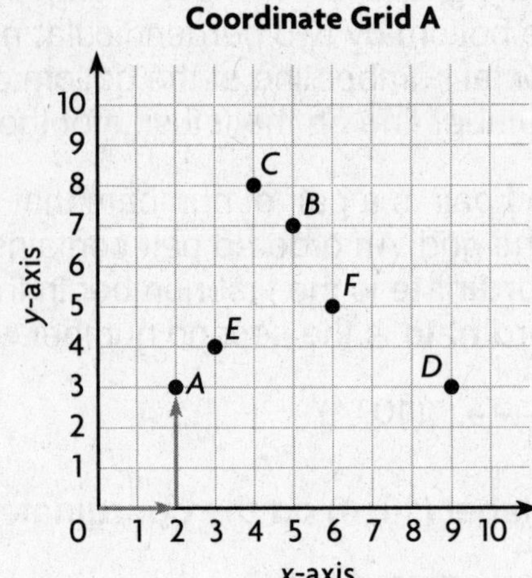

Plot and label the points on Coordinate Grid B.

7. *N* (7, 3)
8. *R* (0, 4)
9. *O* (8, 7)
10. *M* (2, 1)
11. *P* (5, 6)
12. *Q* (1, 5)

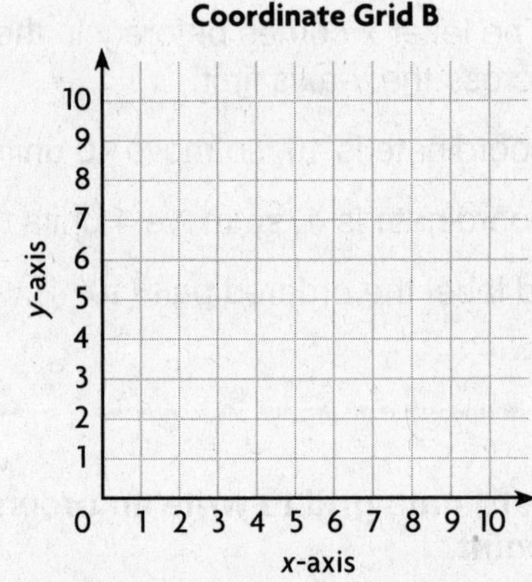

Problem Solving REAL WORLD

Use the map for 13–14.

13. Which building is located at (5, 6)?

____

14. What is the distance between Kip's Pizza and the bank?

____

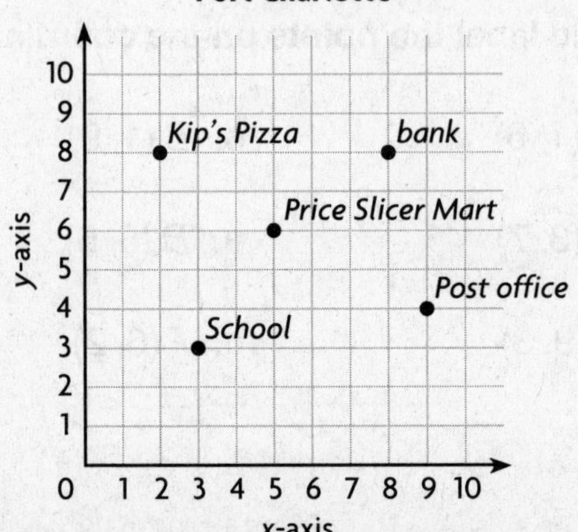

Name ______________________________

Lesson 95

COMMON CORE STANDARD CC.5.G.2

Lesson Objective: Collect and graph data on a coordinate grid.

Graph Data

Graph the data on the coordinate grid.

Plant Growth				
End of Week	1	2	3	4
Height (in inches)	4	7	10	11

- Choose a title for your graph and label it. You can use the data categories to name the *x*- and *y*-axis.
- Write the related pairs of data as ordered pairs.

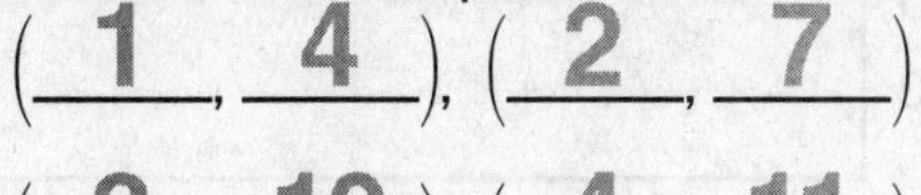

- Plot the point for each ordered pair.

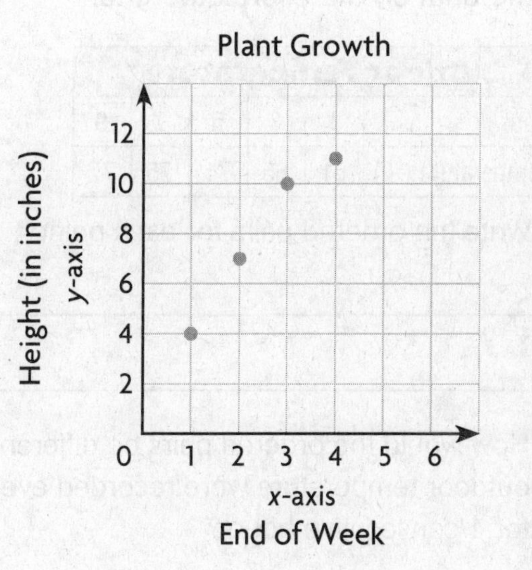

Graph the data on the coordinate grid. Label the points.

1.

Distance of Bike Ride				
Time (in minutes)	30	60	90	120
Distance (in miles)	9	16	21	27

Write the ordered pair for each point.

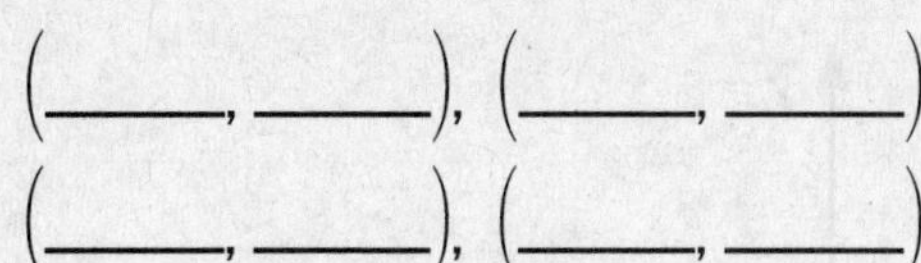

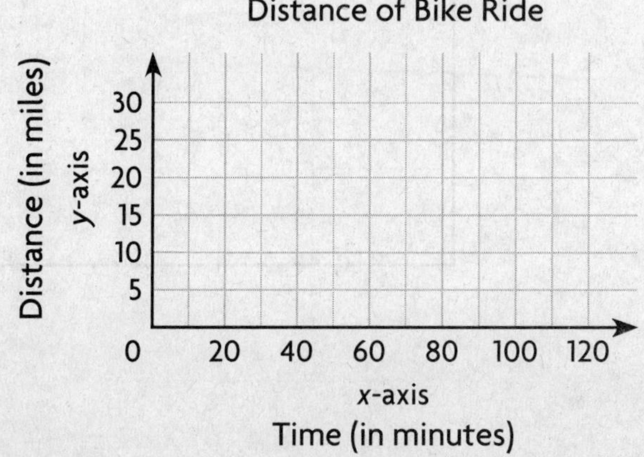

2.

Bianca's Writing Progress				
Time (in minutes)	15	30	45	60
Total Pages	1	3	9	11

Write the ordered pair for each point.

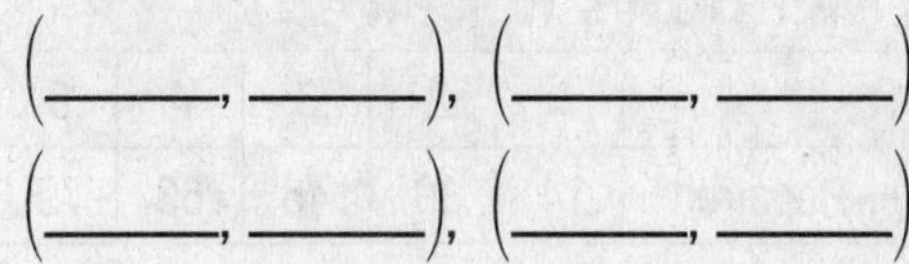

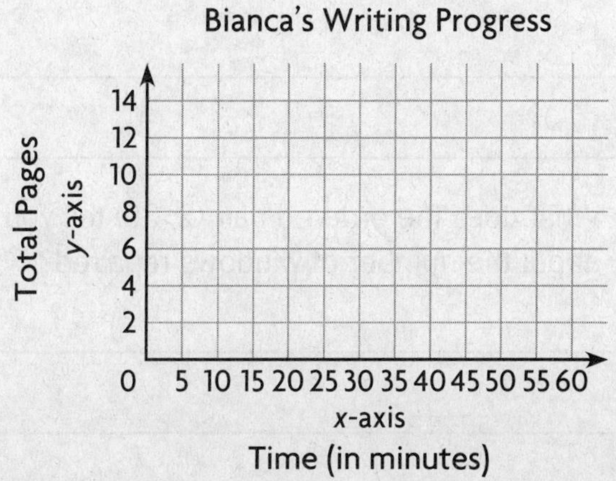

Name ______________________________

Lesson 95

CC.5.G.2

Graph Data

Graph the data on the coordinate grid.

1.

Outdoor Temperature					
Hour	1	3	5	7	9
Temperature (°F)	61	65	71	75	77

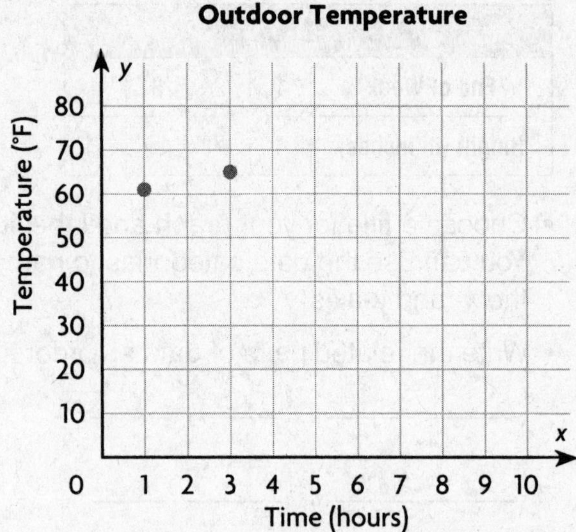

a. Write the ordered pairs for each point.

____

____

b. How would the ordered pairs be different if the outdoor temperature were recorded every hour for 4 consecutive hours?

____

____

____

____

Problem Solving REAL WORLD

2.

Windows Repaired					
Day	1	2	3	4	5
Total Number Repaired	14	30	45	63	79

a. Write the ordered pairs for each point.

____

____

b. What does the ordered pair (2, 30) tell you about the number of windows repaired?

____

____

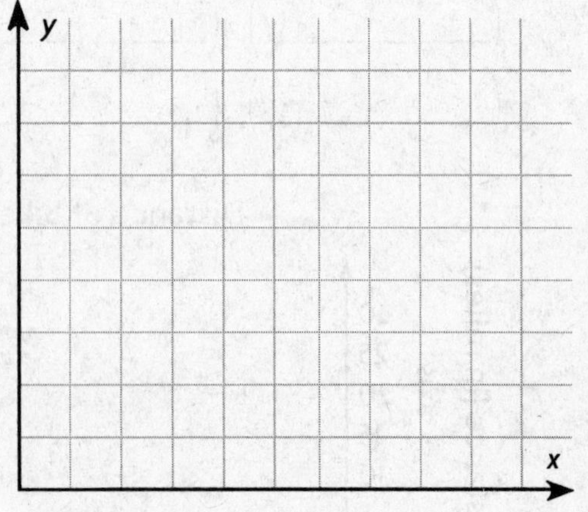

Name ______________________________

Lesson 96
COMMON CORE STANDARD CC.5.G.2
Lesson Objective: Analyze and display data in a line graph.

Line Graphs

A **line graph** uses a series of line segments to show how a set of data changes over time. The **scale** of a line graph measures and labels the data along the axes. An **interval** is the distance between the numbers on an axis.

Use the table to make a line graph.

Average Monthly High Temperature in Sacramento, California					
Month	Jan.	Feb.	Mar.	April	May
Temperature (°F)	53	60	65	71	80

- Write a title for your graph. In this example, use **Average Monthly High Temperature in Sacramento**.
- Draw and label the axes of the line graph. Label the horizontal axis **Month**. Write the months. Label the vertical axis **Temperature (°F)**.
- Choose a scale and an interval. The range is 53–80, so a possible scale is 0–80, with intervals of 20.
- Write the related pairs of data as ordered pairs: **(Jan, 53); (Feb, 60); (Mar, 65); (April, 71); (May, 80).**

1. Make a line graph of the data above.

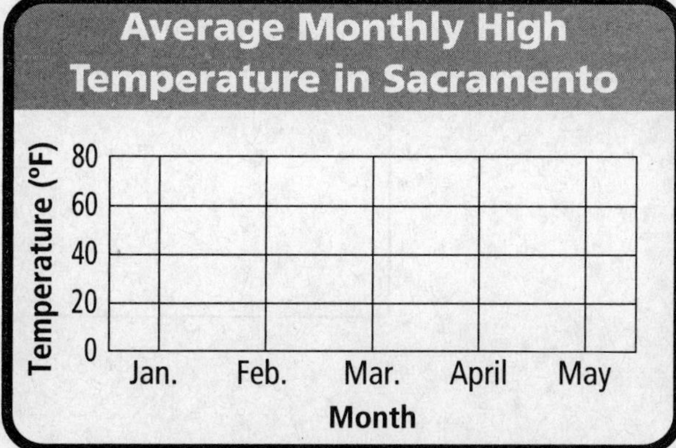

Use the graph to determine between which two months the least change in average high temperature occurs.

____

____

2. Make a line graph of the data in the table.

Average Low Temperature in San Diego, California					
Month	Mar.	April	May	June	July
Temperature (°F)	51	51	60	62	66

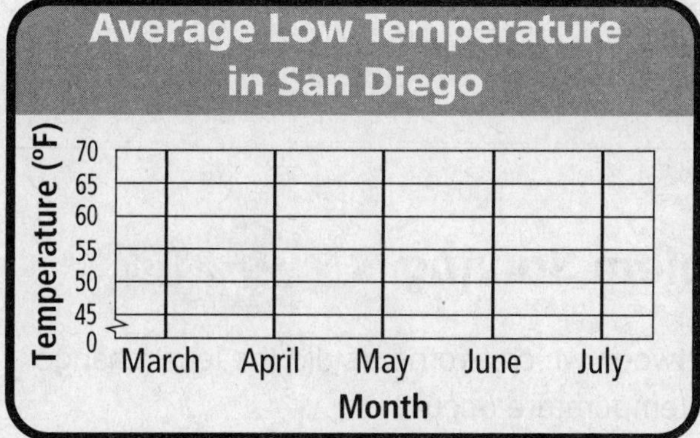

Use the graph to determine between which two months the greatest change in average low temperature occurs.

____

Name ______________________________

Lesson 96

CC.5.G.2

Line Graphs

Use the table for 1–5.

Hourly Temperature							
Time	10 A.M.	11 A.M.	12 noon	1 P.M.	2 P.M.	3 P.M.	4 P.M.
Temperature (°F)	8	11	16	27	31	38	41

1. Write the related number pairs for the hourly temperature as ordered pairs.

   (10, 8);

   ____

2. What scale would be appropriate to graph the data?

   ____

3. What interval would be appropriate to graph the data?

   ____

4. Make a line graph of the data.

   ____

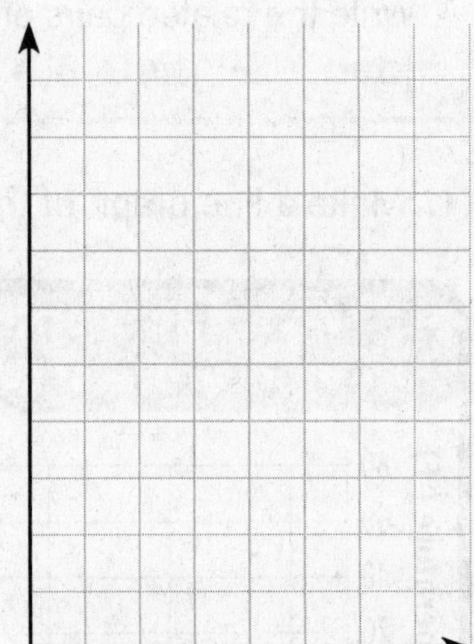

5. Use the graph to find the difference in temperature between 11 A.M. and 1 P.M.

   ____

Problem Solving REAL WORLD

6. Between which two hours did the least change in temperature occur?

   ____

7. What was the change in temperature between 12 noon and 4 P.M.?

   ____

Name ____________________

Lesson 97

COMMON CORE STANDARD CC.5.G.3

Lesson Objective: Identify and classify polygons.

Polygons

A **polygon** is a closed plane figure formed by three or more line segments that meet at points called vertices. You can classify a polygon by the number of sides and the number of angles that it has.

Congruent figures have the same size and shape. In a **regular polygon,** all sides are congruent and all angles are congruent.

Polygon	Sides	Angles	Vertices
Triangle	3	3	3
Quadrilateral	4	4	4
Pentagon	5	5	5
Hexagon	6	6	6
Heptagon	7	7	7
Octagon	8	8	8
Nonagon	9	9	9
Decagon	10	10	10

Classify the polygon below.

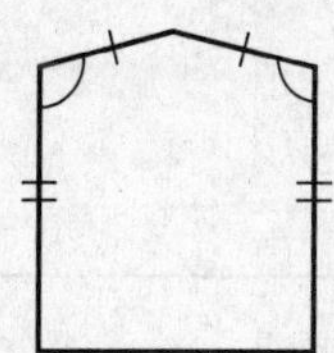

How many sides does this polygon have? 5 sides

How many angles does this polygon have? 5 angles

Name the polygon. pentagon

Are all the sides congruent? no

Are all the angles congruent? no

So, the polygon above is a pentagon. It is *not* a regular polygon.

Name each polygon. Then tell whether it is a *regular polygon* or *not a regular polygon*.

1. 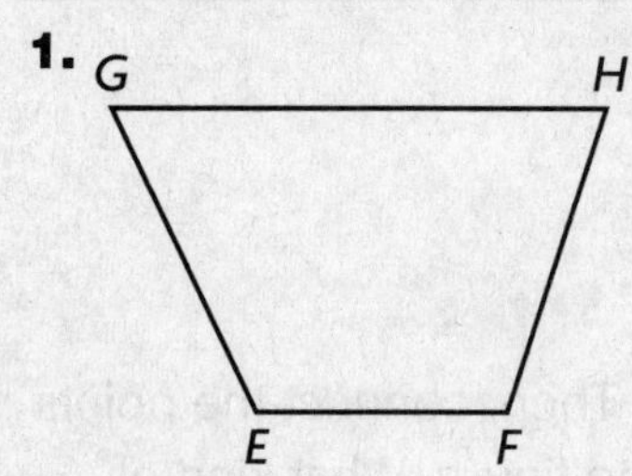

2. 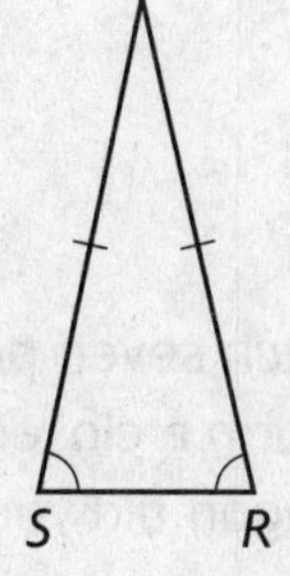

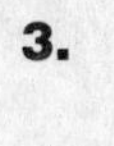

3. 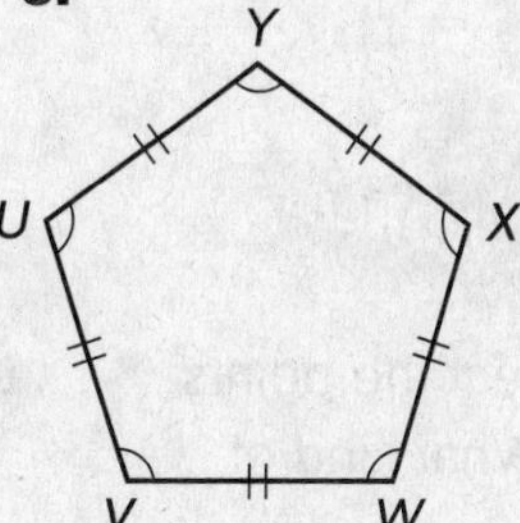

4. 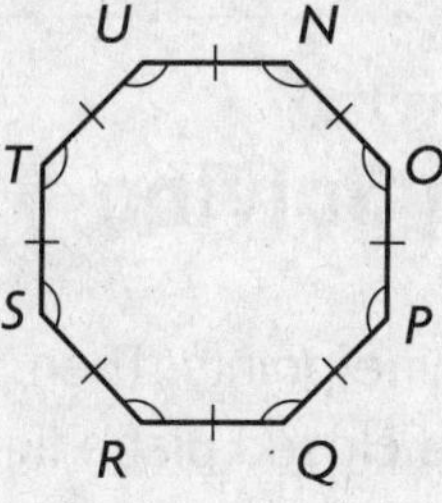

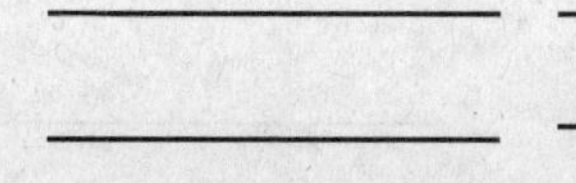

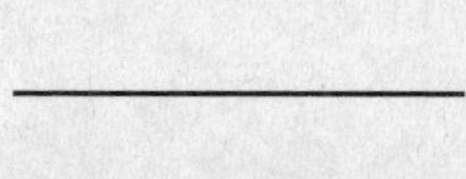

Name ______________________

Polygons

Name each polygon. Then tell whether it is a *regular polygon* or *not a regular polygon*.

1.

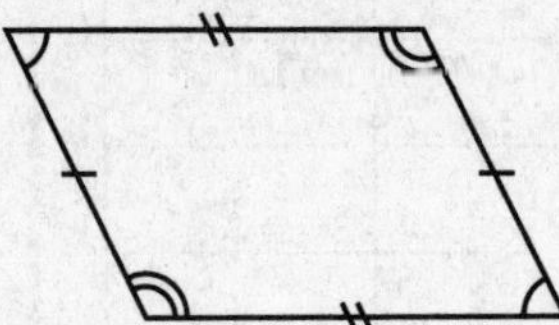

4 sides, 4 vertices, 4 angles means it is a **quadrilateral**. The sides are not all congruent, so it is **not regular**.

2.

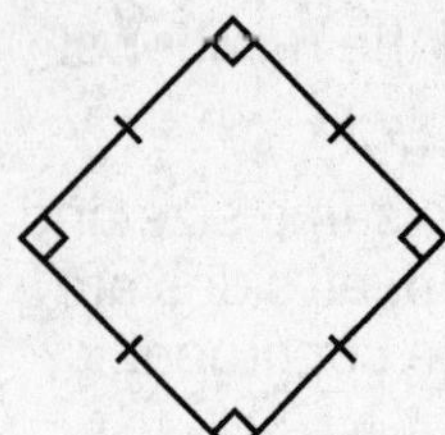

____

3.

____

4.

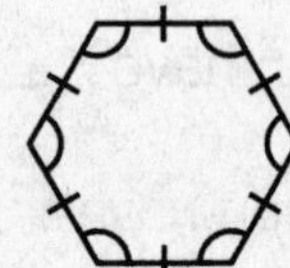

____

5.

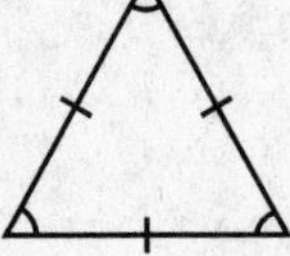

____

6.

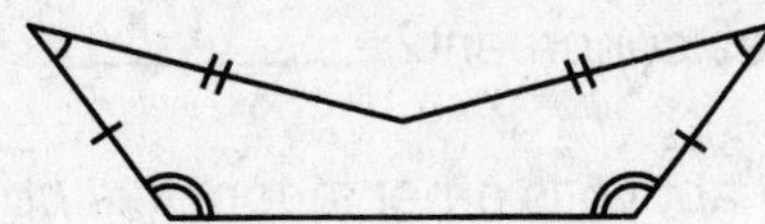

____

Problem Solving

7. Sketch nine points. Then, connect the points to form a closed plane figure. What kind of polygon did you draw?

____

8. Sketch seven points. Then, connect the points to form a closed plane figure. What kind of polygon did you draw?

____

Name ___________________________________

Lesson 98

COMMON CORE STANDARD CC.5.G.3

Lesson Objective: Classify and draw triangles using their properties.

Triangles

You can classify triangles by the length of their sides and by the measure of their angles. **Classify each triangle.**

Use a ruler to measure the side lengths.

- **equilateral triangle**
  All sides are the same length.
- **isosceles triangle**
  Two sides are the same length.
- **scalene triangle**
  All sides are different lengths.

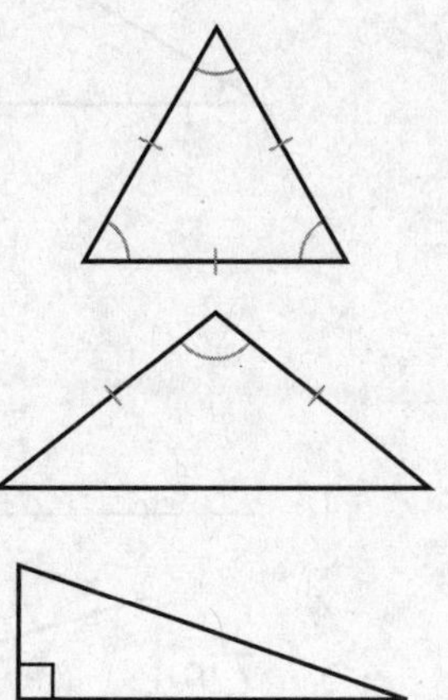

Use the corner of a sheet of paper to classify the angles.

- **acute triangle**
  All three angles are acute.
- **obtuse triangle**
  One angle is obtuse. The other two angles are acute.
- **right triangle**
  One angle is right. The other two angles are acute.

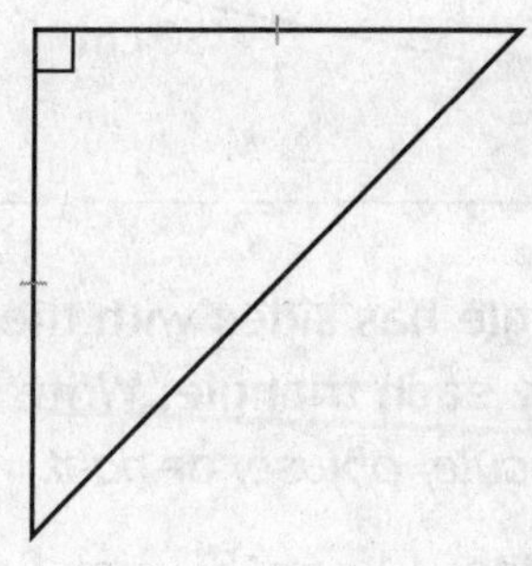

Classify the triangle according to its side lengths.
It has two congruent sides.
The triangle is an isosceles triangle.

Classify the triangle according to its angle measures.
It has one right angle.
The triangle is a right triangle.

Classify each triangle. Write *isosceles*, *scalene*, or *equilateral*. Then write *acute*, *obtuse*, or *right*.

1. 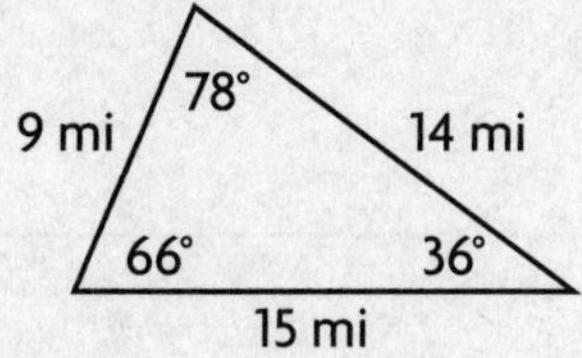

____

2. 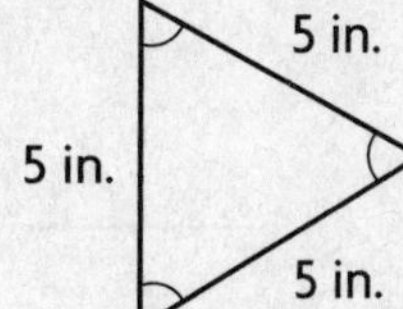

____

3. 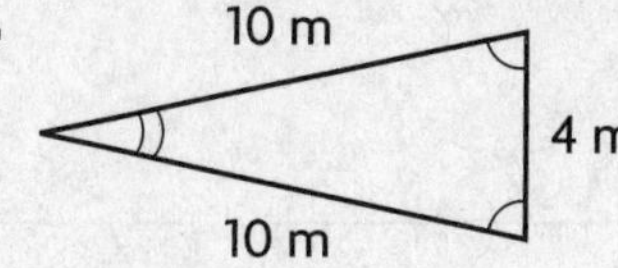

____

4. 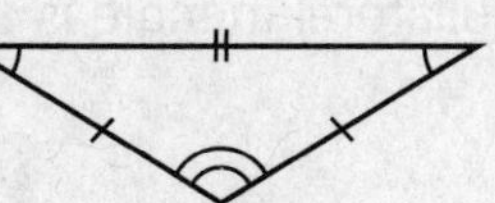

____

5. 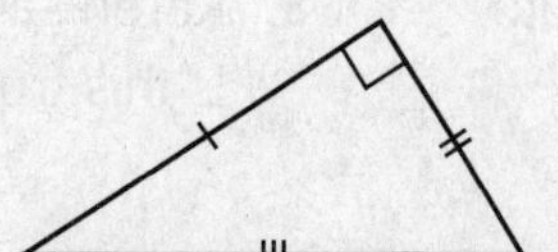

____

6. 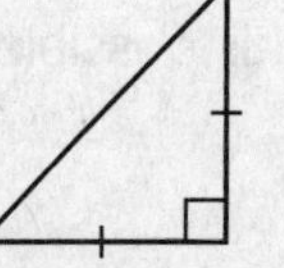

____

Name ______________________________

Lesson 98

CC.5.G.3

Triangles

Classify each triangle. Write *isosceles, scalene,* or *equilateral.* Then write *acute, obtuse,* or *right.*

1.

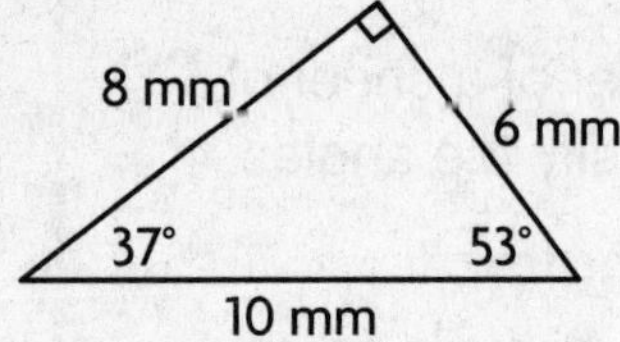

None of the side measures are equal. So, it is

scalene. There is a right

angle, so it is a right triangle.

2.

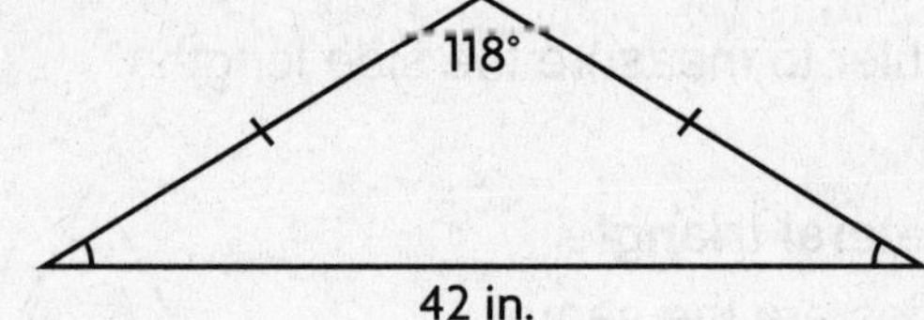

______________ ______________

3.

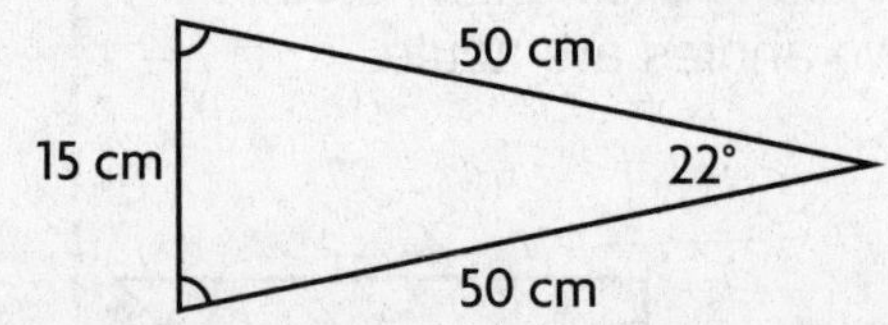

______________ ______________

4.

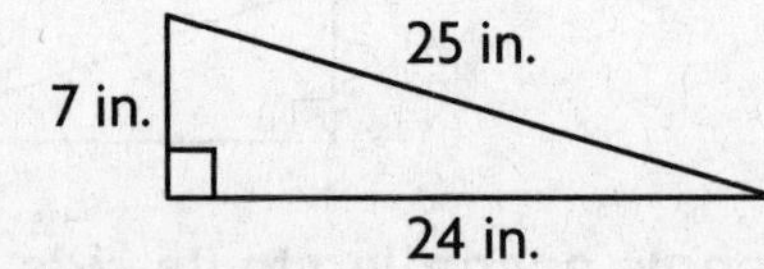

______________ ______________

A triangle has sides with the lengths and angle measures given. Classify each triangle. Write *scalene, isosceles,* or *equilateral*. Then write *acute, obtuse,* or *right*.

5. sides: 44 mm, 28 mm, 24 mm
angles: 110°, 40°, 30°

______________ ______________

6. sides: 23 mm, 20 mm, 13 mm
angles: 62°, 72°, 46°

______________ ______________

Problem Solving

7. Mary says the pen for her horse is an acute right triangle. Is this possible? **Explain.**

____

8. Karen says every equilateral triangle is acute. Is this true? **Explain.**

____

Name ______________________________

Lesson 99

COMMON CORE STANDARD CC.5.G.3

Lesson Objective: Solve problems using the strategy *act it out.*

Problem Solving • Properties of Two-Dimensional Figures

Haley thinks hexagon *ABCDEF* has 6 congruent sides, but she does not have a ruler to measure the sides. Are the 6 sides congruent?

A B C D E F

Read the Problem	Solve the Problem
What do I need to find? I need to determine if sides **AB, BC, CD, DE, EF, and FA** have the **same length**.	Trace the hexagon and cut out the shape. **Step 1** Fold the hexagon to match the sides *AB* and *ED*, sides *FE* and *FA*, and sides *CD* and *CB*. F C A E D B The sides match, so they are congruent.
What information do I need to use? The figure is a **hexagon** with **6** sides and **6 congruent** angles.	**Step 2** Fold along the diagonal between *B* and *E* to match sides *BA* and *BC*, sides *AF* and *CD*, and sides *EF* and *ED*. Fold along the diagonal between *A* and *D* to match sides *AF* and *AB*, sides *FE* and *BC*, and sides *DE* and *DC*.
How will I use the information? I will **act it out by tracing the figure and then folding the figure** to match all the sides to see if they are **congruent**.	**Step 3** Use logic to match sides *AB* and *CD*, sides *AB* and *EF*, sides *BC* and *DE*, and sides *DE* and *FA*. The sides match, so they are congruent.

1. Justin thinks square *STUV* has 4 congruent sides, but he does not have a ruler to measure the sides. Are the sides congruent? **Explain.**

____

2. Esther knows octagon *OPQRSTUV* has 8 congruent angles. How can she determine whether the octagon has 8 congruent sides without using a ruler?

____

Name ________________________

Lesson 99
CC.5.G.3

Problem Solving • Properties of Two-Dimensional Figures

Solve each problem.

1. Marcel thinks that quadrilateral *ABCD* at the right has two pairs of congruent sides, but he does not have a ruler to measure the sides. How can he show that the quadrilateral has two pairs of congruent sides?

He can fold the quadrilateral in half both ways. If both sets of sides match, then they are congruent.

2. If what Marcel thinks about his quadrilateral is true, what type of quadrilateral does he have? ________________

3. Richelle drew hexagon *KLMNOP* at the right. She thinks the hexagon has six congruent angles. How can she show that the angles are congruent without using a protractor to measure them?

____

____

4. Jerome drew a triangle with vertices *S*, *T*, and *U*. He thinks ∠*TSU* and ∠*TUS* are congruent. How can Jerome show that the angles are congruent without measuring the angles?

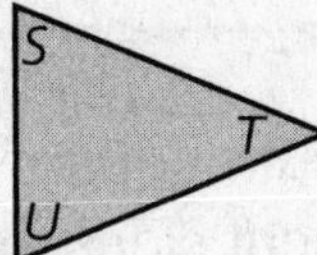

____

____

5. If Jerome is correct, what type of triangle did he draw?

____

Name ____________________

Lesson 100

COMMON CORE STANDARD CC.5.G.4

Lesson Objective: Classify and compare quadrilaterals using their properties.

Quadrilaterals

You can use this chart to help you classify quadrilaterals.

quadrilateral
4 sides

parallelogram
quadrilateral
opposite sides are parallel
opposite sides are congruent

trapezoid
quadrilateral
exactly one pair of parallel sides

rectangle
parallelogram
4 right angles
2 pairs of perpendicular sides

rhombus
parallelogram
4 congruent sides

square
rhombus
rectangle

Classify the figure.

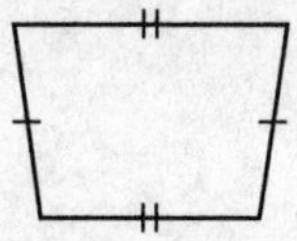

The figure has 4 sides, so it is a *quadrilateral*. The figure has exactly one pair of parallel sides, so it is a *trapezoid*.

quadrilateral, trapezoid

Classify the quadrilateral in as many ways as possible. Write *quadrilateral*, *parallelogram*, *rectangle*, *rhombus*, *square*, or *trapezoid*.

1.

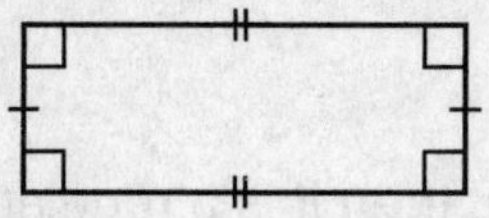

____

____

2.

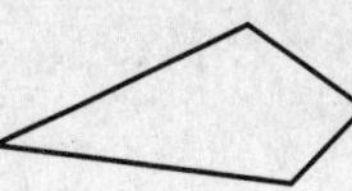

____

____

3.

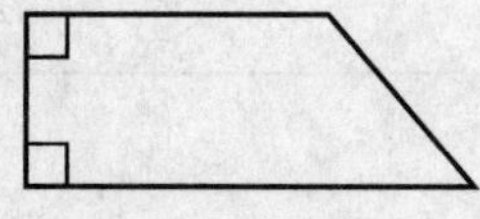

____

____

4.

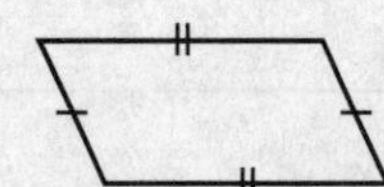

____

____

Name ______________________

Lesson 100

CC.5.G.4

Quadrilaterals

Classify the quadrilateral in as many ways as possible.
Write *quadrilateral, parallelogram, rectangle, rhombus, square,* or *trapezoid.*

1.

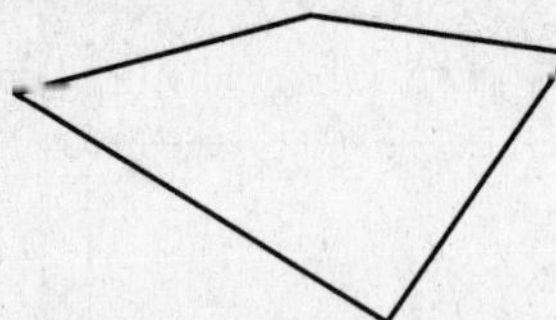

It has 4 sides, so it is a quadrilateral.
None of the sides are parallel, so there is
no other classification.

2.

____

3.

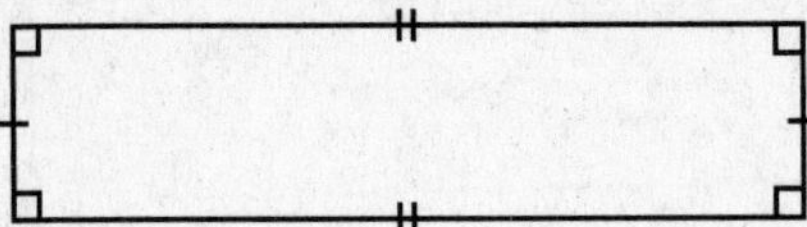

____

4.

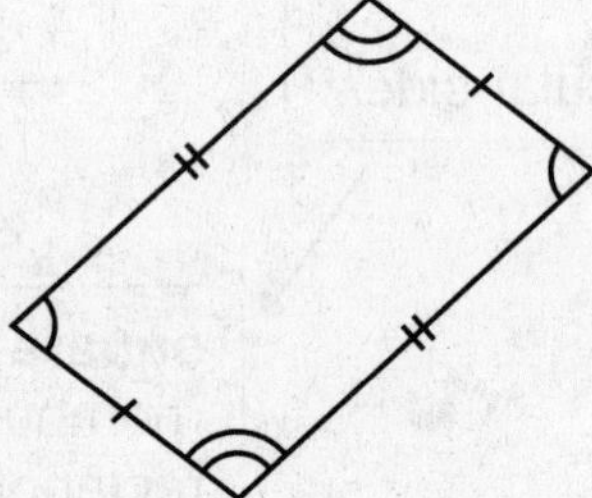

____

5.

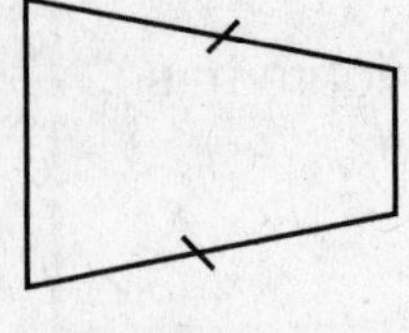

____

6.

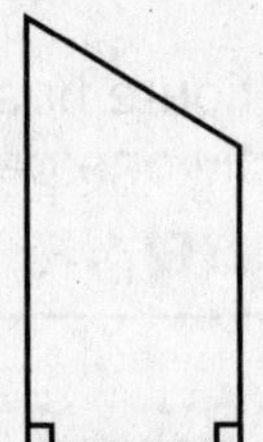

____

Problem Solving

7. Kevin claims he can draw a trapezoid with three right angles. Is this possible? **Explain.**

____

8. "If a figure is a square, then it is a regular quadrilateral." Is this true or false? **Explain.**

____